Scripta Series in Geography

Series Editors:

Richard E. Lonsdale, University of Nebraska
Antony R. Orme, University of California
Theodore Shabad, Columbia University
James O. Wheeler, University of Georgia

Other titles in the series:

W. A. Dando: The Geography of Famine
G. A. Klee: World Systems of Traditional Resource Management
F. C. F. Earney: Petroleum and Hard Minerals from the Sea
M. H. Yeates: North American Urban Patterns
S. D. Brunn/J. O. Wheeler: The American Metropolitan System: Present and
                            Future
L. S. Bourne: The Geography of Housing
J. E. Oliver: Climatology: Selected Applications

Land Use in America

Richard H. Jackson

Department of Geography, Brigham Young University
Provo, Utah

 V. H. Winston & Sons

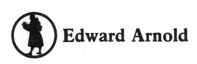 **Edward Arnold**

Copyright © V. H. Winston & Sons 1981

First published 1981 by
Edward Arnold (Publishers) Ltd.
41 Bedford Square, London WC1B 3DQ
and distributed in the United States of America by Halsted Press, a division of John Wiley &
Sons Inc.

British Library Cataloguing in Publication Data

Jackson, Richard H
    Land use in America. – (Scripta series in geography).
    1. Land use – Planning – United States – History
    I. Title
    333.7'0973   HD205

    ISBN 0-7131-6301-1

Library of Congress Cataloging in Publication Data

Jackson, Richard H   1941-
    Land use in America.

    (Scripta series in geography)
    "A Halsted Press book".
    1. Land use – United States.   I. Title.
    II. Series.
    HD205 1980.J33 1981   333.73'13'0973   80-20184

    ISBN 0-470-27063-2

Typeset in America by
Marie Maddalena of V. H. Winston & Sons
Printed in Great Britain by R. Clay (The Chaucer Press) Ltd, Bungay, Suffolk

Contents

Chapter 1   Land Use in America: The Dilemma of Changing Values   1

Chapter 2   The Public Welfare: Implementation of Land Use
             Regulation   27

Chapter 3   The Federal Government and Land Use   47

Chapter 4   The Development of State Land Use Controls   63

Chapter 5   Land Use: A Community Dilemma   87

Chapter 6   Land Use Problems and Micropolitan Areas   119

Chapter 7   Changing Methods of Controlling Land Use   147

Chapter 8   Farmland Preservation: Necessity or Misperception   171

Chapter 9   Implementing the Control of Land Use   195

Chapter 10   Land Use in Tomorrow's America: Today's Dilemma   211

             Index   221

Chapter 1

Land Use in America: The Dilemma of Changing Values

Introduction

The United States of America is one of the world's largest countries. With 3.68 million square miles, the United States ranks fourth after the Soviet Union (8.6 million square miles), Canada (3.85 million square miles), and the People's Republic of China (3.7 million square miles). The vastness of the United States led to the idea that because there was such a surplus of land there was no need to control any but the most extreme forms of land use. In 1800, there were only approximately 5 million inhabitants of the U.S. territory, and concern for preserving the land was low. By 1900, the population had surged to 76 million due to massive migration coupled with a high birth rate, but there were still nearly 30 acres of land for every man, woman, and child in the country. The population growth of the 20th century has now cut this figure to only about 10 acres per person in the U.S. This figure is still high when compared to China (about 2 acres per person) or India (less than one acre per person), but the quality as well as quantity of the land resource base must be considered. If the land resource were divided evenly, a typical American would have 2 acres of cropland, 2½ acres of grass pasture and rangeland, 31/3 acreas of forest land, and 11/3 acres of wasteland, ½ acre of land used for recreation and wildlife, and ¼ acre of roads, airports, and other urban components.

The relative abundance of the American land resource when compared to other areas of the world should not obscure the fact that it is still finite. There are very real limits to the productive capacity of our land resource. Changes in technology may increase the productivity of cropland and forest, but expanding

1

Table 1. The Land of the United States, 1970

State or possession	Area					
	Land		Inland water		Total	
	Square miles	Acres	Square miles	Acres	Square miles	Acres
Alabama	50,708	32,453,120	901	576,640	51,609	33,029,760
Alaska	566,432	362,516,480	19,980	12,787,200	586,412	375,303,680
Arizona	113,417	72,586,880	492	314,880	113,909	72,901,760
Arkansas	51,945	33,244,800	1,159	741,760	53,104	33,986,560
California	156,361	100,071,040	2,332	1,492,480	158,693	101,563,520
Colorado	103,766	66,410,240	481	307,840	104,247	66,718,080
Connecticut	4,862	3,111,680	147	94,080	5,009	3,205,760
Delaware	1,982	1,268,480	75	48,000	2,057	1,316,480
District of Columbia	61	39,040	6	2,840	67	42,880
Florida	54,090	34,617,600	4,470	2,860,800	58,560	37,478,400
Georgia	58,073	37,166,720	803	513,920	58,876	37,680,640
Hawaii	6,425	4,112,000	25	16,000	6,450	4,128,000
Idaho	82,677	52,913,280	880	563,200	83,557	53,476,480
Illinois	55,748	35,678,720	652	417,280	56,400	36,096,000
Indiana	36,097	23,102,080	194	124,160	36,291	23,226,240
Iowa	55,941	35,802,240	349	223,360	56,290	36,025,600
Kansas	81,787	52,343,680	477	305,280	82,264	52,648,960
Kentucky	39,650	25,376,000	745	476,800	40,395	25,852,800
Louisiana	44,930	28,755,200	3,593	2,299,520	48,523	31,054,720
Maine	30,920	19,788,800	2,295	1,468,800	33,215	21,257,600
Maryland	9,891	6,330,240	686	439,040	10,577	6,769,280
Massachusetts	7,826	5,008,640	431	275,840	8,257	5,284,480
Michigan	56,817	36,362,880	1,399	895,360	58,216	37,258,240
Minnesota	79,289	50,744,960	4,779	3,058,560	84,068	53,803,520
Mississippi	47,296	30,269,440	420	268,800	47,716	30,538,240

2

State						
Missouri	68,995	44,156,800	691	442,240	69,686	44,599,040
Montana	145,587	93,175,680	1,551	992,640	147,138	94,186,320
Nebraska	76,483	48,949,120	744	476,160	77,227	49,425,280
Nevada	109,889	70,328,960	651	416,640	110,540	70,745,600
New Hampshire	9,027	5,777,280	277	177,280	9,304	5,954,560
New Jersey	7,521	4,813,440	315	201,600	7,836	5,015,040
New Mexico	121,412	77,703,680	254	162,560	121,666	77,866,240
New York	47,831	30,611,840	1,745	1,116,800	49,576	31,728,640
North Carolina	48,798	31,230,720	3,788	2,424,320	52,586	33,655,040
North Dakota	69,273	44,334,720	1,398	890,880	70,665	45,225,600
Ohio	40,975	26,224,000	247	158,080	41,222	26,382,080
Oklahoma	68,782	44,020,480	1,137	727,680	69,911	44,748,160
Oregon	96,148	61,557,760	797	510,080	96,981	62,067,840
Pennsylvania	44,966	28,778,240	367	234,880	45,333	29,013,120
Rhode Island	1,049	671,360	165	105,600	1,214	776,960
South Carolina	30,225	19,344,000	830	531,200	31,055	19,875,200
South Dakota	75,955	48,611,200	1,092	698,880	77,047	49,310,080
Tennessee	41,328	26,449,920	916	586,240	42,244	27,036,160
Texas	262,143	176,765,760	5,204	3,330,560	267,338	171,096,320
Utah	82,096	52,541,440	2,820	1,804,800	84,916	54,346,240
Vermont	9,267	5,930,880	342	218,880	9,609	6,149,760
Virginia	39,780	25,459,200	1,037	663,680	40,817	26,122,880
Washington	66,570	42,604,800	1,622	1,038,080	68,192	43,642,880
West Virginia	42,070	15,404,800	111	71,040	24,181	15,475,480
Wisconsin	54,464	34,856,960	1,690	1,081,600	56,154	35,938,560
Wyoming	97,203	62,209,920	711	455,040	97,914	62,664,960
Total	3,536,855	2,263,587,200	78,267	50,090,880	3,615,122	2,313,678,080

Source: U. S. Department of the Interior, *Public Land Statistics, 1976*, p. 3 (Washington: GPO, 1976).

population and urban sprawl can offset this. The adequacy of our land resource to meet future demands of the citizenry of the United States will largely center on how well we use it today. Actions which positively or negatively affect the land resource need to be analyzed in terms of both short- and long-term impact. Such analysis is made difficult (if not impossible) by existing land use controls which are diffused among private individuals, business, and local, state, and federal governments. The powers and actions of each are multi-faceted and often overlap.

The federal government, for example, directly manages large land areas (particularly in the West), but also affects land use decisions through government spending and taxation. The effect of federal action on land use may be as local as the construction of a post office in a suburb, or as broad as the multi-state impact of a large water development project. Likewise, states have broad powers which affect land use, including, in some states, specific legislation to regulate land use for selected regions or the entire state. Local government can also undertake an array of actions affecting land use, including land use planning, zoning, capital expenditures, and taxation.

It would appear that American land use is already overcontrolled, and yet in the last decade there has been an upsurge in interest in land use controls. States have passed new legislation, several bills have been proposed for national legislation of land use, and the question of control of land use has become important to all Americans. The basic reason for the increased interest in land use controls is the rapidly growing population that is demanding products and services of the land which are different from those required in the past. If America is to resolve the dilemma of use of its land, it will be necessary to develop workable and acceptable laws and programs to guide decisions which are made concerning the land resource.

AMERICA'S LAND RESOURCE

The total gross area of the United States (including Alaska and Hawaii) is 2,314 million acres (Table 1). It should be noted that about 2% of the total gross area of the country consists of inland water bodies such as the Great Salt Lake. Inland waters are included in Table 1 only if they are ponds or lakes 40 acres or more in area; streams, rivers, or canals 1/8 of a mile wide or wider, deeply indented embayments or other coastal waters behind or sheltered by headlands or islands separated by less than 1 nautical mile of water. (The Great Lakes, Long Island Sound, and Puget Sound are not included as part of the inland waters.)

Approximately one-third of this land is controlled by agencies of the federal government (762 million acres). The Bureau of Land Management controls 60% of the land administered by the federal government, and the Forest Service controls an additional 24%. Other federal agencies administering public lands include the National Park Service, the Fish and Wildlife Service, and the Bureau of Reclamation. In addition, the federal government holds 50 million acres of land in trust for Indian tribes and individuals.[1]

The remaining two-thirds of the United States land resource consists of approximately 1.1 billion acres and is controlled by private individuals and corporations or state and local governments. State, county, and municipal governments received title to 328 million acres of land for support of schools, roads, and other economic development, but only 134 million acres remain in their ownership today.[2] Noteworthy among corporations controlling land are railroad companies. Between 1850 and 1976, slightly more than 94 million acres of public land were granted to railroads as an incentive to expand the rail links of the nation. Although much of this has since been sold by the railroads, they are still major landholders. The balance of the nation's land is controlled by other corporations or individuals.[3]

Land Use in the United States

The land of America is used for a multitude of activities. Land use includes everything the land is used for by residents of the country, from farms of golf courses, houses to fast food establishments, hospitals to graveyards; and all uses are interconnected. The Illinois corn farmer's use of artificial fertilizer affects fishermen on Lake Erie, and the erection of a factory in rural Nebraska precipitates loss of prime corn land to the ubiquitous subdivision. Although land use types are almost limitless, America's land use can be broadly categorized into intensive and extensive types. Extensive land use includes the bulk of the land in the categories of cropland, grazing land, forest land, wasteland, and recreation and wildlife areas. Intensive land uses include urban uses and land for transportation purposes (Table 2).[4]

The cropland resource of the United States is estimated to be at 472 million acres, or 21% of the land area, representing neither the acreage actually harvested each year nor that which could conceivably be used, but land that is now involved in cropland rotation.[5] In any given year, the cropland resource consists of land actually in crops, land used for pasture, and fallow land. The amount of land classified as cropland has not changed significantly in the past few decades, but there have been important changes in individual use components. The record high for land actually used for crops occurred in 1949 when 387 million acres of cropland were planted. Since that time, there has been a general downward trend to 333 million acres in 1969. Land planted remained at this low figure until 1973 when it increased sharply to 354 million acres.[6] The decline in cropland planted was a result of increased productivity in the 1949–1969 era in which productivity per acre increased over one-half. As a consequence, marginal lands were abandoned and other land was diverted into fallow under government programs. Cropland in soil improvement and other government programs ranged from 37 to 65 million acres between 1950 and 1972.[7] After 1973, cropland planted increased dramatically as a result of world demand for foods and associated price increases which cut diverted land to only 8 million acres. By 1974, only 2 million acres of cropland remained in the government-sponsored diversion programs.[8]

Another trend affecting the nation's cropland has been associated with expansion of cropland through reclamation projects. New cropland has appeared in a number of well-defined areas, particularly along the Mississippi River as a result of drainage, in the western states as a result of expanded irrigation, in Florida

Table 2. Major Land Use in the United States, 1969

Major land uses	Acreage[a] (million acres)	Percent of total
Agricultural:		
Total cropland	384	17.0
Grassland pasture and range	692	30.6
Forest land grazed	198	8.7
Farmsteads, farm roads	9	.4
Total agricultural land	1,283	56.7
Nonagricultural:		
Forest land not grazed	525	23.2
Special uses	169	7.5
Urban areas, roads, and other built-up areas	(61)	(2.7)
Recreation parks and wildlife	(81)	(3.6)
Public installations and facilities	(27)	(1.2)
Miscellaneous land	28	12.6
Total nonagricultural land	981	43.3
Total land area	2,264	100.0

[a]It is almost impossible to provide adequate statistics on land use in the United States because of differing definitions of what constitutes forest, or grazing land, or even cropland. Publications of the U.S. Department of Agriculture give differing figures depending on the purpose of the publication. Consequently all figures used here will refer to those developed from the (1969) census of agriculture unless otherwise indicated. Although they have changed in the ensuing decade, they show relative magnitude of uses.

Source: U.S. Department of Agriculture, *Our Land and Water Resources* (Washington: Economic Research Service, 1974), Misc. Pub. 1290, 1974, p. 3.

associated with both drainage and irrigation, and in northern Montana as a result of improved dryland farming techniques. There has also been expansion of cropland throughout the corn belt associated with contouring, drainage, leveling, and other management techniques.

Cropland has also been changed to non-cropland use in the United States.[9] With the exception of the Mississippi Delta states and Florida, the entire south is a region of such cropland "abandonment." Lands "abandoned" were infertile, unsuited for mechanization, or both. The northeastern states have also been the scene of land abandonment as marginal land was allowed to revert to brush, or transferred to other types of uses. Between 1952 and 1972, the nation lost 6% of its taxable farm acreage. In the same period, New England lost half of all its farm acreage, and New Jersey lost 45% (Fig. 1).[10]

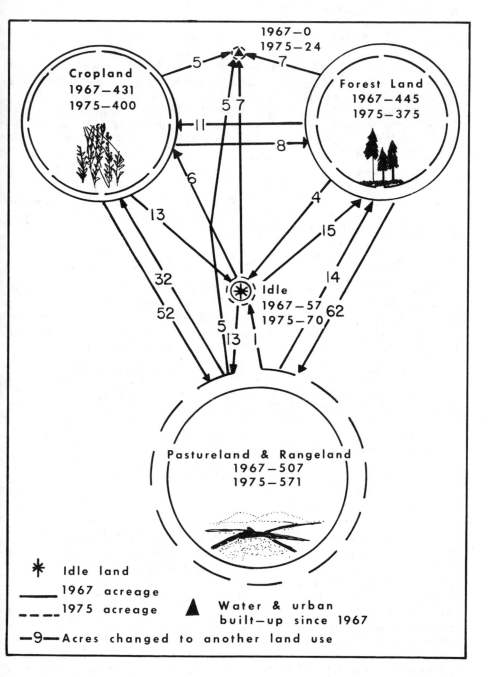

Fig. 1. Changes in land use: 1967–1975.

Pasture and Range

Livestock graze on 890 million acres, or 39% of the land area of the United States. The land used for grazing includes not only grassland, but cropland and forest land which is grazed. The total amount of land used for pasture and range has declined since 1950, but cropland pastured has increased 31 million acres. The 88 million acres of cropland used for pasture contributes half of total pasture land needs.[11] Approximately two-thirds of land used for pasture or range is on private farms. This includes the 88 million acres of cropland pastured, 452 million acres of permanent pasture and range, and 62 million acres of woodland used for grazing. The 288 million acres of non-farmland used for grazing consist of 72 million acres of private or state-owned woodland, 72 million acres of federal woodland, and 144 million acres of federally administered grazing lands, primarily in the more arid western states.[12]

Forest Land

About one-third of the United States (754 million acres) is categorized as forest land by the Census Bureau. The quality of the forest land varies, with one-sixth in Alaska where little timber is harvested for commercial use. There are 633 million acres of forest land in the 48 conterminous states, and an estimated 80% (493 million acres) of this is commercially useful. During the decades of the '50s and '60s, the area of commercially productive forest declined 8.4 million acres (2%).[13] This decline is largely concentrated in the south, especially in the Mississippi Delta region where bottomlands are being drained and forest land transformed into cropland. The most productive forest land is found in the Pacific Northwest and the southern states.

Special Land Uses

Twenty percent (456 million acres) of the land in the United States is classified as land other than cropland, pasture–grazing land, or forest land. Areas unsuited for use in deserts, swamps, tundra, and bare rock comprise 287 million acres, and an additional 169 million acres (8% of the total land resource) are in the special purpose land use category (Table 3).[14] Land in swamps, tundra, and bare rock is low use land. The special use lands include intensive uses such as urban and transport uses, as well as extensive uses such as recreation and wildlife.

There are some 35 million acres of land classified in urban or urban related uses. This includes land in all urban places, plus all land in incorporated and unincorporated places of 1,000 or more population. The land use in the urban category includes residential, commercial, industrial, and transportation uses as well as vacant land within the boundaries of urban areas.[15]

The road system of the United States exclusive of urban areas occupies 21 million acres and includes lands in roadbeds and right-of-ways of systems administered by federal, state, and local governments. This system is quite stable in amount of land utilized, with increases associated primarily with completion of the federal

Table 3. Special Land Uses, 1959, 1969

Special uses	Million acres		
	1959	1969	Change
Urban areas	27.2	34.6	7.3
Transportation areas	24.7	26.0	1.3
Recreation and wildlife areas	61.5	81.4	19.9
Public installations and facilities	27.5	27.4	-.1
Farmsteads and farm roads	10.1	8.4	-1.7
Total	151.0	177.8	26.8

Source: U.S. Department of Agriculture, *Our Land and Water Resources* (Washington: Economic Research Service, 1974), Misc. Pub. 1290, 1974, p. 10.

interstate highway system. The interstate system utilized 1 million acres in 1969, and approximately 100,000 acres per year are added it.[16] "Rural" airports include an additional 1.8 million acres of land, including airports serving large urban areas which are classified as rural because of their location outside of the urbanized area.

THE CHANGING USE OF LAND IN THE U.S.

Land use is not static, but rather a dynamic, interacting system. Changes are occurring in each of the categories of land use which have an impact on the residents of the nation. Those which have received the greatest attention center around the special uses, particularly those related to urban functions. Urban sprawl with its attendant destruction of prime farmland, the second-home phenomenon which destroys the tranquility of highly prized natural environments, and the seeming spread of tract housing over hill and dale have received attention in popular and scholarly works. Examination of the trends in land use in the United States seems to indicate that these problems are less severe than popularly supposed. If so, it is because the statistics are macro in scale. At the micro scale, serious problems of land use are being created by these trends.

The general trend in land use for the past 20 years has involved two facets. The first of these has shifted land from agricultural, forest, or other extensive uses into such intensive uses as roads, airports, and other urban related activities. At the same time, a change has occurred affecting land shifts within the extensive uses, as land is shifted from cropland or forest land to recreation or wildlife activity. During the 1959-1969 decade, an average of 1.2 million acres of rural land per year was shifted to intensive urban related uses. One million acres per year were shifted to extensive uses (Fig. 1).[17]

The trend in land use associated with the 1960s continued in the '70s. Recent estimates indicate that on non-federal lands, 79.2 million acres were removed from cropland use between 1967 and 1975. In the same period, only 48.7 million acres were converted to cropland use, resulting in a net loss of 30.5 million acres of cropland.[18] Pasture land and rangeland increased by 64 million acres as cropland or forest land was converted to pasture use. Forest land declined by about 70 million acres during the 8-year span, and acreage in miscellaneous other uses increased by 13 million acres.[19] An estimated 17 million acres of land were shifted to urban related activities during the same time, and an additional 7 million acres were flooded by reservoirs or used for flood control.[20] In general, it can be said that the land use trends of the 1960s intensified in the '70s, with increasing amounts of land being transformed into urban related uses each year.

The importance of the trends in American land use centers around their impact on the ability of the nation to maintain sufficient land to provide for future food, fiber, and forest products required by the population. When viewed at the micro scale, the amount of land being lost to intensive uses is a small percentage. Only an estimated 600,000 acres of land transformed to urban uses each year comes directly from land used for crops. Although the rate of conversion of land to urban and built-up areas is increasing, the majority of the land affected is not prime agricultural land. Such a micro analysis of land use trends masks important regional differences, however.

The mountain states, the Pacific states, and the northeastern states are regions in which the availability of prime land is limited, and yet these regions are seeing rapid conversion of land to urban uses. The semi-arid mountain states are faced with restrictions of topography which result in serious competition for the use of the more level land, with resultant loss of cropland as their population rapidly increases (Table 4). The Pacific states have been growing rapidly for the past several decades, with a California study indicating 134,000 acres per year converted from agriculture, a rate of change which, if continued, would consume three-fourths of the state's agricultural land by the year 2000.[21]

In addition to loss of land to urban uses, important land use shifts occur as the demand for recreation increases. From 1965 to 1972, participation more than doubled in such activities as camping, picnicking, fishing, swimming, and canoeing. By 1976, the Bureau of Outdoor Recreation estimated a total of 6.8 billion visitor hours on federally administered lands alone.[22] Over 1 million acres

Table 4. Estimated Population Growth in the United States, 1970–1980

Region	1970 population (millions)	1980 population (millions)	Growth (%)
Northeast	49.157	50.3	2.3
North central	56.673	59.0	4.1
South	63.032	72.7	15.3
West	34.947	40.5	15.9
United States	203.810	222.5	9

Source: U.S. Census Bureau, "Population Estimates to 1980" (Washington: Commerce Department, 1978). n.p.

are converted annually to recreation related activities. Increased leisure time, more disposable income, increased concern for the environment, and greater mobility indicate that there will be even greater demands for recreation land in the future. Changes in land use in America and the pressures affecting their use pose important questions concerning how our land resource is controlled, managed, and used.

LAND USE POLICY: ISSUES AND QUESTIONS

The focus of questions concerning land use are: what should be controlled, who should do the controlling, how the inevitable costs associated with such controls will be borne, and what uses should be encouraged. Historically in the United States, land use decisions have been made by a host of individuals, corporations, and government agencies. Since the decision-making process is fragmented, the resultant land use may at best only result in minor benefit to society, or at worst may negatively affect the community, state, or nation. It has been said that "land use is, in fact, the key to all the rest of our environmental problems,"[23] a statement which reflects the critical nature of decisions affecting the land resource. But land use decisions do more than affect environmental problems. Speculative pressure causes loss of cropland to suburbia, exclusionary zoning restricts low income housing to the ghetto, and recreation home developments seriously impair the beauty of large tracts of land. The interconnected nature of all land use decisions necessitates developing a set of criteria for evaluating all land use decisions so that the needs of the individual can be met without the rights of society being abrogated.

Goals of a Land Use Policy

There is broad agreement on what a land use policy should do for the nation. Generally, it can be stated that it should maximize the benefit derived from our land resource to both individual and society. The following list presents some specific objectives designed to accomplish this goal. (The list should be viewed simply as a series of interrelated objectives, not as a ranking of relative importance.) Common objectives concerning our land resource include:

- Maintenance of the land necessary to insure adequate provision of food, fiber, and forest products.
- Preservation of scenic, historic, or other highly valued landscapes to prevent encroachment on areas which comprise the national heritage.
- Protection of individuals and society through restriction of building in floodplains, seismic areas, on steep slopes, or other hazardous areas.
- Provision of adequate land for recreation at the community, regional, state, and national level, including land for intensive recreation activity, wilderness, and open space functions.
- Provision of adequate, decent housing, and community services for all residents of the nation through planned, orderly development to minimize urban sprawl and maximize the quality of life.

—Minimization of pollution of land, air, and water through proper location of industries and disposal sites; and community planning to minimize automobile use with its associated energy demands and pollution.

—Protection of wildlife, wilderness, and fragile environments, including coastal zones, deserts, wetlands, and estuaries.

—Prevention of urban sprawl through maintenance of green belts and open space to separate urban areas, and encouragement to develop unneeded vacant or idle lands within existing built-up areas.

—Protection of the health, safety and welfare of the public by preventing inappropriate land use.

Such objectives are designed to allow rational use of the land, while preventing irrational and socially costly activities through wise land use management. Such management is designed to enhance the quality of life of those who rely on the land resource. Land management does this by affecting three interrelated variables of land use: the relationship of land uses to one another, the relationship of intensive land use to open space, and the timing of development.[24] Without management of these variables to achieve the goal of wise land use, existing problems are perpetuated.

Issues Presented by Land Use Management

Implementation of a management program to reach the land use objectives discussed raises a variety of issues. Central to any discussion of adoption of land use management programs is the question of control. Who will make the decisions and what controls will affect the decision makers? If it is postulated that existing land use problems grow out of the present fragmentation of decision making, at what level should control be centralized? It is normally assumed that the government will play a central role in any management program, but what level of government should have the control? Should it remain at the local level as at present? Will the fragmentation of decision making be lessened? If central control is vested in state or national governments, will the problem be resolved or merely exacerbated by another layer of bureaucracy? How will citizen input be provided and what will be the nature of that input? Since ultimately it is the individual who either benefits or suffers from land use decisions, it is essential that he have a voice in such decisions.

Another series of issues centers around the questions of restrictions of land use. For what purposes, at what price, and by whom should land use be restricted to accomplish the objectives of society? There are competing uses for almost all land, and alternative uses may benefit or hurt different groups. If it is decided that land in the path of urban growth is to be retained for a greenbelt, who will pay the owner for the loss of his development rights? What agency will determine how much hazard is acceptable before building must be prohibited, and what responsibility do government agencies have to inform people of hazards in areas they occupy? The 1977 Utah State Legislature defeated an innocuous bill which would have required classifying land in seismic areas on the grounds it would result in disastrous decreases in property values in areas where developers proposed to build. Was this an abdication of their responsibility?

Related to the issue of restriction of land use is the question of the impact of management on housing. Will land use controls result in even higher costs for housing and push prices even further out of the reach of lower income families?[25] Additional controls on land use may delay construction and drive up costs which are passed on to the consumer. Restrictions on building on prime farmland, flood-plains, or other designated areas may not only increase construction costs, but may create a shortage of land for housing and add additional costs to housing. A corollary to the effect on housing is the effect on jobs. Would land use controls depress the important building industry and increase the unemployment rate?

Since taxation is one of the major existing controls affecting land use, is there a need to modify the tax structure to encourage better use of the land? Can the assessment of land be changed to encourage development of vacant lands within urban areas where services already exist, thus protecting farmland and greenbelts while minimizing the cost to society of providing services? What level and nature of preferential taxation is needed to allow farmers to withstand speculative pressure on lands in the paths of urban growth? If the farmer is taxed at the value of the land for residential use rather than at its value for cropping, he will be forced to allow development of his land. Tax reform is clearly needed, but the extent and nature of that reform is debatable.

Another group of issues affecting a land use policy centers around constitu-tional questions. How much control can be exercised over land use before the government has effectively abrogated the constitutional right to own land? At what point do controls effectively constitute "taking" of private land necessitating reimbursement to the owner?[26] What constitutes the appropriate level of public involvement in land use management and how should responsibility for decisions be allocated among different levels of government? Does the state have a right to dictate standards for control of land at the local level? If so, will this prevent the individual citizen from having the right to affect local land use decisions?

Although not a constitutional issue, a related problem is the question of private versus public objectives for land use. Private objectives are usually concerned only with a temporally and spatially restricted area. The public objective involves a larger view and may conflict with that of the private sector. How can such con-flicts be resolved and who will bear the costs involved? When costs of public action concerning land use are assessed to a specific individual or group but benefits are diffused over an entire region or community, how can the costs be paid? The resident of an urban area in New England may enjoy a drive through the farming area around his town, but his enjoyment does not benefit the farmer. When the farmland is transformed into suburbia, the urban resident has lost the benefit of the scenic countryside. If, however, the farmer is prevented from developing his land in order to maintain a greenbelt around the city for the residents' enjoy-ment, it is the farmer who is the loser. Who should bear the opportunity cost associated with retention of the greenbelt: farmer or resident?[27]

All of the issues discussed above are basically extensions of the fundamental questions of what, when, who, and where as they affect use of the land. The existing land use in America reflects the past decisions concerning these four questions. The decisions in turn are shaped by the attitudes, policies, and controls

affecting the land resource. Any change in these will have profound and fundamental impacts on the land itself. Attitudes toward the land are reflected in the
policies and controls governing land use, and changes in attitudes signal a change
in policies and, of necessity, controls. The underlying attitudes of public and
government determine land use, and these attitudes are deeply rooted in individual
and society. The attitudes were formed over several centuries of American experience; thus suggestions that they be changed may be met with strong resistance.
Development of a coherent, logical land use policy for America, however, requires
that the attitudes of Americans be changed from those which dominated frontier
America's optimistic assessment that a surplus of resources, including land, was
guaranteed by an all-knowing deity, to the sober recognition that we may be enter-
ing an era of scarcity with its concomitant responsibility to wisely husband our
limited and irreplaceable land resource.

THE AMERICAN ETHIC: PRIVATE OWNERSHIP

The fundamental attitude affecting American land use centers around the
right of the individual to own land. This attitude developed with the settlement
of North America by Europeans in the 15th and 16th centuries and represented
a remarkable break with the European experience the settlers had left behind.
In feudal Europe, the right to own land was restricted to the ruling classes, as
ownership of land was the basis of power, wealth, and position. The typical
European peasant was tied to a manorial system with little or no possibility of
ever being anything more than a tenant farmer. The concept of universal land
ownership was unheard of.[28] When settlement of the new world was begun, a
new set of circumstances developed. The land shortage of Europe was replaced
by a land surplus. As the Anglo settlers of Europe occupied this abundant land,
they did not recreate the feudal manor with its dependent serfs. In the new land,
the basic method of land division involved some form of individual, private ownership of land. Settlers were primarily attracted to the New World by the opportunity to acquire land, and there emerged the concept of freehold tenure.[29] The
importance of this means of land disposal cannot be overstated. Inherent in the
granting of land to individuals was the concept of universal private ownership
of land, and this was reinforced by adoption of a simple means of transferring
land by signing a deed or release executing a change in ownership. Concomitant
with ownership of the land were the rights to use that land in the manner desired
by the owner. Consequently, there emerged in America a system of land ownership
completely different from that in Europe, where the Lord of the Manor dictated
the use of the land. In America, each individual was his own "Lord and Master,"
and instead of a dependent peasantry there emerged the independent and in-
dividualistic yeoman farmer.[30] Owner and occupier of his own land, the yeoman
farmer was theoretically independent of outside influences, since he was able
to provide his own food and shelter from the land. Moreover, in order to occupy
the land, the yeoman was faced with the necessity of clearing the forests, building
his own how, and developing his own trails and roads.[31] In the process, the settler

developed traits of self-reliance and initiative. Central to his security and well-being was the land he owned, and the attitude of the settler was essentially that since it was his and he had wrested it from the wilderness, any attempts to dictate its use would be intolerable. This attitude (that the person holding the title to land had the inalienable right to use that land in whatever way he desired) became a central part of the American ethic and remains so today. Anti-government sentiment, opposition to land use controls, exclusionary zoning—all are at least partially the result of the widespread American belief in, and interpretation of, private control of land.

LAND USE CONTROLS IN COLONIAL AMERICA

The emergence of the dominant idea that the individual had a God-given right to own and control his own land occurred against the background of limited, but important land use controls. These controls varied from area to area in the New World and played an important role in both the development of attitudes and resultant land use patterns. Four general areas and types of land division can be recognized in colonial America:[32]

- The Spanish in the southwestern and southeastern United States.
- The French in the St. Lawrence and Mississippi Valleys.
- The New England Village.
- The plantations and dispersed farms of the east central and southern states.

The Spanish System

The Spanish system for occupying the New World included specific details on how land was to be distributed and required establishment of towns according to a specified plan. Details of the Spanish system were not published as *The Laws of the Indies* until 1572, but were in use immediately after Columbus' voyage of discovery. Based on the work of Roman writer Vitruvius (*Ten Books of Architecture*, 30 B.C.) which had been rediscovered by the Spanish in the 15th century, the Spanish plan focused on town morphology, land grants, and the mission system. Towns such as St. Augustine, Florida were established by the Spanish as colonial outposts. Guidelines required that the town focus on a central plaza with church, military garrison, and government buildings around it. The town was laid out on a rectangular grid basis, with provision for individual lots, common grazing area, and individual parcels of land.[33] Beyond the villages established by the Spanish, large tracts of land were given out in the *encomienda* system. The basic premise affecting the land use of these grants was that the individual granted an encomienda was charged with caring for, civilizing, and converting the native occupants of the grant. Thus the Spanish grantee primarily affected the land use by intensification of agricultural activities or relocation of the native inhabitants.[34] Other Spanish institutions affecting the land distribution included the mission and the presidio. The mission was a frontier institution in which the missionaries essentially took the place of the Spanish grantee and attempted to convert and civilize the Indian.[35] As such, they were rigidly controlled and guidelines were specific regarding how the land was to be used.[36] The presidio was a military garrison and often existed coincident with the mission since both represented Spanich response to fear of incursion of British, French, or Russians into the core area of Spanish settlement south of the present United States-Mexican border.[37]

The French Land System

The French used a land system in their North American possessions which was similar to the feudal system then in existence in France. Land was given out in large grants (*seigneuries*) to *seigneurs* who were responsible for ensuring settlement of the grant. The seigneur offered land to potential settlers and in return received small rents and other payments from them.[38] The primary impact on land use of the seigneurial system was associated with its provisions for land division. Individual settlers were granted strips of land extending inland from rivers which were the primary transport available. Concentrated along the St. Lawrence River and its major tributaries, these individual holdings (*routoures*) were usually 384 to 576 feet wide and had a depth averaging nearly one mile.[39] Later, subsequent divisions were made with a road as the focus of the long strips. In theory, this means of land division was cheap since only a starting point was necessary and then subsequent routures could be established by simple measurement along the river. A further advantage was that each routure included access to the river for water, transport, and fishing; pasture lands in the floodplain of the river; cropland on the higher level away from flooding; and forest land for furs, lumber, and fuel on the rugged land removed from the river. These so-called "long-lots" persist to the present in areas settled by the French along the St. Lawrence and Mississippi Rivers.

The New England Village

In the areas settled by the British in New England, land was originally granted as a "town" to a group of men who then distributed the land to those willing to establish a home in the "town" and to assist in its development. Although these New England villages differed from one another in specific details, the general pattern of land division was similar.[40] Within the boundary of the original town grant,[41] a village was established with a commons for grazing, and house lots large enough for house, garden, and outbuildings. Settlers were also given grants of plowland, meadowland, woodland, etc.[42] As the village became crowded, a group from the town would either obtain a portion of the original town grant as the site for a new village, or obtain a new grant from the colonial government and repeat the process. The resultant land use is distinctive in New England and consists of a nucleated village center surrounded by dispersed farmsteads. Land use controls were primarily designed to ensure that the land was actually settled and that the settlers would remain in a compact group. Controls on land use activities within the village proper focused on the necessity of preventing nuisance activities. Thus inns, ale houses, tanneries, and other activities which might affect the health and welfare of the community were at least partially regulated. The primary concern remained that of land division and occupance, however.[43]

Plantation and Farmstead: The East Central and Southern Colonies

South of New England, a variety of land division methods were employed in colonial America. These ranged from the unsuccessful Dutch attempt to recreate the manorial system in New York; to Virginia, and Maryland where land could not be bought during the 17th century but was granted by the government to individuals for meritorious service; to William Penn's plan to populate the country with sturdy yeoman farmers.[44] In each case, land use controls were initially attempted, but as European settlers arrived, their desire to own land often forced abandonment of the plan. Few Dutchmen were willing to become serfs when there was such an abundance of land and they quickly spread across the large grants instead of remaining in compact, manageable groups. Migrants from the Rhine River area of present Germany were interested in acquiring land; often incapable of paying even the relatively minor fees requested by the Pennsylvania colony, they simply settled where they desired. In Virginia and the Carolinas, new settlers were granted a warrant by the authorities which allowed the holder to settle a specified number of acres, and he simply occupied a likely piece of unoccupied land. Upon filing the description of the land, and if no one contested the property, he received title to it in fee simple.[45] The motivation of the settlers was land ownership, and planning and land use controls were incidental. The system which emerged in the middle and southern colonies became the model for the occupance of the balance of America, and is the source of the American ethic of individual ownership and administration of land.

Colonial Cities: Hearth of Land Use Planning

At the same time the land of eastern America was being divided into farms, towns developed throughout the occupied portion. In general, the planning which dictated the morphology of these communities can be described as nonspecific. The New England town, the villages of the central states, and the incipient centers of the south were characterized by winding streets, irregular lot sizes, and random accretions to the initial settlement.[46] There were notable exceptions to this generality, however, and these exceptions became the basis for urban planning in America.

Early planning attempts substituted a regular grid pattern for the irregular pattern. One of the earliest grid communities in the Anglo occupied area was New Haven, Connecticut established in 1748. The important aspects of the plan were its large streets, large, open blocks, and provision for open space.[47] The pattern used in New Haven was similar to that later used by William Penn in Philadelphia in 1783.[48]

Philadelphia is important because it is commonly accepted as the model upon which many other American towns were based. The original Penn plan was a regular, rectangular grid with streets 50 or 100 feet wide, a central square as the focus, and four additional squares preserved in each of the four quarters of the city.[49] Philadelphia's plan was copied with minor variations as settlement proceeded beyond the Applachians. Typically, towns based on Penn's model consisted of the regular geometric grid focusing on a single central square as in the towns of America's midwest. From a planning standpoint, the importance of Philadelphia is that it popularized the grid pattern which was then applied religiously even when topography made it less practical than other forms.[50]

Other colonial cities employed a grid pattern but incorporated circles, diagonals, or more open space to create important variants of the grid plan for land distribution. Noteworthy among these were the plan for Savannah, Georgia and Washington, D.C. Savannah was laid out by James Ogelthorpe in 1733 and is significant because the plan guided growth and development until 1856.[51] The important innovations in Ogelthrope's plan included division of the town into "neighborhoods" of 40 lots with provision for a public square in each. The plan for Washington by Pierre L'Enfant reflected European (particularly French) ideas of the period. The plan was completed in 1791 and consisted of a regular grid pattern over which was superimposed a system of diagonals, squares and radials.[52] Neither Washington nor Savannah was as important as models for subsequent settlements as Philadelphia seems to have been. Savannah was isolated from the main flow of westward migration, and Washington's plan was not as simple as Philadelphia's. Nevertheless, it is important to note the incipient planning in these and other towns of the colonial era, since it was in the towns and cities of America that today's major land use controls finally emerged.

As geographic features, the towns of colonial America never occupied as much as 1% of the occupied land, however, and the beginnings of planning in the colonial towns remained largely dormant after the Revolutionary War.

LAND USE CONTROLS AND FEDERAL GOVERNMENT: 1787–1934

The period following the Revolutionary War resulted in a change in focus in land use, as the government attempted to use and occupy the seemingly inexhaustible lands of the new nation. Four factors negatively affected planning for land use in American cities as expansion occurred in post-revolutionary America. Of prime importance among these was the Jeffersonian ethic, which viewed cities as unwholesome, unhealthy, and dehumanizing.[53] This anti-urban sentiment was widely shared, and with its corallary romanticism of individualism, effectively handicapped any attempts by urban governments to limit or control private land use.

Economic competition among the cities as each attempted to extend their hinterland at the expense of other towns also hindered land use planning. The emphasis of growth, and growth, came through expanded transport systems. Thus the attention and energies of the towns were directed outward in the century following the revolution as roads, canals, and railroads were designed to ensure growth.[54] As a result, control of land within the city was often secondary.

Cities faced another handicap as a result of the revolution. The new constitution which created the states from the colonies resulted in ultimate power over land use resting with state governments. Cities which had had complete authority over land under colonial grants were now limited in their control of actions of individuals with regard to their land.[55]

The final result of the revolution was perhaps the most significant in its effect on American land use. Following the war, the new federal government acquired the lands formerly claimed by the colonies as the new states reluctantly ceded their titled to the national government. Federal control of these lands and resultant acts affecting their disposition fostered speculation and the attitude that private ownership guaranteed omnipotent control of land use.

A Century of Land Distribution: 1787–1887

Demand for land was the motivating force that brought settlers to the New World, and speculation in land was rooted in the colonial era. Following the revolution, speculation increased since absolute control of the land now rested with the new nation's leaders. The first century following the Revolution was a period of cheap land, with controls primarily affecting how and at what price the land was to be distributed. Significant blocks of land were sold to groups of speculators by the new government, often under questionable circumstances.[56] The bulk of the land, however, was distributed to individuals or corporations under regulations which originated with the Ordinance of 1785. The Ordinance of 1785 divided the land into "townships" of 6 miles square which were subdivided into 36 sections of 640 acres. A minimum price of $1.00 per acre was imposed, but the land was to be sold at public auction, presumably in hope that actual prices would be higher. To allow the purchaser of "modest means" an opportunity to obtain land, the townships were auctioned alternately as whole townships and as individual sections. Initially, the government attempted to maintain some control over the land resource as it passed into private hands through reserving in each township four sections for the federal government, one school section, and parts of the mineral and forest resources. Only the school sections were successfully reserved, however.[57] Two critical features of the Ordinance of 1785 affected American attitudes toward land. The surveying system provided a simple means of identifying a parcel of land, and purchasers received title to a specified parcel rather than a subsequently located site. The system greatly facilitated speculation in land since deeds to the land could be easily exchanged. Speculators could now trade in land as easily as they could any commodity.

The century following enactment of the Ordinance of 1785 resulted in significant modification to the government system of land disposal. As many as 5,000 acts dealing with land disposal were ultimately passed by Congress. Only about 100 of these dealt with broad aspects of the public domain, with the balance affecting only small parcels.[58] Major changes affecting the disposal of land from 1785 to the Homestead Act are shown in Table 5.

Table 5. Major Acts Affecting Land Alienation

A. Ordinance of 1785
   1. Land divided into 6 miles square townships with 36 sectors of 640 acres each.
   2. Land to be sold at action.
   3. Alternate towhships to be sold intact at minimum of $1/acre and as sections of 640 acres for *cash*.
B. 1796
   1. Same except that minimum price was raised to $2/acre and half of purchase price could be deferred for one year.
C. 1800
   1. Amended land laws so that ½ section (320 acres) could be purchased.
   2. One-half of purchase price in cash, one-fourth due 2 years from date of sale, one-fourth due 4 years from date.
D. 1804
   1. Minimum lowered to 160 acres (¼ section).
E. 1820
   1. Minimum lowered to 80 acres (1/8 section).
   2. Minimum price lowered to $1.25/acre.
   3. Credit repealed, cash only.
F. 1832
   1. Minimum lowered to 40 acres. (Could obtain a farm for $50.)
G. 1841—Preemption Act. (Log-Cabin Bill)
   1. Granted to anyone who had settled on unsurveyed land the right to purchase the 160 acres he was on at the minimum price when it came up at auction.
H. 1862—Homestead Act.
   1. Any head of family or anyone over 21 could have 160 acres free by living on it and cultivating it for 5 years.

The dominant themes illustrated in Table 5 are the reduction in minimum size of parcels and the reduction in costs of acquiring a parcel of land. The north-eastern states viewed the nation's lands as a source of revenue for the government, but westerners and southerners desired cheap land for farms. It is evident that the South and West prevailed, since a farmer could purchase an 80-acre farm in 1820 for only $100.00. In 1862, of course, it became possible to obtain a farm for only the filing fee and 5 years of residence.

Subsequent to 1862, important acts affecting land use were passed which basically allowed larger homesteads to be obtained in arid regions and/or through special improvements. These included the Timber Culture Act, the Desert Entry Act, and similar measures. In addition, the important acts affecting grants to railroads must be mentioned. From 1850 to 1871, Congress granted land to states with the stipulation that it be used as grants to encourage construction of railroads. To facilitate a transcontinental railroad, Congress concurrently appropriated land directly to railroads willing to undertake construction. Acts of 1862 and 1864 resulted in millions of acres being transferred to the railroads as a subsidy for transcontinental construction (Fig. 2).[59]

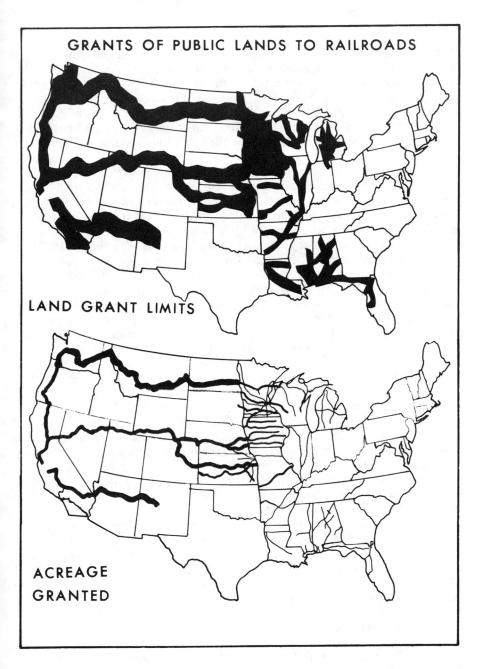

Fig. 2. Grants of public lands to railroads.

The Era of Reservation of Land

Concomitant with liberalized land laws was a movement into the marginal western lands. The Homestead Act was designed to foster occupation of the land by individuals for farming, but much of the land of the West was unsuited for traditional agriculture. The land was more valuable for timber or minerals, and fraudulent entries under the various land acts were common.[60] As early as 1875, the Commissioner of the Land Office stated that there was little land in the West which could be homesteaded and indicated the unlawfulness of many entries.[61]

The first of the acts of the government to reserve the public domain occurred in 1872 when the lands which later formed Yellowstone National Park were withdrawn because of their unique nature.[62] The major reservations of public land occurred after 1891 when an act repealing the Timber Culture Act included a section allowing the President to withdraw public forest lands from entry and establish forest reserves with the land.[63] Between 1891 and 1893, 16 forest reserves totaling 17,500,000 acres were created. Congressional action in 1897 provided for establishment and funding of a service to manage the national forest lands, and by the end of 1897 a total of 20 reserves with 38,897,840 acres had been created.[64] In 1905, administration of the forest reserves was transferred from the General Land Office to the Department of Agriculture and the Forest Service. This was accompanied by withdrawals of additional large acreages from the public domain. By the end of 1906, the Forest Service administered 106,999,138 acres of formerly public lands. During the Roosevelt administration of 1901 to 1909, a total of 141,267,530 acres were reserved as forest lands.[65] Subsequently, only minor additions have been made to forest service land through purchase or exchange.

Although acts associated with forest preserves reserved millions of acres of forest land, other millions of acres in the West without forest were also unsuited to homesteading. This land was arid to semi-arid and was used for grazing of sheep and cattle. Since it was public land, there was little incentive to adequately maintain it, and the western grazing lands became severely overgrazed. In spite of western opponents (who wanted the balance of the public domain to be granted to the states), the Taylor Grazing Act was passed in 1934 to withdraw the western grazing lands from homesteading. Signed into law on June 28, 1934, the bill authorized homesteading only on those areas which would subsequently be shown to be suitable for agriculture and required fees from grazers to be used in managing the lands. In November of 1934 and February of 1935, President Roosevelt used the provisions of the Taylor Grazing Act to withdraw all public land in the United States from homesteading until it could be classified in terms of grazing quality and suitability for homesteading.[66]

The Dawn of Planning in America

Roosevelt's action signalled an end to the era of cheap, surplus land which had hindered development of a national planning ethic. Reservations for forest and grazing purposes were public acknowledgement that land resource was limited and needed careful husbanding. Such an acknowledgement by the government, however, did not result in an immediate change in the attitude of the public. Land ownership was still viewed as synonymous with total control of use. The implementation of rational and uniform planning throughout the nation is a process which has not yet been accomplished.

The planning emphasis which we know today had its origin in the cities of pre-20th century America. The great migration to the new world of the 19th century which affected the homesteading of the public land also fostered urban growth. With little or no control over such growth and large numbers of poor migrants and laborers to house, living conditions for many of the poor were abominable, prompting concern by social reformers which led to the first effective planning acts focused on upgrading housing quality in low income neighborhoods. In New York city, incipient planning acts in 1879 restricted lot coverage from 90% to 85% and mandated a light shaft along the property line between tenement houses. In 1901, lot coverage was reduced to 70% and the light shaft enlarged or replaced by a central court.[67] The provisions of the 1901 Tenement House Act were adopted by other urbanized states and provided one basis for the concept that private land was subject to public restriction concerning use.[68]

During the 19th century, another important movement affecting land use emerged through the efforts of those interested in maintaining and developing parks and other open space to beautify cities and improve urban life. The first large urban park originated in 1853 when land for Central Park in New York city began to be acquired.[69] Under the direction of Frederick Law Olmsted, Central Park was developed into a nationally acclaimed centerpiece for New York city. It quickly became a model for other major cities and fostered the concept of municipal planning.[70] Parks were the outward manifestation of the incipient development of use controls in urban areas. The incipient planning emphasis was reinforced by the Chicago Fair of 1893. Intended as a celebration of the 400th anniversary of the discovery of America by Columbus, the exposition brought together the leading architects of the time to design the buildings for the Jackson Park site selected by Olmsted. Important elements of the plan were an emphasis on classical style structures, the formal nature of the street plan, emphasis on enclosed civic spaces, and statues and monuments. The Chicago Fair was the basis for an emergent planning emphasis which focused on city beautification as a solution to urban ills. This period of planning in America was embodied in classical civic structures, monuments, development of parkways and boulevards, and monumental architecture.[71] It was epitomized in Washington, D.C. where, in 1901, plans for development of the central city were developed with the Washington Monument and Mall as its focus. The widespread publicity associated with development of the plan for the nation's capital fostered adoption of similar planning activities for other cities and further reinforced the idea that planning need only focus on city beautification. With focus on civic centers, parks, and thoroughfares, the so-called City Beautiful Movement dominated concepts of planning in the early 20th century. Although sometimes viewed as a negative force because it ignored the real social ills of the time caused by uncontrolled land use, the City Beautiful Movement was an important precursor of later urban planning. The effect of a century of laissez-faire government control over land and attendant speculative fever effectively prevented rational planning for land use with its attendant impact on individual rights.

> The tendency . . . has been to promote those forms of civic improvement which can be carried out without interfering with vested interests. To improve severe sanitary conditions, to limit the height and density of dwellings, or to prevent the destruction of amenities on privately owned land, may all help to reduce the profits of the speculator . . . . But to purchase large public parks and to develop civic centers adds to the value of the privately owned land and buildings in the city . . . .[72]

This view, from an unnamed "English writer," succinctly points out why civic beautification was popular, while the housing acts of the large cities in the early decades of the 20th century which controlled density and height were bitterly contexted in court.

CONCLUSION

The three centuries between the first permanent settlement in present North America at Jamestown to the beginning of the 20th century are the background against which present day land use controls have developed. The early settlements of the eastern seaboard were the basis for occupation of the new land, a land where abundance obviated the need for planning for its use. The need to occupy the land, and the resultant agrarian economy, minimized problems associated with urban areas in Europe, further handicapping control of land use. A century of government attempts to dispose of the public domain exacerbated the tendency, and the American land ethic which emerged is a force which still affects efforts to implement innovative land use controls.

Following the changes which occurred when the best of the public domain was occupied and the government withdrew the remainder, the long transition to increased public interest in land use began. Industrialization and associated urbanization fostered the city beautiful movement, but also set in motion forces which fueled the movement toward control of land. The 20th century is the scene of this transition in which individual rights are balanced against the rights of society.

NOTES

[1]*Our Land and Water Resources* (Washington, D.C.: U.S. Department of Agriculture, Economic Research Service, Misc. Pub. 1290, 1974), p. 21.

[2]*Public Land Statistics, 1976*, U.S. Department of the Interior (Washington, D.C.: Government Printing Office, 1976).

[3]Ibid.

[4]*Our Land and Water Resources*, op. cit., p. 1.

[5]Ibid., p. 2.

[6]Ibid., pp. 2–3.

[7]Orville Krause and Dwight Han, *Perspective on Prime Lands*, U.S. Department of Agriculture (Washington, D.C.: Government Printing Office, 1975), p. 13.

[8]Ibid., p. 3.

[9]This trend is usually erroneously referred to as "land abandonment." The land is not abandoned, it is converted to woodland, pasture or second home development. Only the cropping is abandoned.

[10]*Conservation News* (National Wildlife Federation, Washington, D.C.), Vol. 43 (1978), No. 1, p. 3.

[11]*Our Land and Water Resources*, op. cit., pp. 7–9.

[12]Ibid.

[13]Krause and Han, op. cit., p. 17.

[14]*Our Land and Water Resources*, op. cit., p. 10.

[15]*Major Uses of Land in the United States* (Washington, D.C.: U.S. Department of Agriculture, Economic Research Service, Agricultural Economic Report No. 247), pp. 16–17.

[16]*Our Land and Water Resources*, op. cit., p. 11.

[17]Ibid., pp. 10–11.

[18]Raymond I. Diderikson, Allen R. Hildebaugh, and Keith O. Sihmude, *Potential Cropland Study*, Soil Conservation Service, Statistical Bulletin No. 578, 1977, p. 1.

[19]Ibid., pp. 10–11.

[20]Ibid.

[21]*State Open Space and Resource Conservation Programs for California*, California Legislature, Joint Committee on Open Space Lands, April 1972.

[22]*Environmental Quality, 1977. Eighth Annual Report of the Council on Environmental Quality* (Washington, D.C.: Government Printing Office, Dec. 1977), p. 80.

[23]"Planning the Second America," *Washington Post*, Nov. 20, 1971.

[24]See Elizabeth H. Haskell, "Land Use and the Environment: Public Policy Issues," *Environment Reporter*, Monograph No. 20, Bureau of National Affairs, Vol. 5, No. 28 (1974), p. 3.

[25]Marion Clawson, *Suburban Land Conversion in the United States: An Economic and Governmental Process* (Baltimore: John Hopkins Press, 1971), p. 320.

[26]Fred Bosselman et al., *The Taking Issue: An Analysis of the Constitutional Limits on Land Use Control*, Comment in *Environmental Quality*, July 1973.

[27]Haskell, op. cit., pp. 19–24. This is an excellent discussion of fundamental policy issues affecting land use decisions.

[28]Richard F. Babcock and Fred P. Bosselman, "Land Use Controls, History and Legal Status," in Randall W. Scott, editor, *Management and Control of Growth*, Vol. I, (Washington, D.C.: The Urban Land Institute, 1975), pp. 196–210. For a discussion of land division in Europe, see John Fraser Hart, *The Look of the Land* (Englewood Cliffs, N.J.: Prentice-Hall), pp. 25–44.

[29]Ibid. Freehold tenure is simply the legal term for individual, private ownership.

[30]Henry Nash Smith, *Virgin Land: The American West as Symbol and Myth* (New York: Vintage Books, 1950), pp. 153–156.

[31]Ibid., pp. 141, 152.

[32]This is a general differentiation which of necessity has simplified a much more complex system of land occupance. It is intended to provide only a broad overview of the regional differences in land use and land controls of the period.

[33]Hart, op. cit., p. 47.

[34]John F. Bannon, *Bolton and the Spanish Borderlands* (Norman: University of Oklahoma Press, 1964), p. 190.

[35]Ibid.

[36]R. Louis Gentilecore, "Missions and Mission Lands of Alta California," *Annals of the Association of American Geographers*, Vol. 51 (1961), pp. 46-72.

[37]Bannon, op. cit., pp. 32-64, discusses the defensive nature of Spain's settlements in what is now the United States.

[38]Richard Colebrook Harris, *The Seigneurial System in Early Canada: A Geographical Study* (Madison: University of Wisconsin Press, 1966).

[39]Ibid., pp. 166-167.

[40]Sumner Chilton Powell, *Puritan Village* (New York: Anchor Books, 1965).

[41]Hart, op. cit., p. 51. Town grants varied in size but approached a 6-mile-square size.

[42]Powell, op. cit., p. 113.

[43]John W. Reps, *The Making of Urban America* (Princeton, N.J.: Princeton University Press, 1965).

[44]Ray Allen Billington, *Westward Expansion: A History of the American Frontier*, 2nd ed. (New York: Macmillian, 1960), pp. 44-45, 68-69.

[45]Hart, op. cit., p. 54.

[46]Reps, op. cit., p. 128.

[47]Reps, op. cit., pp. 128-130.

[48]Reps, op. cit., p. 129. Reps suggests Penn may have modelled his plan on that of New Haven, but stresses that this is only a hypothesis.

[49]Albert Cook Meyers, editor, *Narratives of Early Pennsylvania, West New Jersey, and Delaware, 1630-1707* (New York: Charles Scribner and Sons, 1912), pp. 242-44.

[50]Reps, op. cit., pp. 172-174; Richard C. Wade, *The Urban Frontier* (Chicago: University of Chicago Press, 1964), p. 27.

[51]William I. Goodman, editor, *Principles and Practices of Urban Planning* (Washington, D.C.: International City Manager's Association, 1968), p. 9.

[52]Reps, op. cit., pp. 248-256.

[53]Henry Nash Smith, op. cit., p. 144.

[54]Wade, op. cit., pp. 187, 190-193; Goodman, op. cit., p. 13.

[55]Goodman, op. cit., p. 13.

[56]Malcolm J. Rohrbough, *The Land Office Business* (London: Oxford University Press, 1968), p. 11.

[57]Ibid., pp. 8-9.

[58]Clawson, op. cit., p. 23.

[59]Billings, pp. 643-645.

[60]Roy M. Robbins, *Our Landed Heritage: The Public Domain, 1776-1970* (Lincoln: University of Nebraska Press, 1976), pp. 236-254.

[61]Louise E. Poffer, *The Closing of the Public Domain* (Stanford: Stanford University Press, 1951), p. 9.

[62]Ibid., p. 15.

[63]Ibid.

[64]Ibid., p. 17.

[65]Ibid., p. 66.

[66]Ibid., pp. 220-224.

[67]Goodman, op. cit., pp. 16-17.

[68]Arthur Gallion and Simon Eisner, *The Urban Pattern*, 2nd ed. (Princeton, N.J.: D. Van Nostrand, 1963), pp. 67-69.

[69]Goodman, op. cit., p. 18.

[70]Reps, op. cit., pp. 336-339.

[71]Reps, op. cit., p. 502.

[72]John Nolen, *New Ideals in the Planning of Cities, Towns and Villages* (Boston: Marshall Jones Co., 1927), pp. 133-134.

Chapter 2

The Public Welfare: Implementation of Land Use Regulation

Introduction

The precursors of land use regulation were associated with efforts to regulate population density in city tenements in the late 19th and early 20th centuries. The social reformers who argued for such regulation maintained that the costs to society of crowded, unhealthful slums were sufficient to justify imposition of regulations which restricted landowners' use of the land. Implicit in such arguments is the recognition that an individual is free to pursue his own actions only insofar as they do not harm others. The need to protect the welfare of the public, however, faced intense opposition from speculators, developers, and other vested interests. The opposition of these interests is understandable, since they were the ones who had to bear the costs of regulations which tended to restrict the use of the land. The conflict between economic costs and benefits on one hand, and social costs and benefits on the other, remains a primary issue in land use regulation at the present time, and has fostered acrimony, debate, and court cases as America has attempted to resolve the issues surrounding public and private rights and needs.

PUBLIC NUISANCE

The earliest acts of cities which restricted certain uses of land were based on the concept of "nuisance" activities. Nearly all colonial towns had provisions affecting location of activities which might constitute such a nuisance. Annapolis,

Maryland, for example, established 20 lots east of the original city to be used by tradesmen, as a result of a 1695 law prohibiting certain types of land use:

> ... that when any baker, brewer, tailor, dyer, or any such tradesmen, that, by their practice of their trade, may any ways annoy, or disquiet the neighbors or inhabitants of the town, it shall and may be lawful for the commissioners and trustee .... to allot and appoint such tradesmen such part or parcel of land, out of the present town pasture, as .... shall seem meet and convenient for the exercise of such trade, a sufficient distance from the said town as may not be an annoyance thereto .... [1]

Odors from tanneries, slaughter houses, or from similar activities were obviously unpleasant and restriction of their location was accepted as a logical act of government. Extension of the concept of "nuisance" to include the problem associated with slums in the late 19th and early 20th centuries was a revolutionary change whose legality was not so obvious, however. The concept of nuisance as developed from English common law embodies major principles which limits its use as a tool for remedying problems associated with land use. It has been suggested that nuisance regulation is insufficient to control land use because: [2]

> – The nuisance must be a physical influence which arises on one property and crosses to other properties. This includes noise, odors, and physical dangers such as fires. This excludes from regulation many land use activities which have a dramatic impact on the community.
> – The right to regulate uses as nuisances is designed to protect property rights from invasion and as such it is unclear what protection is provided tenants who are not property owners.
> – Nuisance restrictions are absolute in that they prohibit a specific use, and when a court case results in a declaration of an activity as a nuisance, buildings and other capital investment may be lost. Consequently courts have traditionally ruled on individual cases rather than declaring additional classes of actions as nuisances. Thus, it is possible to prohibit nuisance activities only after they have been in existence and shown to be a nuisance.

These limitations make nuisance regulation inadequate as a general tool for land use control. In spite of the limitations caused by these characteristics, the concept of nuisance remains a form of land use regulation, but one which is today normally used only in specific cases.

ZONING: PRIMARY TOOL OF LAND USE REGULATION

In response to the pressures associated with urbanization,[3] American cities developed an alternative to the traditional common law nuisance doctrine. This alternative was initially based on the idea that the nuisance law could logically be extended to allow municipalities to use their police power to regulate all aspects of land use.[4] Police power is the inherent right of a municipality to govern the community in order to provide for the "health, safety, morals, or general welfare" of the community. Out of this extension of police power grew what sometimes has been described as the "tool" of land use regulation—zoning.

The first American zoning laws were developed in Washington, Los Angeles, and Boston and involved regulation of land use and/or size of buildings.[5] Height restrictions of 60, 90, and 130 feet were set for various structures of Washington, D.C. in 1899, to "protect the visual dominance of the capital."[6] Boston passed a similar ordinance in 1904, which was upheld in 1909 by the U.S. Supreme Court.[7] In 1909, Los Angeles zoned seven areas as industrial zones, with the balance of the community essentially zoned residential. But New York city has the distinction of having the first comprehensive zoning ordinance, created in 1916. The impetus for this zoning act came from retail garment merchants in the Fifth Avenue area. At the time, manufacturers of the garments maintained their sewing factories in "lofts" above the retail outlets to minimize transport costs. Retail merchants were concerned because when the laborers had a lunch break or went to and from work it not only created congestion in the streets but led to an undesirable mingling of the lower class workers with the shoppers. The solution seemed obvious, to limit the height of new buildings in the retail district along Fifth Avenue to 125 feet, which they felt would allow retail activity but would not provide cheap space for lofts.[8] The concerns of the Fifth Avenue Association ultimately led to creation of a commission which drafted the New York zoning ordinance of 1916, the first comprehensive zoning ordinance to be adopted by an American city.[9] New York's ordinance set specific requirements for land use districts, area or lot coverage, and height of buildings, all of which were subsequently held valid by the courts.

The concept of zoning to control land use within their boundaries immediately became popular in other American cities. By 1917, it was reported that because of New York's success, 20 additional cities or municipalities had either implemented, or were considering implementing, zoning of their land.[10] By 1922, one observer reported that "zoning has taken the country by storm" and that the existence of 20 enabling acts, 50 ordinances, and progress in developing 100 district zone plans was evidence of its growing popularity.[11]

Euclidian Zoning

Amid the rush to control land use activities by zoning there were some who questioned whether the new tool did not, in fact, deny constitutionally guaranteed rights to property. Local and state courts heard numerous cases challenging the new zoning laws, but not until 1926 did the Supreme Court of the United States rule on the question of the constitutionality of zoning. The Village of Euclid, Ohio was a suburb of Cleveland with less than 10,000 inhabitants when it passed a zoning ordinance in 1922. The ordinance divided the town into six land use districts, three classes of height districts, and four classes of area districts.[12] The Ambler Realty Company owned 68 acres which fell into three different districts, ranging from two-family to unlimited industrial activity. Since part of the property abutting on the main street (Euclid Avenue) was in the most restrictive zone, Ambler Realty felt that the value of the entire property, which was being held for speculative purposes, was diminished.[13] The realty company challenged the constitutionality of zoning on the ground that it violated the 14th Amendment to the Constitution, which protects against property being taken without due process of law. Ambler's contention that zoning was not legal was upheld by the trial court but was ultimately rejected by the Supreme Court in 1926. The Supreme Court ruled that communities have the power to pass and enforce laws and regulations designed to further the general welfare of the community as part of their police power, and that zoning was a logical part of that power.[14] Zoning, like the nuisance laws, attempted to protect property from adverse effect from neighbors. The Supreme Court decision resolved the question of validity of zoning and indicated that the "scope of the police power is elastic and capable of expansion to meet the complex needs of an urbanizing society."[15] This latter point has been the basis for increasingly restrictive controls on land use in the United States, but the former was the basis for wholehearted adoption of zoning in the country. By the end of 1927, 45 states had adopted some form of zoning laws, and by the end of 1930 47 states had granted authority to zone to municipalities. In the 48th, the existing state constitution granted home rule to larger cities, which was interpreted as granting them the right to zone.[16]

The basis for the power to zone in all but the one state was the various enabling acts passed by the state legislatures. Following the development of the Federal Government after 1776, power had been removed from individual cities and towns and vested in the new state and national governments. These powers were shared with the towns through state constitutions, statutes, and enabling acts.

The Standard Enabling Act for Zoning

The enabling acts which granted power to zone to communities were initially very similar. Almost all are based on the Standard State Enabling Act which was published by the U.S. Department of Commerce in 1926, prior to the Supreme Court's decision in the Ambler vs. Euclid decision. This act was adopted with minor modifications by the various states following the court's ruling, and its major aspects are indicated in the first three sections:[17]

> Section 1. Grant of Power. For the purposes of promoting health, safety, morals, or the general welfare of the community, the legislative body of cities and incorporated villages is hereby empowered to regulate and restrict the height, number of stories, and size of buildings and other structures, the percentage of lot that may be occupied, the size of yards, courts, and other open spaces, the density of population, and the location and use of buildings, structures, and land for trade, industry, residence, or other purposes.
>
> Section 2. Districts. For any or all of said purposes the local legislative body may divide the municipality into districts of such number, shape, and area as may be deemed best suited to carry out the purposes of this act; and within such districts it may regulate and restrict the erection, construction, reconstruction, alteration, repair, or use of buildings, structures, or land. All such regulations in one district may differ from those in other districts.
>
> Section 3. Purposes in View. Such regulations shall be made in accordance with a comprehensive plan and designed to lessen congestion in the streets; to

secure safety from fire, panic, and other dangers; to promote health and the general welfare; to provide adequate light and air; to prevent the overcrowding of land; to avoid undue concentration of population; to facilitate the adequate provision of transportation, water, sewerage, schools, parks, and other public requirements. Such regulation shall be made with reasonable consideration, among other things, to the character of the district and its peculiar suitability for particular uses, and with a view to conserving the value of buildings and encouraging the most appropriate use of land throughout such municipality.

The key element of the enabling act is, of course, the grant of power to cities to zone. In essence, the acts granted control over the height, bulk, and area of buildings constructed after enactment of zoning regulations. The purposes of these controls were to minimize the problems of congestion, including traffic congestion, fire hazard, loss of access to sunlight due to shading by tall buildings, and control of population density; to insure provision of urban services; and to promote the general welfare of the public.

Of primary interest in the enabling act legislation for the various states is the reiteration of the sections in the Standard Enabling Act requiring zoning regulations to be based on a comprehensive plan and granting of power to divide the city into districts with different uses and regulations. Based on a cursory examination of only these two aspects of the enabling act, it would appear that any community adopting a zoning ordinance would of necessity have a carefully thought ...ing districts reflect. In actuality, the zoning ordinances ...ommunities tended to consist of a map dividing the com- ...s without a comprehensive plan for land use, streets, sewers, ...other facets affected by such zoning. Although not necessarily ...omprehensive plan, the courts historically tended to rule that exis- ... of the zoning map was an indicator that comprehensive planning was being undertaken.

The language of enabling acts is general, and early zoning ordinances tended to be as general. Restrictions were primarily designed to protect residential areas from the incursion of incompatible uses. In practice, even the modest requirements of the early zoning acts have received numerous challenges in court. The consensus of opinions in such cases differs from state to state; but in general, for zoning ordinances to be upheld, they must meet the following minimum requirements.

- Zoning ordinances must meet requirements of the nation's constitution and must conform to the state enabling act.
- Zoning requirements must be uniform within a district and there must exist a reasonable basis for classifying a district as different from surrounding areas.
- Zoning should apply to the entire city, not to restricted parcels of land.
- Regulations must be reasonable when applied to an individual parcel of land and provide for a reasonable use of that property.

The problem with both the standard enabling acts and the short list above is interpretation. What constitutes a "reasonable use"? What is "adequate light and air'"? What constitutes "undue concentration of population"? What is the "most appropriate use of land"? It is in attempting to answer such questions that zoning regulations have encountered their greatest opposition. The regulations have reflected the particular viewpoint of the governing body in power when it was drawn up as modified by pressures from vested interests. As applied to the entire city, they may have been gratefully received by the public, but when such ordinances came into conflict with the individual's ingrained view of his private property they were often regarded as unfair or illegal interferences with individual freedom. This view of zoning has changed little even today. As one author noted, "The intriguing fact about the citizen as decision-maker in the area of such dominant social overtones is that the hoary political labels of 'conservative' and 'liberal' are meaningless when we talk about zoning."[18] Consequently, the near uniform adoption of zoning has not necessarily created rational planning. As commonly adopted, the dominant characteristic of zoning ordinances consisted (and usually still consists) of emphasis on use districts. These use districts normally are divided into residential, commercial, industrial, and special use categories in varying degrees of subdivision. On the surface, this seems a reasonable type of division since it separates suburban areas (with their children) from the dangers of the activities in the industrial zones. Similarly, by keeping commercial activities out of residential zones, traffic is minimized on suburban streets. In addition, by restricting types of uses, property values are maintained. If a neighborhood consists of middle income, single family houses, allowing construction of multi-family units within it could result in lowered property values. Therefore, zoning not only protects the safety of the community but contributes to the general welfare by maintaining property values and the associated tax base.

The difficulties presented by such zoning involves several factors. First, such use zones tend to create exclusive districts. If a use zone is categorized as single family residential, how can a neighborhood convenience store, which would actually benefit the inhabitants, be allowed? Exclusion of the store not only deprives the residents of a convenience, but minimizes the potential for variety in the urban landscape. Second, in practice the use zones of traditional zoning have primarily been used as a means to maintain the integrity of the middle income, single family residential district. Although maintenance of property values is a perfectly legitimate goal of planning, protection of the middle-class residential area from incursion of low income housing is discriminatory.

Zoning, which has historically been the most widely used method of control of land use in America, has also been the most severely criticized land use control. The problems associated with zoning discussed above have been the focus of this criticism. Books concerning faceless American suburbs are numerous, and many authors have decried the homogeneity of the city resulting from the exclusive nature of use districts.[19] Individuals have decried the restrictions placed on their property, maintaining that they constituted illegal "taking" of property rights without just compensation. This issue is still the subject of court cases, and points out the inherent conflict which develops when it is necessary to discriminate between the public welfare and individual rights.[20]

INDIVIDUAL AND SOCIETY: THE PROBLEM OF DEFINITION

The need to protect the public from adverse actions of individuals is obvious. Equally obvious is the need for municipal governments to provide certain services for the residents within their jurisdictions. Both of these impact on the individual's use of his land in a variety of ways. First, it is possible for governments and certain private organizations[21] to acquire use and possession of an individual's property through the power of eminent domain. Eminent domain is the right of specified agencies to take an individual's land for the benefit of society in general. The right of eminent domain rests with the state or officially delegated authorities on the local level. For instance, a new road may cut through a farmer's fields, and although he is unwilling to sell his property, the power of eminent domain allows the government or agency in question to acquire it in spite of his opposition. Eminent domain requires, however, that the landowner who has had his land taken through condemnation receives just compensation. As long as the purpose for acquiring the property through eminent domain is recognizably necessary for the benefit of the public, and the owner receives fair market value for his land, direct condemnation is usually accepted. Its use is relatively rare since it may place the municipality or other condemning party in the unenviable position of appearing as an adversary against its own citizens, whom it is supposed to serve.

More important (from the standpoint of the average landowner) than the potential of condemnation under powers of eminent domain is the impact of zoning regulations which do not take title to the land, nor pay the landowner for loss of value to the property, but restrict use of the property and thus affect its value. Justification for government control over land use which affects value lies in the need to promote the health, safety, morals, or general welfare of the society in question. Few would contest the necessity of restricting property owners from engaging in activities which cause distress to entire neighborhoods because of noise, odor, danger, or pollution. It is apparent a parcel of land in a residential area should not be used for heavy industrial activities, but what is less apparent is the extent to which that parcel can be regulated for the public good. Is it in the public good to prevent a widow from maintaining a commercial activity in a residential zone in the form of a seamstress operation? Suppose the residential land in question is located adjacent to a busy street and its value for residential use is thus diminished, but it has potential as a commercial site. Is it in the public good to insist that its use be restricted to residential purposes? Herein lies the fundamental problem involved in all land use controls. The owners of the property in question, if they sell their property, are being required to sell at a reduced value, thus sustaining a loss. The neighboring residents who desire to prevent commercial encroachment will have their property values maintained but will bear none of the direct cost involved in the action which maintained the value. Does the public good override the individual's right to use his/her property? Does the diminishment in value of the property in question constitute an illegal taking? Variations on this question are numerous, but they all pose the problem of:

Definition: What is the extent of land use restriction acceptable under the rubric of "public health, safety, morals or general welfare"?

Equalization: To what extent can zoning action reduce the value of my land without the result being confiscatory ("taking") in nature?

SOCIAL VERSUS INDIVIDUAL COSTS: THE EARLY PERIOD

Thes problems were early recognized, and in 1928 the Supreme Court decision in the Nectow case set the standard against which future questions were measured. In the Nectow case, the landowner challenged the zoning ordinance because it placed the westerly 100 feet of a 29,000 square foot industrial tract in a residential zone. The landowner challenged the zoning ordinance on the grounds that, as applied to this property, it effectively deprived him of any reasonable use and thus constituted an uncompensated "taking." The Supreme Court ruled in favor of the landowner because, as applied to his property, the ordinance failed to "promote the health, convenience, and general welfare of the part of the city affected."[22] Subsequently, the Supreme Court was not to hear zoning related questions per se until the 1970s, leaving the interpretation of social benefit versus individual rights to local zoning boards and local, state, and district courts. In general, the trend during the years since the ruling on Nectow has been toward acceptance of an ever broader interpretation of the "public good" with concomitant increase in municipal controls. Numerous examples of this general trend could be cited, but the following are indicative.

In 1938, an owner of vacant land on Linden Boulevard in Brooklyn, New York wanted to build a gasoline station. The area was in a transitional stage between historic agricultural practices and on the verge of development. Until 1928, the land had been zoned as "unrestricted," at which time it was changed to residential. The owner pointed out that there was no residential development along the street at that time and that a gasoline station would thus not affect the health, morals, safety, or general welfare of the people. The only justification for zoning the area residential would be in controlling future development. The owner maintained that it would be at least 10 years before such development would occur and in the interim he would be unable to sell his land for the residential use allowed in the zone, hence the zoning ordinance resulted in an illegal "taking" of his property. In addition, because of the presence of a city incinerator, open sewage discharge, and related activities in the vicinity, it was questionable whether the land would ever be suitable for residential use. The court ruled that the zoning ordinance deprived the owner of any productive use of his property and was not valid.[23] It is interesting to contrast this example with one from California in 1970.

Because of persistent filling of the marshes and tidelands around San Francisco Bay, public concern over the future of the Bay environment in the late 1960s led to the formation of the Bay Conservation and Development Commission (BCDC) to develop a plan for use of the Bay. After 3 years of intensive study, the plan for the Bay with its associated regulatory procedures became state law in 1969. Although the regulations were based on the need to maintain the environmental quality of the Bay, they also considered the need to prevent increased population congestion, minimize traffic, and maintain the general scenic attractiveness of the Bay for residents and tourists alike. A landowner who had tideland property which was partially submerged but unnavigable even at high tide desired to continue to fill his land to bring it above the water level. Although the application was only to fill the property, it would then presumably be used for construction purposes. In its unfilled state, the property, which cost the owner $40,000, was only usable if dredged to permit boating or other water related use. In the case of *Candlestick Properties v. BCDC*, the judge ruled that the owner could be restricted from filling the property. Although the potential value of the land was significantly reduced, the costs to society of allowing filling superceded the owner's right to do as he desired with his property. The court ruled that the value to the public of the existing San Francisco Bay justified the severe restrictions on the individual.[23]

A similar example of the increasing willingness of courts to interpret the concept of public good in a broader context (in the recent past) is exemplified in *Consolidated Rocks Products v. City of Los Angeles*. The landowner operated a rock quarry in a district which had numerous rest homes and sanitariums for asthma patients. A city ordinance prohibited further removal from the quarry because of the impact on the health of patients caused by the dust and noise of quarrying. It was shown that for all intents and purposes there was no viable use for the quarry land. Nevertheless, the California Supreme Court upheld the ordinance and prohibited quarrying operations.[24] Although the land use in question in this latter example was essentially a nuisance activity, it is indicative of the extent to which the California courts have been willing to restrict individual rights in order to benefit society. Other states have not necessarily interpreted the phrase "public health, safety, morals, or general welfare" in identical fashion, but generally it can be said that within the last decade there has been increasing regulation of land use without compensation to the owner, as the courts have seemed to conclude that there is a need for increasing government regulation.

The most obvious of these increasing regulations are those affecting environmental quality wherein the impact of changing land use has broad impact on society in general. Numerous examples of how increasing regulation occurs could be given, but the experience of Florida is representative.

PROFITING FROM THE SWAMP: SUBDIVISION DEVELOPMENT IN FLORIDA

The development of southern Florida into a retirement center and the subsequent subdivision of large expanses of swampland is illustrative of the conflict between private rights and public needs as well as the increasing restrictions being imposed on private developers. With acceptance of the concept of mandatory retirement in the United States, and associated development of social security and private retirement pensions after the Great Depression of the 1930s, large numbers of retirees were freed from requirements to live near a job. Such freedom

Table 6. Selected Large Developments in Florida

Name	County	Developer	Acreage	Residential units	Projected population	1974 population
Cape Coral	Lee	GAC Corp.	61,000	100,000	300,000	16,371
Golden Gate Estates	Collier	"	112,000[a]			-0-
River Ranch Acres	Osceola	"	49,356[a]			10
Remuda Ranch Grants	Collier	"	60,000[a]			
Poinciana	Osceola/Polk	"	47,300	70,000	250,000	-0-
Port Charlotte	Charlotte/Sarasota	General Development	100,840	190,677	500,000	28,500
Port LaBelle	Hendry/Glades	"	31,530	50,000	130,000	10
Port St. Lucie	St. Lucie	"	48,480	83,100	220,000	9,500
Port Malabar	Brevard	"	43,500	70,449	185,000	6,750
Deltona	Volusia	Deltona Corp.	17,500	36,000	109,400	10,866
Spring Hill	Hernando	"	16,400	34,500	100,000	4,600
Citrus Springs	Citrus	"	15,300	33,000	95,600	1,085
Sunny Hills	Washington	"	17,100	34,000	98,500	175
Marion Oaks	Marion		15,000	33,280	96,500	-0-
Royal Trails	Lake	Royal P.B. Colony Inc.	11,000	5,800	16,500	-0-
Coral Springs	Broward	Coral Ridge Properties	13,000	53,000	130,000	6,715
Rotunda West	Charlotte	Cavanaugh Comm. Corp.	26,000	65,688	164,000	520
Lehigh Acres	Lee	Lehigh Acres Dev. Inc.	60,000	28,500	80,000	4,394
Palm Coast	St. Johns/Flagler	IT&T	100,000	250,000	750,000	600
Compass Lake	Jackson	Compass Lake Dev. Corp.	12,000[a]			
			857,306	1,137,994	3,225,500	90,086

[a]Held in underdeveloped acreage in 1974.

Source: Luther J. Carter, *The Florida Experience.* Washington, D.C.: Resources for the Future, 1974, pp. 32–33. (Used by permission.)

of movement was recognized by developers after World War II and was the basis for the development of numerous second-home communities in Florida. These were new communities created in southern Florida, where the subtropical climate could be used to attract future retirees. Many of the subdivisions are located in environmentally sensitive marsh, swamp, and coastal wetlands and require dredging and drainage to be useable. Most of the land sold between 1950 and 1975 was sold sight unseen to out-of-state buyers. Some of the developments were on small lots suitable only for a single home, but most were sold as 1- to 5-acre parcels with the implication that the purchaser could subsequently resell a part. Profits were large, with one company reporting in its promotional literature that in the period of 1957-1961 alone they had sales of one-quarter billion dollars.[25] An indication of the scale of developments of 10,000 acres or more in Florida as of 1974 is shown in Table 6. The sheer impact on Florida's population alone, if all of the lots platted were to be developed, would be over 2.5 million people. It should be remembered also that the lots in the developments are in addition to those being developed in existing communities. But the problem of land development in Florida is not only of mounting population. The problem of Florida's growth is compounded by the fragile nature of its lands, many of which are affected by developments. The pressures from population have led to development in environments which are entirely unsuited for such development. The wetlands of Florida are of ecological and economic importance. They act as both water reservoirs and water purifiers. The surface movement of underground water from north to south in Florida allows dirt and pollutants to be filtered out. The water storage capacity and flood control benefits of Florida's wetlands are perhaps even more important as surface water runoff during wet periods is diffused over millions of acres of marshland causing no damage so long as the wetland is undamaged by man. During the dry season, the water in storage in the wetlands is essential for residential, commercial, and agricultural use.

Unfortunately, the development of lots in these areas causes irreparable damage to the wetland environment. Drainage canals have been constructed to lower the water level so that the land is above the water surface, but such drainage destroys the water storage role of the wetlands. Equally as important is the destruction of the wetland environment. A process known as dredging and filling is used in which hydraulic dredges suck up sediment from the bottom, and/or draglines scoop up the marsh, and deposit it in ridges to create an interfingering of canals and land. An estimated 60,000 acres, or 80%, of Florida's wetlands have already been lost to this process (Fig. 3). Where the land is covered with trees, as in the mangrove swamps, bulldozers and huge machines (known as tree crushers) flatten the trees into the mud in conjunction with the dredging operations. The destruction of the mangroves is particularly costly in shallow waters in the intertidal zone. Mangrove roots catch sediment and slowly build up the land. Additionally, the root zone is the home for shellfish and other young fish until they are large enough to move into the open gulf. Decaying mangrove leaves enrich the bottom sediments which serve as the diet for numerous organisms. The trees themselves serve as the rookeries for numerous species of birds.[26] As much as 20% of Florida's total estuarine environment (390,400 acres) has declined in productivity or has

Fig. 3. Building lots resulting from dredge and fill.

been destroyed. As much as 2 acres of wetlands can be destroyed for every acre that is actually dredged and filled. Between 1950 and 1973, 275 square miles of estuarine habitat were actually subjected to dredging and filling.[27]

The impact of dredging and filling on water availability and quality is equally alarming. The canals and water may stagnate because of law water velocity. In addition, pollutants are dumped into them in the form of municipal and industrial wastes, storm waters from residential areas, and pesticides from agricultural lands. The polluted canals in turn pollute the ground water of the aquifers through which they flow. Since most of the developments are in areas with shallow water tables, such pollution is a significant problem. It is compounded by the fact that many of the developments obtain their water supply from wells, and rely on septic tanks to dispose of wastes. The canals also affect the quality of water available, draining the rainwater off before it has a chance to infiltrate into the ground, causing water shortages in south Florida.

The epitome of these problems is found in the Golden Gate Estates development in the Big Cypress Swamp (Fig. 4). The Golden Gate Estates is a subdivision of 113,000 acres in the Big Cypress some 15 miles east of Naples, Florida. The property was divided into 1¼-, 2½-, or 5-acre parcels. Purchasers were assured by salesmen that these lots could be further subdivided.[28] The property was sold not as unimproved swamp, nor as improved subdivision, but as "semi-improved" land. The improvements consist of a grid of canals and roads crisscrossing a large

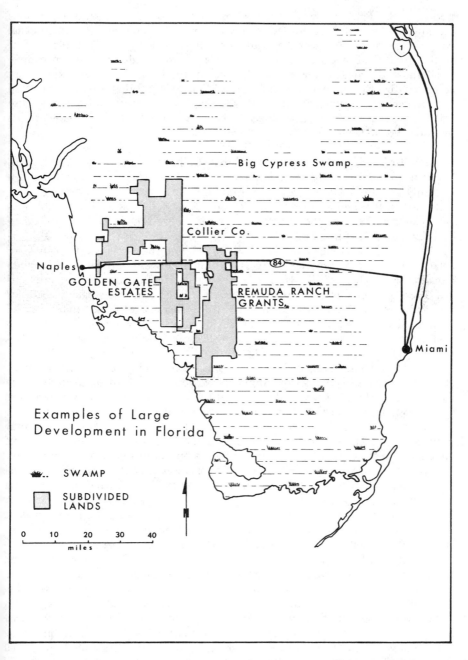

Fig. 4. Examples of large land developments in South Florida.

section of the Big Cypress. The canals were built according to county regulations and lowered the water table 6 feet below the ground level. The $26 million canal system, constructed to meet the regulations, drain enough water into the Gulf of Mexico from Golden Gate Estates to provide for the needs of 4 million people. In addition, the area of the swamp drained by the canals has dried out and has become a fire hazard. It has been predicted that by 1990 the development could become a barren wasteland.[29] Repairing the damage is almost impossible because tens of thousands of lots have already been sold to individuals scattered across the country who would have to agree to changes.

The Golden Gate Estates project affects not only the developed area, but much of the rest of the Big Cypress and west coast. Collier County, particularly Naples, has suffered from drought several times in the 1970s. The water table has fallen markedly and the county faces water shortages. In addition, the lowering water table makes the aquifer subject to the intrusion of sea water. This problem is particularly acute along the coast, and such towns as Naples are then forced to drill new well fields further inland.

The expense of subdividing the swamp did not end with the Golden Gate Estates. The development company (Gulf American) also offered the Remuda Ranch Grants scheme (Fig. 4). This consisted of 60,000 acres divided into 2½- and 5-acre parcels sold as unsurveyed "ranches." The purchasers paid $1,000 per acre and received rights to hunt and fish in the area, use of some limited "club" facilities, and assurances that the land lay in the path of progress.[29] Sales were stopped in 1969 after Gulf American merged with General Acceptance Corporation, but numerous parcels had already been sold.

The continuing division of the swamps and the increasing scale of development in other central areas of Florida ultimately led to development of greater government control. The Golden Gate Estates met Collier County's zoning requirements. Other developments in Florida met their local zoning and subdivision regulations. Too often, however, compliance with the regulations meant greater environmental damage. Construction of roads and canals in the Golden Gate Estates was much more harmful than the sales of unimproved swampland in Remuda Ranch Grants. As a result of the seeming inability of local ordinances to control the large developments, state action was ultimately taken to protect Florida's land and water. In 1972, the actions of concerned groups and individuals culminated in passage of Florida's Environmental Land and Water Act, which ostensibly allowed protection of critical areas within the state. Because of limitations on areal extent of lands so designated, and the need to act quickly to save the Big Cypress, in 1973 the Florida legislature passed the special Big Cypress Act. This allowed the state to use its powers of eminent domain to acquire critical lands in the Big Cypress and initiated land use regulations, and allowed the carbinet to act on both the proposed regulations and proposed boundaries at the same time.[30]

Implementation of the proposals for the Big Cypress met resistance from local residents who viewed state action as an unwarranted invasion of their property rights. Public resistance resulted in a reduction of the area designated as critical from 650,000 acres to 285,000 acres outside of the National Preserve. Land use restrictions were also reduced so that instead of restricting modification to a parcel, a maximum of 10% could be so modified.[31] Even with the reduction, the resultant control of Florida's Big Cypress represented a dramatic change and is indicative of the increasing expansion of the concept of public welfare. As will be discussed in a later chapter, the legislative package passed in Florida in 1972 has become the basis for controlling developments having regional impact. As such, it represents the ever increasing control exercised by governments over private lands and their use.

COMPREHENSIVE PLANNING

Where the original concept of zoning was simply an extension of the nuisance act designed to protect neighborhoods from incompatible activities, land use regulations, typically through zoning, now attempt to provide for the broader interests of society. Some states utilize state land use controls to insure that local zoning and other land use regulations in fact meet the needs not only of the individual community, but of the broader region. Most states still rely on local control of land use, however, with its associated plethora of governing agencies. Over 10,000 governments in the U.S. have zoning ordinances, and over 8,000 have some form of subdivision controls.[32] With such an enormous number of governing bodies, the extent to which resultant ordinances actually protect the needs of the public is questionable. Traditional Euclidian zoning has long been criticized because of its exclusive nature. In protecting a specific neighborhood from encroachment of noncompatible uses, zoning often prohibits low income families. Single family residential areas traditionally oppose entrance of higher density (i.e., lower cost) housing on the grounds that it will lower the value of the property in the neighborhood. Such discriminatory action has been accepted in the past by courts so long as communities based their zoning on a "comprehensive" plan which indicated the present land use of the city and provided a basis for its future development. The existence of such a comprehensive plan has been accepted as proof that in fact the zoning provides for all groups and is therefore not discriminatory.

> This fundamental conception of zoning has been present from its inception. The almost universal statutory requirement that zoning conform to a "well considered plan" or a "comprehensive plan" is a reflection of that view . . . . Without [a comprehensive plan], there can be no rational allocation of land use. It is the assurance that the public welfare is being served and that zoning does not become nothing more than just a Gallup poll . . . .[33]

The comprehensive plan is recognized by the courts as the justification for zoning. It is sometimes referred to as a general plan, or a master plan, but the latter term is misleading since it is often used to apply to only a portion of a comprehensive plan, as a "master street plan". The comprehensive plan should have the following characteristics:

> —It should be "comprehensive" in that it deals with all geographic areas of a community or region and all of the factors which affect its physical development.

—It should be "general." That is, it summarizes policies and proposals upon
which future development will be based but does not spell out detailed regulations or specific locations.

—It should be "long range" and deal with the problems and possibilities over a
10- to 30-year period rather than only current issues.[34]

It is important to reiterate that the comprehensive or general plan is not the
zoning ordinance. Rather, the zoning ordinance is based upon it. Traditionally,
the comprehensive plan has not been viewed as legally binding upon property
sinze the zoning ordinance interpretation of the comprehensive plan is the actual
regulatory device. This view of the comprehensive plan is changing. In Oregon,
for example, the case of *Baker v. City of Milwaukie*[36] resulted in a court decision
preventing zoning changes which result in more intense use of the land than was
projected in the comprehensive plan.[37] Similar rulings indicate the importance
of the general plan in shaping the development of community or region.

The comprehensive plan normally contains at least three major elements: the
land use plan, the circulation pattern, and projection of community facilities.
Preparation of such a document will require analysis of the following:

a. Present population, past trends in population, and projections of future
   population.
b. Analysis of the economic base of the community and projections of future
   developments.
c. Examination of existing public facilities and future needs for same (including
   schools, libraries, fire and police, etc.).
d. Analysis of existing categories of land use and demands for future types of
   land use.
e. Analysis of existing housing stock and future demands.
f. Examination of the existing and required transport and circulation system.
g. Analysis of existing utilities and projection of future needs and expansion.
h. Potential impact on the community of changes in land use (including both
   positive and negative social costs).

Comprehensive plans need not be restricted to the above items, but normally
at least these items will be included. In addition, each plan would include maps
(or sometimes drawings) showing the major elements of the plan. For example,
maps of present and future land use, housing quality, and road systems are normally included.

The basis for comprehensive planning of the type described above was the
Standard City Planning Enabling Act. Published in 1928 by the U.S. Department
of Commerce, it became a model for state enabling acts. Unfortunately, although
the 1928 Act emphasized comprehensive planning, its need was often overlooked
in the rush to adopt zoning ordinances after *Ambler v. Euclid*. Not until passage
of the Housing Act of 1954 by Congress did comprehensive planning begin to be
emphasized. The 1954 Act required each applicant for urban renewal funds to
have a workable program of redevelopment, including a comprehensive plan. The
great impetus for preparation of at least nominal "comprehensive plans" grew out
of the "701" program associated with the 1954 Act, since it provided matching
matching funds for comprehensive planning by local governments.[38] Since that

time, additional government programs related to open space, public housing, water quality, and other issues have required the use of, and conformance to, comprehensive plans.

Comprehensive planning has been undertaken by thousands of communities, and yet the resultant zoning has failed to adequately regulate land use. The Golden Gate Estates and similar developments are but the most flagrant example of poor land use actions in spite of planning and zoning. Some have maintained that the concept of comprehensive planning is nonattainable. The complexities of the interrelationships affecting modern urban centers are so great that it is impossible to effectively plan for all of its components. Although it is possible to make population projections, and to examine their effect on the economy, public services, and land use, such projections may be invalidated by future events. Changing attitudes and values on the part of the public may make even the underlying goals of the comprehensive plan obsolete.[39]

Such criticism of comprehensive planning should not be allowed to obscure its value. Even critics recognize that the following favorable results occur from the comprehensive planning process.

- Public debate can result in inputs into the planning process which allow adequate resolution of the fundamental priorities upon which a comprehensive plan rests.
- Data on potential impacts of alternative courses of action can be collected and made public, allowing the public to recognize the results associated with alternative futures.
- Analysis of public and private costs and benefits associated with plan alternates can lead to greater intergovernmental cooperation.
- It is possible that public recognition of the social costs of speculation, and other poor land use, may result in institutional changes. Such changes are necessary to prevent the immense private profits associated with land speculation a la the Florida experience from frustrating good planning practices.[40]

One of the major problems handicapping effective comprehensive planning is zoning. Zoning remains the primary tool of implementing the comprehensive plan, and yet some authors have pointed out that zoning may be inimical to comprehensive planning. Where the comprehensive plan requires long-range, general, value-based viewpoints, zoning requires immediate resolution of urgent demands related to specific sites. While the comprehensive plan attempts to evaluate the interrelationship of land uses to prevent unwarranted social costs, zoning is interested in specific parcels of property and may not consider the impact on the rest of the system of changing its use.[41]

Another criticism of comprehensive planning is that it is normally related only to one community. Consequently the plan may ignore regional needs and interests. A good example of this occurred in Washington Township, New Jersey. Washington Township is a small, single family residential community located in Bergen County, New Jersey, occupied by middle to upper income residents. Little commercial development and no industrial or multi-family residential uses existed in 1973. The zoning ordinance required 2-acre lots on a 30-acre parcel which a developer desired to use for multi-family units. Since only 100 acres were available for development in the community, it was questionable whether other land would become available for multi-family use. The issue was compounded by the fact that there were few moderately priced rental units in the region. In 1970, the region had 72,000 people and all of the communities restricted the construction of rental units. Of eight communities, five excluded all multi-family residences. Because of regional impacts, the courts ultimately forced Washington Township to rezone the 30 acres to allow construction of multi-family units as dense as 9 units per acre.[42] Such action is indicative of the increasing interest in regional needs as opposed to those of the community only.

CONCLUSION

Beginning with the nuisance controls of early colonial towns, American land has been subject to control to protect or further the general welfare of the public. Zoning became the dominant form of control in the early 20th century, but while zoning ostensibly benefited the public, that benefit was very uneven. In actuality, zoning became a means for maintaining middle and upper income neighborhoods at the expense of lower income families who are effectively zoned out by high land costs. Adoption of comprehensive plans did not improve the situation because of the multitude of individual governments doing such planning. The increasing recognition of regional interests in the comprehensive planning process is the beginning of a mandate for land use controls to supplement local zoning. The impetus for such change has come from numerous institutions. Some states have adopted state controls. Federal agencies have increased their support for, and encouragement of, planning which will further the interests of broader sectors of the public. Both actions represent the continuing evolution of American attitudes toward the land.

NOTES

[1] "An Act for Keeping Good Rules and Orders in the Port of Annapolis," as quoted in John W. Reps, *The Making of Urban America* (Princeton, N.J.: Princeton University Press, 1965), p. 106.

[2] Norman J. Williams, *The Structure of Urban Zoning* (New York: Buttenheim Publishing, 1966), pp. 11–12.

[3] See Seymour I. Toll, *Zoned American* (New York: Grossman Publishers, 1969) for a discussion of the attitudes of the time which affected development of zoning.

[4] Richard F. Babcock, *The Zoning Game* (Madison: University of Wisconsin Press, 1966), p. 4.

[5] Williams, op. cit., p. 60.

[6] Arnold W. Reitze, Jr., *Environmental Planning: Law of Land and Resources* (Washington, D.C.: North American International, 1974), p. 19.

[7] Charles M. Haar, 1st ed., *Land-Use Planning* (Boston: Little, Brown and Co., 1959), p. 148.

[8] S. J. Makielski, Jr., *The Politics of Zoning: The New York Experience* (New York: Columbia University Press, 1966), pp. 11–13.

[9] Richard C. Fordham, *Measurement of Urban Land Use* (Cambridge: University of Cambridge, 1974), p. 24.

[10] Haar, op. cit., p. 148.

[11] Ibid.

[12] Haar, op. cit., pp. 156–157.

[13] Richard F. Babcock and Fred P. Bosselman, "Land Use Controls, History and Legal Status," in Randall W. Scott, editor, *Management and Control of Growth*, Vol. I (Washington, D.C.: The Urban Land Institute, 1975), p. 199. The test of the court's decision can be found in Haar, op. cit., pp. 156–164.

[14] Haar, op. cit., p. 161.

[15] Babcock and Bosselman, op. cit., p. 197.

[16] Haar, op. cit., p. 165.

[17] U.S. Department of Commerce (1926), reprinted in Reitze, op. cit., p. 21.

[18] Babcock, op. cit., p. 20.

[19] Jane Jacobs, *The Death and Life of Great American Cities* (New York: Vintage Books, 1961). A classic on the need to have diversity of activity in the various areas of a city.

[20] Fred P. Bosselman, David Callies, and John Banta, *The Taking Issue: A Study of the Constitutional Limits*, in Randall W. Scott, editor, *Management and Control of Growth*, Vol. 1 (Washington, D.C.: The Urban Land Institute, 1975), pp. 256–274, discusses the concept of taking.

[21] Certain private universities, for example.

[22] *Nectow v. City of Cambridge*, as quoted in Babcock and Bosselman, op. cit., p. 198.

[23] *Alverne Bay Construction Co. v. Thatcher*, 278 N.Y. (1938). The entire case is quoted in Haar, op. cit., pp. 170–174.

[23] Frank Broadhead and Roselyn Rosenfield, *Open Space Zoning Handbook*, prepared for the Assembly Select Committee on Open Space Lands, California Legislature, April 1973, pp. 16, 39.

[24] Ibid., p. 39.

[25] Luther J. Carter, *The Florida Experience* (Washington, D.C.: Resources for the Future, 1974), p. 29.

[26] Leslie Allan, Beryle Kuder, and Sarah L. Oakes, *Subdivisions in Florida*, Vol. 2 of *Promised Lands* (New York: INFORM, Inc., 1977), p. 57.

[27] Ibid., p. 59.

[28] Carter, op. cit., pp. 232–240; Allan et al., op. cit., pp. 63–64.

[29] Allan et al., op. cit., p. 63.

[29] Carter, op. cit., pp. 247–248.

[30] Ibid., p. 248. At the same time the state was acting to protect the Big Cypress, the federal government was considering establishment of a Big Cypress National Preserve, a 570,000 one-tract tributary to the Everglade National Park.

[31] Ibid., pp. 249–254.

[32] Marion Clawson, *Suburban Land Conversion in the United States: An Economic and Governmental Process* (Baltimore: John Hopkins Press, 1971), p. 98.

[33] *Udall v. Haas*, 21 N.Y. 2d at 469, 235 N.E. 2d at 900 (1968) as quoted in Robert H. Welson, *Zoning and Property Rights* (Cambridge: Massachusetts Institute of Technology, 1977), p. 28.

[34] T. J. Kent, Jr., *The Urban General Plan* (San Francisco: Chandler Publishing Co., 1964).

[35] William I. Goodman, editor, *Principles and Practices of Urban Planning* (Washington: International City Manager's Association, 1968), p. 353.

[36] Milwaukie, Oregon is a suburb of Portland.

[37] Charles M. Haar, 3rd ed., *Land-Use Planning* (Boston: Little, Brown, and Co., 1976), p. 438.

[38]Goodman, op. cit.

[39]Lawrence W. Libby, "Comprehensive Land Use Planning and Other Myths," *Journal of Soil and Water Conservation* (May–June, 1974), pp. 106–108.

[40]Ibid., p. 108.

[41]Donald A. Woolfe, "Zoning Is Doing Planning in," *Practicing Planner* (June, 1976), pp. 10–13.

[42]Melvin R. Levin and Jerome G. Rose, "Suburban Land Use War: Skirmish in Washington Township," in Randall W. Scott, editor, *Management and Control of Growth*, Vol. I (Washington, D.C.: The Urban Land Institute, 1975), pp. 507–513.

Chapter 3

The Federal Government and Land Use

Introduction

Comprehensive planning for land use in cities received a great impetus from the federal government (as discussed in the previous chapter). Such encouragement of planning is only one of many ways in which the federal government affects land use in the United States. In general, the following categories of actions of the federal government can be recognized as affecting land use:

- Public spending as related to transportation and other public facilities.
- Direct land ownership and resultant control.
- Indirect control through programs which may encourage or require land use planning for recipients of federal funds.
- Direct regulatory control through national legislation.

Each of these categories has broad impact on the land resource of the United States. Such impact can be as specific as the decision to locate a post office, as broad as policies affecting building on flood plains throughout the nation, or as explicit as government regulation of land use on federal lands.

THE PUBLIC LANDS

The lands which are owned by the federal government are controlled by nearly 70 separate civilian and military agencies, commissions, corporations, and bureaus, including such diverse agencies as the International Boundary and Water Commission

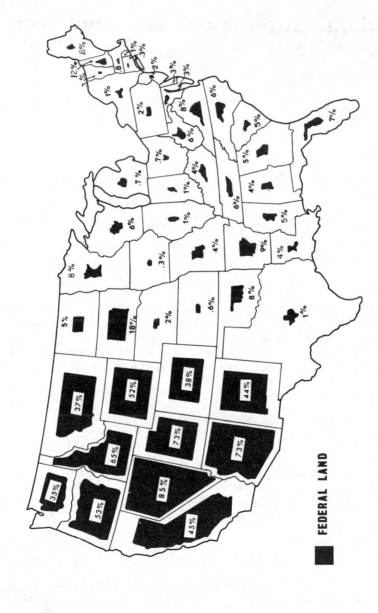

Federal Ownership as a Proportion of State Area

■ FEDERAL LAND

Fig. 5. Federal ownership as a proportion of state area.

48

(122,062 acres), the Bureau of Mines (13,082 acres), and the Training and Employment Service (1.5 acres).[1] The extent of federal ownership is highly variable, with the eastern states having the lowest percentage and western states the highest (Fig. 5). The extremes range from three-tenths of 1% of the state land in Connecticut to over 96% in Alaska. These lands came into federal control either as part of the federal domain which never left federal ownership, or as the result of subsequent acquisition for a variety of purposes.[2]

Relatively few agencies of the government control the majority of the federal lands. The most important of these agencies are:

Bureau of Land Management (BLM), Department of the Interior (470,174,318 acres)

Forest Service, Department of Agriculture (187,507,971 acres)

Various elements of the U.S. Department of Defense (30,760,867 acres)

Fish and Wildlife Service, U.S. Department of the Interior (30,281,190 acres)

National Park Service, U.S. Department of the Interior (25,084,750 acres)

Water and Power Resources Service (formerly Bureau of Reclamation), U.S. Department of the Interior (7,551,590 acres)

The control of land use in these federal lands is determined by the agencies, according to the mission (and interpretation of same) set for each agency by legislation. The Forest Service is charged with managing its land on the basis of a "multiple-use" concept. This policy is based on the Multiple Use–Sustained Yield Act of 1960.[3] The underlying goal of the multiple-use concept is to maintain the productivity of the land while insuring continual production of the renewable resources associated with the forests, including outdoor recreation, grazing, watershed, timber, and fish and wildlife. The 1974 Forest and Rangeland Renewable Resources Planning Act requires the Forest Service to prepare and implement long-term planning for the lands in their jurisdiction. The first of these plans covers the 1976 to 1980 period and is to be revised each decade. Land use regulation by the Forest Service has been the focus of criticism by a host of groups who use the land. Timber interests maintain that Forest Service policies lead to artifically high prices for timber and timber waste. Environmental groups argue that the Forest Service caters to the timber interests and pays inadequate attention to the other users of forest land. Western states and local governments are concerned about their watersheds in the national forests as well as the economic impact of Forest Service actions in managing the land.[4]

The Bureau of Land Management (BLM) administers the largest extent of public land. Lands which BLM manages are concentrated in the American West, with over 60% in Alaska alone. Most of the land administered by BLM was withdrawn from homesteading under the Taylor Grazing Act. The use of BLM lands has historically been oriented to grazing activities, but mining and outdoor recreation activities are also important uses. Controversy over use of BLM lands focuses on such issues as overgrazing, impact of strip-mining on the environment, and destruction of western environments by off-road vehicles. Criticism has been leveled against the BLM by stockmen because of restrictions on grazing, by conservation groups, due to overgrazing caused by grazing fees that are too low; by recreational users who are critical of restrictions on the use of the public land; by mining interests who are critical of leasing regulations; and by environmental groups who feel mining regulations are too lenient. The critical federal regulation affecting BLM administered lands is associated with the Federal Land Policy and Management Act of 1976 which requires land use planning for all BLM land. The planning is to include an inventory of public lands and their resource and other values upon which to base plans. Comprehensive plans must be developed for each grazing unit administered by the BLM. As of 1980, only a few have been completed, but BLM is in the process of preparing Environmental Impact statements, designating roadless areas, and evaluating the potential of areas under its jurisdiction. Such planning is threatened by the action of the 1978 Nevada legislature which declared that federal ownership of land within its borders was illegal. Other western states have followed suit, and as of 1980 the legal counsel of western states was challenging the federal government in court in efforts to resolve the issue. It is highly doubtful that the western states will gain control over federal lands in their states, but their action may result in greater state input into the planning for federal lands.

The Fish and Wildlife Service administers less than one-tenth as much land as the BLM. The primary land use is associated with the National Wildlife Refuge System which consists of more than 340 game refugees and national wildlife refugees as well as some 100 fish hatcheries.[5] The lands controlled by the Department of Defense are used for purposes associated with army, navy, and air force bases.

The National Park Service is primarily concerned with recreation land uses although not all of their 23 million acres are available for recreation uses. The Park Service recognizes three general categories of lands: recreation areas, historical areas, and natural areas. In practice, all of the national parks, monuments, recreation areas, seashores, scenic parkways, wildlife, and scenic rivers are used for recreation to a greater or lesser extent. Conflict over land use in areas under the jurisdiction of the National Park Service focuses on issues relating to type and intensity of recreation activity, maintenance of the quality of the natural environment, and provision of services on park land by private concessionaires.

The Water and Power Resources Service (formerly Bureau of Reclamation administers lands and waters associated with various reclamation projects. A significant portion of the 7.5 million acres under their administration is in reservoirs. For example, in Utah the Water and Power Resources Service controls 1.3 million acres, of which 161,390 acres are contained in the Lake Powell reservoir on the Colorado River which is 186 miles long. The land use of their land is primarily related to recreation, fish and wildlife, and water management.

Impact of Federal Ownership

In total, the federal government directly controls one-third of all land of the United States. Although this land is essentially an area of extensive uses, federal land use policies and actions are of significance to the entire populace of the nation. Some of the impact of federal actions is obvious. Decisions limiting visitors to popular parks such as Yellowstone or Yosemite have direct consequence on a potentially large segment of the public. Other decisions may affect only a limited segment of the public, as Forest Service policies concerning leasing of individual or group recreational sites on public lands.[6] Regulation of the national resources on public land potentially affects broad segments of the economy. Controversy over expansion of areas designated as wilderness in the Uintah and Rocky Mountains of the west and in Alaska involves the question of access for potential exploitation of petroleum and other minerals. Restriction on clear cutting of timber poses questions of costs of lumber and lumber related products for the entire public.

The list of impacts of land use actions on federal lands is long, but they can be categorized into three broad, nonexclusive categories:

> Type 1: Impacts on the entire nation.
> Type 2: Impacts on western states because of the interconnected nature of western environments which do not neatly fit the arbitrary land ownership pattern.
> Type 3: Impacts of a local nature related to quasi-land use controls which extend beyond jurisdictional boundaries.

All land use actions on federal land may involve components of each of these three, but generally such actions can be categorized on the basis of dominant impact. Actions affecting recreation use of federal land are perhaps the best example of type 1 effects. Although it can be argued that local residents often are the dominant recreational users on federal lands, the recreational opportunity provided by these lands is a national heritage and thus policies and practices affect all residents.

The effect of federal land use actions on western states such as Utah, Nevada, and Alaska is profound. Normally, the land under federal control is essential for continued use of that land which is in private control. The federal land is often the source of water for urban and agricultural uses, water which is critical for continued occupancy of the land. In addition to critical water needs, the agricultural economy of western states is partially tied to federal land use because of need for summer or winter grazing lands. In the arid and semi-arid west, with its limited biomass production, few ranches have the large expanses of land necessary to support their livestock operations. This is particularly true where the prevalent agriculture system consists of small irrigated farms which also maintain a few livestock, as in Utah and Idaho.[7] In addition, western economies are impacted by federal land use controls which affect recreation use and resource exploration and exploitation. Providing services for recreation users is often the dominant economic activity for towns near national monuments, parks, and historic sites. Additionally, the granting or refusal of permits to operate large developments, such as ski resorts, utilizing federal land can have significant repercussions in the local economy and society. Of particular concern to western states is the impact of federal land use regulations on the development of energy resources. Large deposits of coal located on BLM land, for example, are suitable for strip mining, and restrictions which affect their exploitation are viewed as handicapping economic growth in the west.[8]

In addition to the impacts of water and economic relations are those in which the controls on federal lands extend beyond its borders and directly restrict actions on private lands. An example of this is in the Grand Teton National Park area of Wyoming. As the park has expanded through time, it has surrounded "islands" of private land. Since the federal government has the power of eminent domain, it could force the owners of this property to sell. But rather than further alienate westerners who already resent the dominant role of the federal government in land ownership, the government allows owners to continue to use the land, though they are restricted from additional construction on their property. Such restrictions are greeted with hostility, and actions of local managers of federal land may increase tensions. In the case of the Tetons, one owner's cabin burned down and he was prevented from rebuilding. Teton National Park, although eager and willing to purchase the property, is cast in the role of villian and the case has been seized upon as an example of unwarranted harrassment of private landowners by federal agencies.

Federal land use controls which affect more than just a few parcels of private land is associated with the Sawtooth National Recreation Area in Idaho (Fig. 6). The Sawtooth Mountains are a scenic area of south central Idaho. They have been used for scattered mining, lumbering, and ranching activities but retain much of their pristine quality. Some 216,000 acres of the total 754,000 acres of the Recreation Area were originally designated as a wilderness area, but access to the Sawtooth is through a ranching area in the Sawtooth valley. There are 25,200 acres of private land in the valley in the form of scattered ranches, the rural communities of Salmon and Stanley, and several incipient second-home developments.[9] These latter were areas plotted into lots as small as 25 feet wide for trailers. In order to maintain the quality of the recreation experience in the Sawtooth, the management plan controls the use of all of the land in the valley. Existing homes in the summer-home subdivisions have been removed, the lots have been purchased, and Stanley has been designated as the community in which future homes and commercial activity will be permitted. Since it is assumed that visitors to the recreation area have pre-conceived notions of what a western ranching area should be like, guidelines have been issued which call for replacing barbwire fence with post and pole fences; use of "earthy" colors of brown, gray, and tan in buildings; removal of surplus equipment in ranch yards, and replacement of sheet metal roofs because they detract from the aesthetic quality of the pastoral ranch scene. The communities and counties involved are under mandate to prepare comprehensive plans, and appropriate zoning ordinances, to insure compliance with the Sawtooth plan.[10]

Antagonism to such direct federal regulation of private lands is shared by the private landowners, county governments, and local communities in the area. The legislation that established the Sawtooth National Recreation Area which allows a federal agency to impose quasi-zoning controls on private land is the exception, however. Normally, federal government affects land use on private lands indirectly.[11]

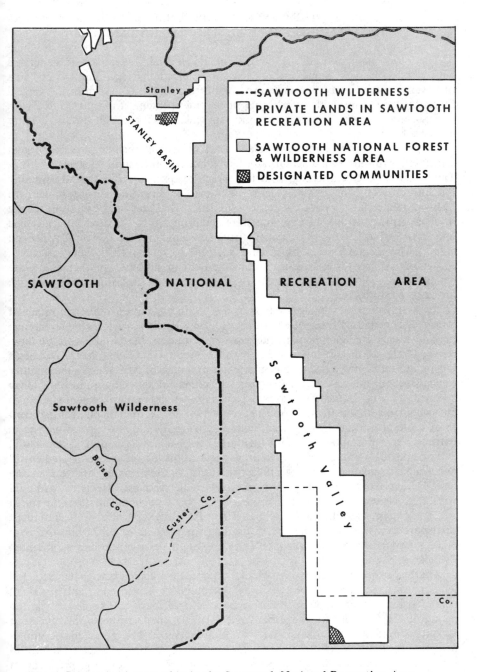

Fig. 6. Private land ownership in the Sawtooth National Recreation Area.

The following labels appear on the map:

Stanley

STANLEY BASIN

SAWTOOTH   NATIONAL   RECREATION   AREA

Sawtooth Wilderness

Sawtooth Valley

Boise Co.

Custer Co.

Co.

Legend:
- SAWTOOTH WILDERNESS
- PRIVATE LANDS IN SAWTOOTH RECREATION AREA
- SAWTOOTH NATIONAL FOREST & WILDERNESS AREA
- DESIGNATED COMMUNITIES

THE POWER OF THE PURSE:
THE EFFECT OF FEDERAL SPENDING ON LAND USE

The major indirect land use control of the federal government is associated with public spending. Some authors have maintained that spending by all levels of government is in fact the single most important land use control in the United States.[12] Among the indirect controls of federal spending, those associated with transportation, water and sewage, housing and urban renewal are particularly important.

One of the major examples of the impact of federal spending on land use is associated with the implementation of the Federal Interstate System in 1956. This began a process affecting land use which continues to the present. Initially, the impact of the interstate system was twofold: direct conversion of land to highway and indirect effect on contiguous land. The land used by the interstate itself is large, with one mile of interstate requiring up to 48 acres of land. The interstate and other transport system utilize 26 million acres of rural American land.[13] The second impact is on land adjacent to, or served by, the interstate. The interstate has fostered urban sprawl, growth of suburbs, and increased commercial and industrial development in the urban-rural transition zone through increased accessibility.

As a consequence of undesirable land use and other detrimental environmental impacts associated with the interstate, subsequent legislation has fostered planning of land use in conjunction with highway construction. Most important of these has been the National Environmental Policy Act (NEPA) of 1969. Control of federal aid for highways was one of the major programs of NEPA, and subsequently Environmental Impact statements were required for federally funded highway construction. In 1974, the Federal Highway Administration issued guidelines for such impact statements. "Any action that is likely to precipitate significant foreseeable alterations in land use; planned growth; development patterns; traffic patterns, transportation services; including public transportation; and natural and man-made resources . . . " requires preparation of an impact statement.[14] Such impact statements serve as an important part of the planning process affecting land use since they nominally provide data on the land use effects of road construction. Planning for land use is also affected by section 134 of the Federal Aid for Highways Act which requires that after July 1, 1965 the Secretary of Transportation was not to authorize funding for projects in urban areas of over 50,000 population unless "such projects are based on a continuing comprehensive planning process."[15]

Another major federal action which has affected land use is that associated with housing. Section 701 of the Housing Act of 1954 provided funds for small communities to prepare comprehensive plans in anticipation of some day participating in the federally funded urban renewal program. Over time, this has been expanded until no city was eligible for funds unless it had prepared a comprehensive plan upon which urban renewal was based. As the concept of urban renewal also expanded to include provision of low income housing, preservation of historic areas, as well as traditional slum clearance, such requirements have had a significant impact on urban land use.[16] The Department of Housing and Urban Development is presently authorized to fund up to two-thirds of the comprehensive planning process. Amendments of 1974 required that by August 22, 1977 all funded comprehensive plans include a land use element.[17]

THE NATIONAL ENVIRONMENTAL POLICY ACT

Another group of indirect land use controls exercised by the federal government is associated with the National Environmental Policy Act which was signed into law on January 1, 1970 (NEPA). The basic requirements of NEPA focus on the necessity of providing an Environmental Impact Statement (EIS) for any action of a federal agency whose actions significantly affect the quality of the human environment. Although initially directed at federal agencies, this mandate has been expanded to include not only action undertaken directly by the agencies, but also "federal decisions to approve, fund, or license activities which will be carried out by others."[18] The Environmental Protection Agency (EPA) was established to carry out the goals of the NEPA. The impact of the EPA on land use is not restricted to the boundaries of the project under consideration. The courts have rules that the information provided in an EIS must be such that rational decisions can be made by the public and local governments as well as by the agency involved.[19] The impact of NEPA on land use is diverse. Environmental impact statements are required for reclamation projects; activities of the Forest Service and BLM; licensing and siting of power plants; permits to dredge or fill anywhere within the waters of the United States, and similar actions.

AIR POLLUTION AND LAND USE

Another action growing out of the environmental concern of the late 1960s and early 70s in the United States is the Clean Air Act of 1970. The act required that standards of air quality be set for several major air pollutants. The significance of the act for land use is that it required states to develop programs for complying with the national air quality standards. As part of the process involved in encouraging states to reach the national standards, all regions of each state are to be designated as Class I, II, or III air quality, where I is least polluted and III is most polluted.[20] The impact on land use results from attempts to either raise the quality of the air or to prevent degradation of existing high quality air. Under the Clean Air Act, the EPA is required to review all proposed new construction which might lead to further degradation of air quality. Specific types of land uses which might affect air quality are regulated in accordance with the class of air affected. Thus, a 5,000 megawatt power plant might be allowed in Class III regions, but not in Class II. A 1000 megawatt power plant is acceptable in a Class II region, but not a Class I. Designation of air quality regions as I, II, or III will have a significant impact on the land uses which occur within them. The EPA by law designates all of a state's areas with air quality higher than the national standard as Class II air until the state develops it own regional designations and associated plan to upgrade its air quality.[21]

WATER POLLUTION AND LAND USE

Just as the Clean Air Act has important implications for land use, so the Federal Water Pollution Control Act Amendments of 1972 provided clauses of significant import to land use. The basic purpose of the 1972 amendments was to reduce water pollution by controlling point and non-point sources of pollution. Point sources include sources which are localized in space such as factories and sewage treatment plants, while non-point sources are those which tend to be random, such as storm waters and runoff from an agricultural area. The impact of the amendments on land use is broad since it affects a host of land use activities, but the most important portion of the 1972 amendments in terms of impact on land use is Section 208. Section 208 provides the means for developing the programs necessary to achieve the goal of having the best possible pollution control technology in operation by 1983. Section 208 requires control of point and non-point pollution sources through regulation, including land use regulation and management. To attain the goal of the 1972 water amendments, plans must be established for each area of a state to regulate land use, provide adequate sewage treatment, and control activities which affect pollution of water. Central to the requirements are the need for each state to have a continuing planning process, and the necessity of a state agency to oversee Section 208 planning since ultimately the state is responsible for all 208 planning within its boundaries. In terms of land use control, this is significant since it requires state agencies to assess existing state and local regulations to determine how well they provide for water management programs as well as establish what additional regulatory programs are needed.[22]

LAND USE AND THE COASTAL ZONE

The coastal areas of North America are among the most intensively used lands of the continent. Geographically, they provide advantageous locations for many of man's activities, including cities, industries, and recreation. The same geographic characteristics which make coastal locations useful to man also result in environments which are highly susceptible to degradation by those activities. To minimize damage to critical coastal locations useful to man also result in environments which are highly susceptible to degradation by those activities. To minimize damage to critical coastal environments, the Coastal Zone Management Act of 1972 (CZMA) was passed by Congress. The act makes federal funds available to states to help them prepare and impement comprehensive plans to control land use in the coastal zone.[23] The critical portions of the CZMA are Section 305, which provides two-thirds of the funds for the planning process, and Secion 306, which provides similar funding for the implementation of the plans. Participation of the states under the CZMA is voluntary, but all 34 states which have coastal zones (including those adjacent to the Great Lakes) have applied for funds.[24] As of 1979, 13 states had received approval for their plans, and an additional 7 anticipated approval by the end of the year.[25] Only two states seemed in danger of losing funding for lack of progress in planning for land use in the coastal zone. Illinois was denied further funding in 1979 because its legislation failed to pass the necessary legislation to establish a control zone management program in the state.[26] Texas has the seventh largest coastline in the U.S., but public opposition to the concept of strict regulation of the coastal zone through quasi-zoning regulations has handicapped efforts to develop a coastal zone management program and the state may lose funding by the end of 1979.[27] But even in these two states, federal funds from the CZMA have been used for planning purposes for the past 6 years.

The CZMA defines the coastal zone as the coastal waters (including the zone of transition zone between land and water occupied by marshes, tidal flats, beaches, and wetlands) and an indeterminate amount of the adjacent land. The inland limit of the coastal zone is defined as that necessary "to control shorelands, the users of which have a direct and significant impact on the coastal waters."[28] Planning for the area which is ultimately designated as the coastal zone in each state must include the following in order for the state to receive federal funding for the planning:

1. Identification of the coastal zone boundaries.
2. An inventory and designation of areas of particular concern.
3. Guidelines establishing priority of land use in particular areas.
4. A definition of what shall constitute permissible land and water uses within the coastal zone which have a direct and significant impact on the coastal waters.
5. An indentification of the means by which a state intends to control the land uses within the coastal zone.
6. The organizational structure that would implement the management program, including state, regional, and local aspects.[29]

Once a state has prepared a management plan, it must be approved by the National Oceanic and Atmospheric Administration, Office of Coastal Zone Management, which administers the CZMA.

Of central importance to land use controls are the provisions of the 1972 act which require control of land use in the coastal zone. The act provides for three alternative types of control, but all are indirect forms of federal control of land use. States may opt for direct state regulation of coastal lands, local regulation in accordance with state standards, or local regulation subject to state review. Whichever option of control the states select, the land use regulations must be administered according to the management plan approved by the Office of Coastal Zone Management (OCZM).

It is too early to critically assess the full impact of the CZMA of 1972 on land use, but the following general statements can be made. The act does not include any means of enforcing preparation of an acceptable management plan. The fact that all 34 eligible states are participating should not be construed as evidence of state control of land in the coastal zone in all. These states are receiving funds for the planning and implementation process, but should either plan or management program fail to meet OCZM standards the only thing OCZM can do is withhold future funding.

FEDERAL CONTROL OF THE FLOOD PLAIN

Floodplains, like coastal zones, are areas with geographic characteristics which have led to concentrations of man's activities. Accessibility provided by rivers, level land, and abundant water has contributed to development of cities, towns, and suburbs on the floodplain. Land use activities associated with urban and suburban use of the floodplain create problems when floods destroy life and property. Since the floodplain is a part of the dynamic system of a river it will flood inevitably, and historically, residents of such flood prone areas were unable to obtain any insurance to protect them against loss. When floods occurred, the federal government became responsible for providing millions of dollars in assistance to residents of the flooded areas in the form of aid to victims of a natural disaster. In response to the damages and associated costs of flooding, the government has funded massive flood control programs whose dams, levees, and assorted structural components were designed to protect against all but the worst floods. Unfortunately, the net effect of these structural solutions has resulted in the potential for even greater flood related damage and destruction. Construction of a dam has been viewed as a panacea for flooding, and the floodplains below dams have consequently received even more urban-related development. The illusion of permanent protection afforded by flood control structures, and associated development of floodplains, has meant increasing destruction and greater costs to the federal government. In response to increasing costs, Congress passed the National Flood Plain Insurance Program in 1968. This program provided flood insurance which was subsidized by the government and encouraged regulation of land use to minimize flood damage.

Since few flood-prone communities volunteered to participate in the program, Congress passed stronger regulation in the form of the Flood Disaster Protection Act of 1973. This act provides important regulations affecting land use in the floodplain. Specifically, it states that no federal assistance can be granted for the acquisition or construction of property in identified flood hazard zones after July 1, 1975 unless the community involved is participating in the National Flood Insurance Program. This action requires communities to adopt land use regulations for their floodplains which meet the federal criteria in order to participate in the program. In addition, the act requires that federal agencies which "supervise, approve, regulate, or insure banks, savings and loan institutions, or similar institutions" must prohibit loaning money on real estate in identified flood hazard zones unless they participate in the National Flood Insurance Program.[30]

The potential impact on land use regulation of such sanctions is evident. In essence, they prevent any bank or savings and loan institution from loaning money for construction in floodplains unless the community regulates the land use to prevent damage from floods. When fully implemented, the Flood Insurance Program will significantly affect land use in floodplains which are prone to flooding. It should be noted that the extent of the floodplain designated as flood-prone is that part subject to what is known as the "100 year flood." The "100 year flood" is a misnomer since it is actually simply a probability measurement, i.e., the area designated as flood prone is that area which lies below the water level which has a 1 in 100 chance of being equalled or exceeded in any given year.

OTHER FEDERAL REGULATIONS

A number of other programs of the federal government affect the American land. There are over 850 federal programs which provide some type of assistance or regulation for state and local governments, and over 130 of them have a direct impact on land use.[31] One of the more important is Section 404 of the 1972 Federal Water Pollution Control Act which charges the U.S. Army Corps of Engineers with the responsibility for controlling dredging and filling activities as they affect the waters of the United States. The act requires an impact statement before permits will be issued for such activities when they affect navigable waterways, freshwater wetlands adjacent to navigable rivers, and coastal wetlands affected by periodic flooding that are contiguous to navigable waterways.[32] As a result of court actions by environmental groups, the 1972 Act has been extended to all waters of the United States. In practice, this means the Corps of Engineers will regulate dredge and fill operations of all types except those associated with normal agricultural and silvicultural activities.[33] Thus the Corps becomes an important regulator of land use activities in wetlands and land adjacent to other water bodies.

Another important act which affects land use in certain areas is the Wild and Scenic Rivers Act of 1968. This originally designated all or portions of eight rivers and adjacent lands as part of a National Wild and Scenic Rivers System (Table 7). An additional 27 rivers were designated as possible additions to this system. Subsequently, 16 other rivers have been designated part of the system (including some of those originally considered for possible addition) and an additional 43 have been added to the potential list. The act provides for protection of the rivers and their immediate environments through funding acquisition of land along the system rivers, prevention of construction on the river, and guidelines for zoning regulations of communities along the designated rivers. The latter point specifies that zoning ordinances in communities along the rivers in the system must prohibit new commercial or industrial uses along the banks and protect the river bank lands through setback, acreage, and frontage requirements.[34]

The federal role is somewhat restricted in that the government is not allowed to purchase more than an average of 100 acres of land per mile of river. The federal government may not take land by eminent domain if 50% or more of the acreage along the river is privately owned, or in any existing town and city with zoning which protects the river. The federal government is authorized to purchase scenic

Table 7. Rivers of the National Wild and Scenic Rivers System

Name	Date
Clearwater, Middle Fork, Idaho	1968
Eleven Point, Missouri	1968
Feather, California	1968
Rio Grande, New Mexico	1968
Rogue, Oregon	1968
Saint Croix, Minnesota and Wisconsin	1968
Salmon, Middle Fork, Idaho	1968
Wolf, Wisconsin	1968
Lower Saint Croix, Minnesota	1972
Chattooga, North Carolina, South Carolina, and Georgia	1974
Rapid, Idaho	1975
Upper Middle Snake, Idaho and Oregon	1975
Allagash Wilderness Waterway, Maine	1970
Little Miami, Ohio	1973
Little Beaver, Ohio	1975
New River, North Carolina	1976
Middle Delaware, Pennsylvania and New Jersey	1978
Pere Marguette, Michigan	1978
Rio Grande, Texas	1978
North Fork American	1978
Upper Delaware, New York and Pennsylvania	1978
Missouri, South Dakota and Nebraska	1978
Skagit, Washington	1978
St. Joe, Idaho	1978

Source: American Rivers Conservation Council, July 1978, p. 1–5; Oct., 1978, p. 1–2.

easements, allowing them to regulate subdivision, removal of vegetation adjacent to the river, distance of new dwellings from the river, and industrial and commercial development.

It would be impossible to list all of the federal activities and agencies which have some impact on land use, but other important ones affecting restricted areas include the Bureau of Outdoor Recreation, The Wilderness Act, the National Scenic Trails Act, Regulations Governing Use of Off-Road Vehicles, and the Land and Water Conservation Fund Act. Of necessity, this listing is fragmentary, but it is indicative of the broad range of land use activities affected by various federal activities.

CONCLUSION

Taken together, the extent of federal control over land use in the United States is of fundamental importance. In general, these controls can be characterized as indirect. With the exception of lands actually owned and administered by federal agencies, the federal impact on land use is essentially carried out through programs which provide incentives to state and local governments to plan. Funds for water and air quality, protection of coastal zones, open space preservation, etc. encourage land use regulation but do not mandate compliance with federal guidelines unless the state or local units accept the funding. Because of the importance of such funding to local communities, however, the regulations upon which funding is contingent have a near universal impact in the United States.

The importance of the federal role in land use control continues to increase. As states proceed in the process of complying with the various provisions of the NEPA and associated acts, the impacts on land use are increasingly affecting each individual in the country. The logical conclusion of increasing control would be a national land use act of some type, but it is questionable whether such legislation will be proposed in the near future. There was great interest in such an act in the early 70s, but 1975 was the last year in which national land use legislation was actually proposed. With increasing resentment of federal government and federal regulation in the late 1970s, it is doubtful whether new legislation which is perceived to have such a broad societal impact as a national land use act can be passed. For the time being, therefore, the role of the federal government will probably continue to be indirect.

NOTES

[1] *Public Land Statistics, 1976* (Washington, D.C.: Government Printing Office, 1977), pp. 14–30.

[2] Elaine Moss, editor, *Land Use Controls in the United States* (New York: Dial Press for Natural Resources Defense Council, Inc., 1977), p. 225.

[3] U.S. Code, Vol. 16, Sec. 528–531.

[4] Daniel R. Barney, *The Last Stand* (New York: Grossman Publishers, 1974). Report on the National Forests prepared by the Ralph Nader Study Group. *The Last Stand* provides a detailed and critical analysis of the management practices of the Forest Service.

[5] Moss, op. cit., p. 229.

[6] Jon A. Kusler, *A Perspective on Flood Plain Regulation for Flood Plain Management* (Washington, D.C.: Department of the Army, 1974), pp. 12–21.

[7] Charles Peterson, *Look to the Mountains* (Provo, Utah: Brigham Young University Press, 1977) discusses the impact on small farms of increasingly restrictive land use controls on federal lands in Utah.

[8] *Environmental Quality, 1977*, Council on Environmental Quality (Washington, D.C.: Government Printing Office, 1977), pp. 23–24.

[9] "Sawtooth National Recreation Area," Hearings Before the Subcommittee on Parks and Recreation, 92nd Congress, S. 1407 and H.R. 6957 (Washington, D.C.: Government Printing Office, 1972), p. 16.

[10] Ibid.

[11] "Federal Land Planning: The Indirect Approach." (Washington, D.C.: Resources for the Future, 1976), pp. 17–18.

[12] Marion Clawson and Burnell Held, *The Federal Lands: Their Use and Management* (Lincoln: University of Nebraska Press, 1957), p. 34.

[13] *Environmental Quality: 1974*, Council on Environmental Quality (Washington, D.C.: Government Printing Office, 1974), p. 39.

[14] Moss, op. cit., p. 177.

[15] Ibid., p. 184.

[16] William I. Goodman and Eric C. Freund, *Principles and Practices of Urban Planning* (Washington, D.C.: International City Manager's Association, 1968), pp. 485–506.

[17] Moss, op. cit.

[18] Ibid., p. 19.

[19] *Guidelines for Air Quality Maintenance Planning and Analysis*, Environmental Protection Agency (Research Triangle Park, N.C.: Office of Air Quality Planning and Standards, 1974–1975), 13 volumes, Vol. 1, *Designation of Air Quality Maintenance Areas*.

[20] Moss, op. cit., p. 58.

[21] Ibid., pp. 71–75.

[22] U.S. Code, Vol. 16, Sec. 1451.

[23] Bradley E. Spicer, De Witt H. Braud, and John M. Bordolon, "States Interest in Land Use," in *Land Use: Tough Choices in Today's World* (Ankeny, Iowa: Soil Conservation Society of America, 1977), p. 409.

[24] U.S. Code, Vol. 16, Sec. 1453 (a).

[25] Moss, op. cit., pp. 101–102; Spicer et al., op. cit., p. 410.

[26] *The Christian Science Monitor*, March 2, 1979, p. 6.

[27] *Planning*, April 1979, p. 9.

[28] *The Christian Science Monitor*, op. cit.

[29] Moss, op. cit., pp. 121–122.

[30] Spicer et al., op. cit., p. 406. A good overview of federal actions affecting land use can be obtained by reading Elaine Moss, editor, *Land Use Controls in the United States* (New York: Dial Press for Natural Resources Defenses Council, 1977); Arnold W. Reitze, Jr. *Environmental Planning: Law of Land and Resources* (Washington, D.C.: North American International, 1974), and Mary Robinson Swe, editor, *Environmental Legislation* (New York: Praeger Publishers, 1976).

[31] Spicer et al., op. cit., pp. 408–409.

[32] Moss, op. cit., p. 86.

[33] *Flowing Free: A Citizen's Guide for Protecting Wild and Scenic Rivers* (Washington, D.C.: The River Conservation Fund, 1977), pp. 64–76 for the entire act.

[34] Ibid., pp. 10–12.

Chapter 4

The Development of State Land Use Controls

Introduction

The increasing role of the federal government in control of land use in the United States is but one manifestation of the changing attitudes towards control of private property. A corollary to the growth of federal input into land use control has been the increase in state land use control related programs and regulations. The extent and nature of land use control at the state level varies, but in general it has tended to be advisory rather than regulatory. All states have regulations, at either state or municipal levels, which provide for zoning regulation. All states have some form of state agency or agencies, program, or regulations dealing with some types of land use activity, many of which have been in existence for decades. The major problem with state land use controls is their fragmented nature and incomplete or overlapping territorial jurisdiction.[1] For example, in California at least 17 separate state agencies or institutions are involved in land use management. These include such disparate groups as the Department of Transportation, the Department of Fish and Game, the State Energy Resources Conservation and Development Commission, and the Public Utilities Commission.[2] As a result of the fragmentation of functions, land use regulation in most states has been carried on at several levels with little coordination between the various agencies or levels of government involved. Few states have a coordinated, comprehensive state land use planning process. The fragmentation of control coupled with the varying degree of regulation resulted in movements in several states in the 1960s and 1970s to expand the state role through either direct regulation of land use by one energy, or regulations of specified types of activities at the state level.

The factors which have caused states to more actively enter into control of land use are similar to those which have prompted federal action affecting land use. It has been suggested that there is a need for the state to intervene in land use decisions in four distinct areas:[3]

(1) When there are problems that cross the boundaries of existing levels of jurisdictions and do not confine themselves neatly to municipal or county entities.
(2) Where there are problems created from the actions of a local body which may result in a negative impact on the interest of the broader public.
(3) When there are lands which have limited local controls that do not effectively protect the land resource of the state.
(4) Problems or conflicts involving implementation of state policies or fund.

Examples of instances when each of these needs for state intervention are required are numerous. In western United States, for example, there is at the present a tremendous increase in exploitation of mineral resources, especially those related to energy. Construction of large power plants with associated mining activity rarely is concentrated in a single town or city. The effect on a community which becomes the bedroom community for coal miners when the coal mines and power plant are outside of the city boundaries is catastrophic. Small towns in southeastern Utah have seen their populations quadruple in a period of years, and yet there has been no effective mechanism to allow the communities impacted by the increased population to benefit from the taxes generated by the power plants and mining activities. In such an instance, the need for state action is obvious.

Using the same example, it is possible to see how the needs and interests of the local Utah residents can result in actions which negatively affect not only the rest of the state, but of the nation. Southeastern Utah was the initial proposed site of a multi-thousand megawatt power plant (the Intermountain Power Project). Local citizens favored the project since it would bring jobs and population migration to an area which had experienced economic stagnation and population decline for the previous half century. The impact of the power plant, however, would have resulted in degradation of air quality in a number of national parks and monuments. In this instance, federal regulation of air quality prohibited construction of the plant, but the need for state regulation remains, since a new site has been proposed farther to the west in the deserts of western Utah. The present site at Lyndell, Utah is in a rural area with extremely sparse population (the biggest city has less than 4,000 population); it is removed from federal jurisdiction, but will have an adverse effect on the already densely populated and pollution-plagued Wasatch front. Again the rural residents affected are in favor of the plant, but there is no mechanism to protect the interests of the state beyond the boundaries of the project area.

In similar fashion, since the proposed power plant is to be developed in a rural area, which historically has had no growth problems, it is occurring in an area without effective controls. In February of 1979, the county affected by the Intermountain Power Project, Millard County, hired its first planner.

The final type of issue justifying state action in land use is obvious. When state policies are not necessarily perceived as in the best interest of local communities, there is little incentive for such communities to implement them. Thus the need for state control.

The issues which could conceivably foster development of a state land use control act are not new. These same issues have existed since the beginning of the States, but the past decade has resulted in forces which have strengthened the need for state intervention in land use. Urban sprawl with its attendant impact on agricultural land has accentuated the problems caused by the conflict of interests between local jurisdiction and regional or state interests. Costs associated with providing transportation, roads, schools, police protection, and the other hosts of services demanded by urban dwellers are not always fully provided by the local community. Furthermore, problems of congestion, crime, and other undesirable consequences of expanded urbanization may impact the entire state.

The rising interest in the environment during tha past decade has further focused the need for state controls. Increased urbanization, industrialization, and unplanned development has resulted in severe degradation of the environment. Consequently, there has been a demand for controls which would effectively prevent further environmental degradation associated with growth. Since it is the areas which have already urbanized that most commonly recognize the need for environmental protection, while the rural areas which have been the scene of economic depression or stagnation view growth and industrial development favorably, a regional conflict develops when those in the urban white collar sector demand state controls to prevent degradation of the pristine rural areas.[4]

Concern for the loss of the prime agricultural land of the United States has emerged as one of the major issues affecting the interests of the entire state. States which have enacted land use regulation have normally made preservation of their agricultural lands one of the central issues of their legislation. Urban sprawl, with its attendant wasteful and seemingly insatiable demand for land, has fostered an increasing awareness of the need to protect the prime agricultural lands which remain. Coupled with this concern for the prime agricultural lands is the recognition that certain areas are of unique or irreplacable character and must be protected against actions which would cause their loss to the broader public. Central to this issue is the question of public versus private rights. Some state legislation is based on the argument that certain unique lands are a state or national heritage and their development and use is of concern to a broader group than the owners or local jurisdiction.

Taken together, the interest in urban sprawl, environmental problems, prime agricultural lands, and unique settings has greatly affected demands for state regulation. These issues are compounded when a state is faced with rapid development and growth, particularly if that development and growth benefit a local community to the detriment of the entire state. For example, the development of condominiums along California's coastline effectively prevents the broader public from access to the beach, and thus becomes a state-wide concern.

All of these issues have affected the demand for state regulation of land in the United States. As of 1978, less than one-fourth of the states had comprehensive land use acts. Those that do have comprehensive acts may include direct regulation of land use, or they may be restricted to the identification of those areas or uses which are of more than local concern (Table 8). Although they represent a minority of the states, those which have adopted state land use acts are significant because they are indicative of the development of a sentiment which favors land use controls at the state level.[5]

The emergence of state-wide land use acts has been referred to as the "Quiet Revolution."[6] This revolution involves realization that the traditional land use regulation in the United States, zoning, has serious weaknesses. Although the right to zone is normally based on state-enabling acts, zoning has developed as a local regulatory device. The thousands of local jurisdictions in the United States each engage in zoning which will benefit themselves. Problems of state-wide concern have not been adequately resolved by traditional zoning and, consequently, states have been forced to reexamine land use regulation.

Many states have adopted legislation in the 1970s designed to allow greater state participation in the planning process. The legislation varies, but in all cases local communities retain an important role in planning.[7] The purposes of state legislation is generally to provide regulation in areas previously excluded from local zoning; to encourage more comprehensive planning through formulation of land use policies, and guidelines; or to provide economic support for planning activities. Analysis of the land use regulations adopted by several states is indicative of the broad array of types of land use legislation presently being adopted.

Table 8. Land Use Activities Regulated by State Permit

Type of activity	Number of states
Waste disposal	44
Waterways, wetlands, floodplain, coastal zone, or submerged land	36
Fresh water use	35
Mining	32
Air quality control	29
Water quality	24
Energy plant/transmission lines	23
Transportation	21
Other	35

Source: Richard A. Mann and Mike Miles, "State Land Use Planning: The Current Status and Demographic Rationale," *Journal of the American Planning Association*, Vol. 45 (1979), (pages 48–61 inclusive).

HAWAII AND THE QUIET REVOLUTION

The first state in the United States to create a state land use act was Hawaii. Hawaii's state land use control program was implemented in 1961 and remains the strongest in the United States insofar as asserting direct state implementation and review over local government actions.[8] The factors which led to the development of a state land use control program in Hawaii are illustrative of both the forces affecting the adoption of land use controls in other states and the unique geographical nature of Hawaii. The state of Hawaii consists of 122 islands in the Pacific, with the bulk of the population concentrated on the southeastern margin of the island chain in four major islands. Eighty percent of the population of Hawaii resides on the island of Oahu on only 9% of the land of the state.[9] This concentration of population on Oahu has existed for decades and was considered in the years after World War II as Hawaii prepared for statehood.

The unique geographical situation facing Hawaii, which partially prompted the development of a state land use plan act, are related to its island nature and climate. Because of the temperate climate, Hawaii had developed an industry based on production of plantation crops of sugar cane, pineapple, and pine. Relatively little of the land on the islands of Hawaii is suitable for either farming or building, and thus the uses of land for agriculture and residential came into conflict. More than half of Oahu is too steep for residential land use, and since the best farmland is also the easiest to build upon, there emerged a desire to protect the farmlands of Hawaii.[10] Consequently, when Hawaii had its first state legislature, it passed Act 187 of 1961 which became known as the State Land Use Law. The major feature of the act was establishment of a Land Use Commission (LUC), appointed by the governor and charged with the responsibility of classifying all lands in Hawaii into three districts: conservation, urban, and agriculture. (Later a fourth category, rural, was added to the districts.) The act required that after the land had been classified into a specific category, any change in classification must be made by the state LUC.[11]

In essence, the Hawaii plan became a de facto state zoning ordinance since classification of land was by the state, and any changes in classification could come only through the approval of the state land use commissions. The significance of this act was not initially recognized by the people of Hawaii in their enthusiasm about statehood. Not until the pressures of growth became such that subdivision of the plantation lands with subsequent development of resorts or subdivision homes became highly profitable did any real pressure develop against the land use act. In the late 1960s and 1970s, however, there was great pressure to make changes from agricultural and conservation lands to development categories as a result of Hawaii's growing population and increasing role as a tourist destination.[12]

In practice, the land use program seems to have primarily existed to protect the agricultural land of the state upon which the state's economy has historically been based. Of the state's four million acres, only 400,000 are designated as prime agricultural land, and it is these lands and the associated grazing land and non-prime cropland which have been protected by the state act.[13]

The state land use program of Hawaii has proceeded under the direction of the LUC. The LUC is composed of nine private citizens, the director of the Department of Land and Natural Resources, and the director of the Department of Planning and Economic Development. Proposals to change the designation (i.e., zoning) of a parcel of land come before the LUC in two ways:[14]

(1)   The comission is mandated by the legislation which established it to reevaluate all of the land use zones every 5 years.
(2)   The commission can act on application for changes in classifications, including changing boundaries, or the law's terminology, at any time between reviews, as it so determines.

Designation of land into a specific district is based on the existing and projected needs of the state. Urban districts consist of all existing urban land and sufficient reserve land to accommodate anticipated urban growth for the next 10 years. Rural districts are those having low-density residential developments on lots ½ acre or larger, but this designation applied to only a tiny fraction of Hawaii's land. Agricultural districts are those that include lands already being farmed and grazed plus lands classified as arable by the University of Hawaii's Land Study Bureau. Conservation districts are the forest reserves which had been established in the territorial period of Hawaii, with additions which were justifiable on the grounds that they were necessary to protect against flood, erosion, and other environmental problems.[15]

As the state land use act with the broadest coverage, and the longest duration, Hawaii's act has been extensively studied by others as they consider possibilities of adopting their own form of state controls. An analysis of the Hawaii experience leads to the conclusion that the basic intent of Hawaii's legislation of 1961 was to provide a truly comprehensive planning process for all of the state of Hawaii. Unfortunately, it has not been possible to fully realize the benefits which Hawaii's law could have provided. Although the LUC is given the charge of controlling changes in the zoning of the state's lands, there have been few clear-cut policies to guide them in their decision making, and too often they have been the focus of pressures for development which have resulted in changes which are detrimental to the comprehensive land use of the state. As a study team from Oregon State University noted, "Although procedures were established, the commission was given no guidance in law on the relative emphasis to place on such major controversies as tourist related development versus the preservation of natural and scenic attractions, or agricultural land versus the supply of land for reasonably priced living accommodations."[16] Because of the lack of specific guidance, amendments to the Land Use Act made in 1975 provide guidelines to direct the LUC in its decisions concerning redistricting.[17] In spite of these amendments, outside observers conclude that there has been too little coordination between state and local entities in the planning process and the resultant actions of the LUC in reclassifying lands, and the actions of county and municipal governments in regulating existing classified land, have resulted in piecemeal actions. Studies by the American Institute of Architects concluded that inadequate planning procedures in Hawaii had resulted in "a climate of confusion . . . . and inaction."[18]

Although Hawaii's pioneering effort to develop a workable state land use control program has not been as successful as its early sponsors might have hoped, it is important because it antedated, by at least a decade, serious efforts by other states to develop comprehensive state regulation of land use. The unfortunate aspect of the Hawaii experience is that the legislation establishing state planning provided the potential for developing a wise management plan for the land of the state, but this potential was never realized because the process of classifying lands into one of the districts became accepted as planning. Ideally, as in all zoning schemes, the land use districts should have been based on policy guidelines which in turn should have been based on the needs and demands of the public. Instead, land was classified into districts and this was viewed as the planning process, just as zoning per se has too often been viewed as planning in cities when in fact zoning should be the manifestation of planning. Once zones of land use were created, little effective planning has taken place.

Many other states have adopted some type of legislation or commission which can be classified as land use planning. Most of the states, however, have simply appointed commissions to study the need to set up land use controls, or have developed state land use agencies to provide information on alternative planning techniques, legal constraints and options, and dispense funds for planning, but do not actually control the land use, as in the Hawaii experience. Other states have adopted land use controls which relate to only a portion of the lands in the state. Normally, these actions are aimed at specific environments classified as critical environments, such as coastal zones, mountain zones, etc. (Table 8). An analysis of some of the more important state land use activities is illustrative of the type of land use controls being adopted by states other than Hawaii.

OREGON: AN INCIPIENT STATE LAND USE LAW

Oregon's experience with planning is illustrative of the process by which other states have moved in the direction of planning at the regional and state level. In 1919, the state legislature granted zoning power to municipalities, but required that they be in accordance with a general plan. In 1947, counties in Oregon received the right to zone, but zoning was to reflect the goals in their comprehensive plan. This is basically similar to land use controls developed in other states in this period. From the time of settlement until 1919, only nuisance activities were controlled. From 1919 to the early 60s, land use was directed through zoning regulation. Other types of regulation were adopted in the late 1960s and early 1970s, as increasing concern for the environment and the livability of the state prompted public interest in controlling land use within Oregon's boundary.

From 1960 to 1970, the population of Oregon's urban areas increased 28%.[19] Although the percentage increase was high, the actual number was relatively small since there are only slightly more than 2 million people in Oregon. The distribution of population, however, generated concern about growth and environmental degradation in the state. Of the total population of Oregon, some 70% reside in the Willamette Valley. There are some 7 million acres in the Willamette Valley, but only an estimated 2 million acres are suitable for immediate development. Roughly 1½ million people reside in the valley. The present population represents a 100% increase since 1940, and it is projected to increase to 2½ million people before the turn of the century.[20]

In addition to the increased urbanization of the Willamette Valley, Oregon was also faced with condominium development, recreational development, and general sprawl along its coastal zone which were resulting in pollution to the shoreline and estuaries, as well as limiting access to the beaches. To the east in the more arid regions of eastern Oregon, an additional problem was the subdivision of rangeland for resale as recreational homesites and/or investments. A 1972 study revealed that 160,000 acres of the arid lands had been divided into parcels averaging 4 acres in size.[21] The combination of pressures of suburbanization in the Willamette Valley, subdivision of the rangelands of the east, and urban sprawl and recreational development along the coast prompted increased interest in controlling land use at other than the local level.

Against this backdrop, Oregon began to move towards a state land use law. In 1969, Senate Bill 10 was passed; it was designed primarily to preserve the prime agricultural land of the state, particularly in the Willamette Valley. The law required that all cities and counties of Oregon prepare a zoning ordinance to regulate the land within their boundaries. Such zoning was to be based on a comprehensive plan, and the bill required that all counties and cities complete their comprehensive plan and associated zoning (or at least make satisfactory progress) by the end of 1971, or the governor of the state could develop the plans for them.[22] Although Bill 10 was an important beginning, it suffered because it provided no standard for evaluating the comprehensive plan upon which zoning was to be used, nor did it provide for coordination between contiguous cities and counties as they made their plans and regulations. In addition, the legislation did not provide any funding by which the planning could be accomplished. As a result these weaknesses and the increasing developments in Oregon, a land use bill for the entire state was subsequently considered.

Oregon's efforts to control its land were set against a background of legislation of the late 1960s which had moved in the direction of insuring public rights. Bills had been passed in the state which provided access to the beaches up to the line of vegetation for all people; a program to remove pollution and clean up the Willamette Valley had been undertaken with good success; and in 1971, the Oregon Coastal Conservation and Development Commission had been created by the legislature to coordinate the planning process in coastal areas. Perhaps more importantly, in 1965 a Clean Water Act was passed which required permits for any type of discharge into water bodies. This had prepared Oregonians for the concept of permits from state entities in association with land use related activities. Against this background, a bill was introduced to the Legislature in 1972, Senate Bill 100, which would have created a strong and comprehensive state planning program. Although the initial bill was subsequently changed and revised to enable it to be passed, it still has the potential for providing a comprehensive land use program for Oregon. As finally passed, the bill mandates the following:

(1) Properly prepared and coordinated comprehensive plans for cities, counties, regional areas, and the state as a whole are to be developed and adopted by the appropriate governing bodies at the local and state levels;

(2) Establishment of the department of Land Conservation and Development to develop state-wide planning goals and guidelines, administer a permit system for activities of state-wide significance, and prepare inventories of land uses;

(3) Preparation of state-wide planning guidelines;

(4) A review process for comprehensive plans to insure conformance with state-wide planning goals;

(5) Coordination of planning efforts of state agencies to assure conformance with state-wide planning goals and compatibility with city and county comprehensive plans;

(6) Widespread citizen involvement and input in all phases of the process;

(7) Preparation of model zoning, subdivision and other ordinances and regulations to guide state agencies, cities, counties and special districts in implementing state-wide goals;

(8) Review and recommendation for designation of areas of critical state concern.

In order to carry out these activities, the Department of Land Conservation and Development, composed of the Land Conservation and Development Commission (LCDC), its director and subordinate officers, and employees, was required to follow through with the elements mandated by the act. The bulk of the responsibility for planning was placed at the local level. The LCDC provided model zoning subdivision and other ordinances, but it is the local jurisdictions who are responsible for implementing them. To insure that they do so, the land use act required that each county and city in the state:

(1) prepare and adopt a comprehensive plan which was consistent with the state-wide planning goals and guidelines approved by the commission, and

(2) that they enact zoning, subdivision, and other ordinances and regulations for implementation of their comprehensive plans which were consistent with the state-wide goals and guidelines. Counties, in addition, are responsible for coordinating the planning activities of cities, counties, special districts, and state and federal agencies within their area. If counties so choose, this coordination function can be carried out by a special area-wide body.[23]

The LCDC is given authority to review and approve or disapprove the local comprehensive plans. Approval is based on conformance with state guidelines, and when a local government does not adequately prepare comprehensive plans, the Department of Land Conservation and Development is directed to intervene and prepare comprehensive plans, and bill the local government for the cost. Should the local government not pay the associated cost, the Secretary of State pays the department from the local government's share of cigarette and liquor taxes. As of March, 1980, only 4 of Oregon's 36 counties have had their plans approved by the LCDC.[24]

To the extent that the provisions of the comprehensive plans are followed, Oregon's land use act has great potential for changing the land use pattern of the state and directing land use for the benefit of all of its inhabitants. To insure that the comprehensive plans are followed, the Land Use Act of 1973 required that all cities and counties adopt subdivision ordinances consistent with the adopted comprehensive plan. This requirement does not set a lower limit on size of parcel to be divided, thus insuring that all subdivisions are covered by the comprehensive plans. Although Oregon's law seemingly provides excellent control of land use in the state, it is questionable how effective it has been. The comprehensive plans do provide guidance, but as with most comprehensive plans, the day-to-day decision making process often subverts the original planning goals.

FLORIDA AND THE PROTECTION OF CRITICAL AREAS

Oregon's land use act, as originally proposed, called for creation of critical areas which included all of the coastal land; all areas within one quarter mile of local, state, and federal parks, recreation areas, and primitive wilderness areas; and scenic highways that were to be controlled to within 1,000 feet of the highway in rural areas or 200 feet in urban areas. As finally accepted by the Senate, however, this concept had been reduced to the more palatable statement which simply said that it was to review and recommend to the legislative assembly the designation of areas of critical state concern.[25] Florida, by contrast, did not attempt to pass a state-wide land use program. Rather, Florida's program was oriented from the beginning toward those areas which were of most critical importance (discussed in an earlier chapter). Compared to Oregon, the problems which prompted development of a state-regulatory act in Florida were gargantuan. Florida had been a boom state in terms of population growth in the 1960s and early 70s. Not only has the population grown at a phenomenal rate, but it has primarily been a result of people coming to the area because of the unique climatological and geographical features of Florida. Its mild winters and abundant recreation has made it the fastest growing state for much of the past two decades. The impact of this growth was particularly profound in Florida because of two factors:

(1) The fragile nature of most of Florida's environment because of its low-lying topography and reliance on underground water movement, and
(2) The nature of the growth which often came in the form of large planned unit developments.

The second factor is particularly important since it meant that instead of a town growing gradually as new homes or small subdivisions were added to it, a county could find its population quadrupled by the emergence of one single project. For example, the Fort Lauderdale area could double its present population of nearly 1 million by completion of only 25 proposed projects, 3 of which have plans for over 100,000 people each.[26]

Since the bulk of Florida's growth has historically taken place in the warmer tropical environments of southern Florida, it has had a dramatic impact on the environment. As discussed in an earlier chapter, the dredge and fill operations associated with such development have had a significant impact on not only the area being developed, but on the entire South Florida region. Of central concern to those interested in the land use issue in Florida has been the problem associated with construction on the wetlands. This has been of particular concern because of the movement of underground waters southward through the Florida Peninsula to maintain the Everglades and Big Cyprus swamp areas.

Because of rapid growth and related environmental problems, Florida has attempted some innovative land use controls in the past few years. Laws regulating Florida's land are largely a recent pheonomena as Florida did not grant right of zoning authority to all of its counties until 1967. As late as 1973, less than one half of the counties of Florida had exercised any type of land use control.[27] In the 70s, however, as local governments became concerned about growth, Florida communities adopted many regulations in their efforts to minimize the negative impacts of growth. For example, Dade County enacted a moratorium on growth in much of the county, and Boca Raton voters passed an act requiring that the city of 32,000 be zoned to accommodate no more than 100,000, an action subsequently ruled illegal. Against this backdrop of increasing local concern for growth and associated environmental problems, Florida enacted a state act entitled The Environmental Land and Water Management Act of 1972.[28] The primary features of the 1972 law are as follows:

(1) The Environmental Land and Water Management Act calls for control of critical environmental areas and large-scale developments (developments of regional impact) by joint state and local regulations;

(2) The Water Resources Act established five regional water management districts which would regulate use of Florida's water;

(3) The Land Conservation Act authorized issuance of $240 million in state bonds for purchase of environmentally endangered lands and outdoor recreation lands (this required voter approval which was received in November of 1972 by a three to one majority);

(4) The Florida Comprehensive Planning Act requires the state to provide for orderly land development through providing long-range guidance for social, economic, and physical growth of the state based on appropriate goals, objectives, and policies.

In 1975, another act mandated all local governments to engage in comprehensive planning and to join with appropriate public bodies to coordinate with the state government to achieve comprehensive planning on a state-wide basis. The state does not have power to override local decisions, but only to review the local and area plans for conformance to state comprehensive plans. However, if the local and area levels have not accomplished comprehensive planning by July 1, 1979, the state government will provide any minimal planning necessary to assure comprehensive state-wide planning. This deadline can be extended for up to 2 years, but if it is not met by the end of this time, the state may establish requirements for subdivisions and zoning in areas without comprehensive land use planning.[29]

The Florida Land Use Law combines the 1972 and 1975 acts and is administered under the direction of the Florida cabinet. The cabinet consists of six independently elected state officials who, in conjunction with the Governor, designate areas of critical environmental concern and act as the appeal board for developments of regional impact. By law, no more than 5% of the state can be designated as critical environmental area, but within this limitation three classes of areas of critical importance can be designated:[30]

(1) Areas having a significant impact upon the environmental, historical, natural, or archaeological resources of regional or state-wide importance;
(2) Areas significantly affected by or having a significant effect upon an existing or proposed major public facility or other area of major public investment;
(3) Areas of major development potential which may include a proposed site of a new community designated in a state development plan.

Regulation of the critical areas involves both state and local control. The Florida cabinet designates the boundaries of the critical area and establishes principles for its development; local governments then must adopt development regulations which comply with the principles. Should the local regulations be unsatisfactory, or should the local government not act, the cabinet can produce a regulation itself. Regulations are administered by the local government under the supervision of the cabinet, who is represented by the division of state planning. If enforcement of the regulations is improper, the division of state planning can use court action to enforce proper protection.[31] As of 1979, only three areas had been designated "areas of critical state concern": the Big Cypress area, the Florida Keys area, and the Green Swamp. Four other areas had been considered for designation as critical areas, but alternative management strategies were suggested instead[32] (Fig. 7).

A second area of major state input into regulation of land use in Florida is in the area of large-scale developments or developments of regional impact. According to the 1972 act, if a development affects more than one county it is of regional impact. In 1973, specific developments of regional impact were designated:[33]

(1) an airport;
(2) a race track or sports stadium;
(3) power plants larger than 100 megawatts;
(4) high voltage electrical transmission lines which cross county boundaries;
(5) hospitals serving more than one county;
(6) manufacturing plants or industrial parks with parking for more than 1,500 cars;
(7) mining activities disturbing more than 100 acres annually;
(8) large port facilities or oil storage tansk;
(9) a post-secondary educational campus of more than 3,000 students;
(10) a shopping center with more than 49 acres of parking of more than 2,500 cars;
(11) housing developments, mobile parks, or subdivisions larger than 250 units in low-population counties or larger than 3,000 units in populous counties.

In practice, the control of developments of regional impact (DRI) consists of a developer making application for his project to the local governing body.[34] The developer submits an application (in essence an environmental impact statement of his project), and the local government then schedules a public hearing. At the same time, the developer sends a copy of his proposed development to the

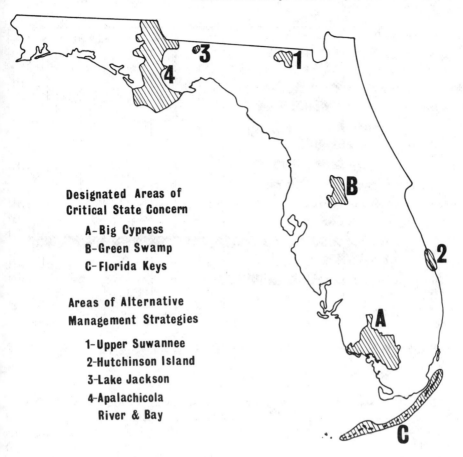

Designated Areas of
Critical State Concern

A-Big Cypress
B-Green Swamp
C-Florida Keys

Areas of Alternative
Management Strategies

1-Upper Suwannee
2-Hutchinson Island
3-Lake Jackson
4-Apalachicola
    River & Bay

Fig. 7. Areas of special management in Florida.

appropriate regional planning agency. In Florida, there are 10 regional planning agencies covering all of Florida's counties. The regional agency has 50 days to review the application and return to the local government a "report and recommendations on the regional import of the proposed development."[35] The local government must consider the regional findings and recommendations, but is not bound by any of them. If the local government approves a developer's proposal, it issues "a development order." It is at this point that state control becomes involved. If the division of state planning or the regional planning agency feels that the local government has approved a project which will have a negative impact on the region, they can then appeal the proposed project to the Florida cabinet. If the development was not approved by the local government, the developer can also appeal to the cabinet. The results of the first 5 years of Florida's

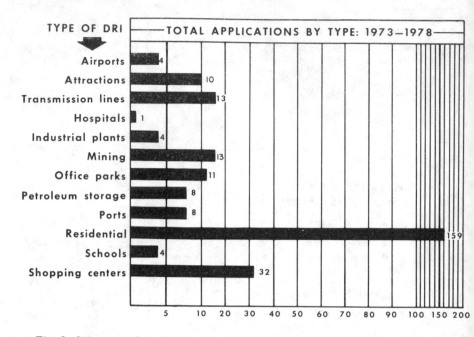

Fig. 8. Summary of applications for developments of regional impact: 1973–1978.

program of managing large developments are shown in Figure 8. By the end of June 1978, 257 applications had been received which included 993,270 residential units and 32 regional shopping centers. By June 30, 1978, the local governments had acted on 179 applications. Of these, 141 (79%) were approved, 24 (13%) were approved with conditions, and 14 (8%) were denied. At the local level, the approval rate increased from 88% in 1973-74 to 100% in 1977-78, representing the increasing recognition by developers of the need to plan for developments so that they can meet the standard. Of the 179 development orders issued in the 5-year period, 38 were appealed to the Florida Land and Water Adjudicatory Commission, including 6 of the 8 denials, 2 of 3 approved, and 30 of those approved with conditions. Only 28 of the appeals actually proceeded, and 21 of these were resolved through compromise before reaching the Commission. In only one case did the Commission reverse a local government's approval of a DRI.[36]

With the enactment of the 1975 Comprehensive Plan Act in Florida, which required all local governments to prepare comprehensive plans, it would appear that Florida is well on its way to controlling land use of state-wide concern. Although the state does not have the power to change local comprehensive plans, it does have the power to provide them if local governments do not do so themselves, and has the power to enforce the state regulation requiring that all land use regulations adopted by a community be consistent with its adopted comprehensive plan. However, on November 22, 1978, the State Supreme Court of Florida ruled that the first of the critical environmental areas which had been designated, the 322,000 acre Green Swamp, was invalid because the 1972 act of the legislature had been unconstitutional. The court ruled that the 1972 Land and Water Management Act was too far-reaching. Although the governor of Florida called the legislature into session in December of 1978 to provide stopgap legislation to protect the critical areas until the 1979 legislature could reexamine the 1972 act, it appears that Florida's Land and Water Management Act may need to be rewritten. Although it is unclear what direction the Florida legislature will move in reacting to the 1978 judicial ruling, it is unlikely that the state will abandon its land use regulation role.

VERMONT: CONTROLLING LEISURE HOME DEVELOPMENT

Vermont, in many ways is the antithesis of Florida. Vermont is primarily a rural state, with only 32% of the population residing in urban areas. Having only two cities with a population of over 15,000 people, Vermont is the most rural state in the Union. It is the third smallest state in the nation and had a growth rate of 14% during 1960–1970. Such growth may not appear alarming, but it represented the greatest growth rate in the past century for the state and represented a major addition to the state's 1960 population of 390,000.[37] In addition, the type of growth that was occurring was of major concern to the residents of the state. A high proportion of the development consisted of second home developments concentrated in scenic mountain or coastal areas. Local regulation was inadequate to control the problems associated with large-scale recreational developments, whether associated with the seashore or ski resort areas. As late as 1975, only about 40% of the municipalities in the state were zoned, although the state enabling legislation authorized full planning, zoning, and subdivision control by municipalities.[38]

To combat the problems associated with rapid growth in those areas which were perceived as most suitable for recreational development, the state developed comprehensive land use legislation in 1970. Act 250 passed by the Vermont legislature in that year created a state-wide regulatory system for much of the residential development and provided for a three-phase planning process. The essential elements of the planning process were to include:

(1) a first phase consisting of inventory of present land use and capability for land development;
(2) a second phase to establish a land capability and development plan to provide the planning principles to guide economic development, define protection of natural resources, transportation needs, and energy conservation in the state;
(3) a third phase to provide for a state-wide land use plan which would designate areas for conservation, agriculture, development, and other land uses.

Phase two was completed in 1973 and provides the guidelines presently regulating development throughout the state. Phase three was defeated by the 1974 and subsequent legislatures.

The 1970 act, entitled the Vermont Environmental Control Act, remains in force and does provide state regulation of land use activity. The act has state-administered environmental criteria which must be met by all projects beyond a certain size. These include:[39]

(1) subdivisions of more than 5 lots;
(2) construction of more than 10 housing units;
(3) development of commercial or industrial property of more than 1 acre in towns without zoning or subdivision regulations;
(4) all construction regardless of size above 2,500 foot elevation;
(5) any state or municipal construction on more than 10 acres.

In order to encourage local land use controls, the legislature has excluded state regulation of housing developments having a minimum lot size of 10 acres or more, and commercial or industrial developments of 10 acres or less if the project is inside a town with local zoning and subdivision regulations.[40] Vermont uses a unique permit process to regulate the activities listed above. The state is divided into nine districts and the governor appoints three local residents as commissioners for each region. These commissioners decide whether or not to grant permits for developments and subdivisions covered by the law. A review process exists in the form of an independent regulatory body, the Environmental Board, consisting of nine members who are lay citizens appointed by the governor.[41] A developer applies to the local district commission for approval of the activities listed above. In ruling on a proposal, the district commission considers the following:[42]

(1) Will the proposed development result in undue water or air pollution?
(2) Does the proposed development have sufficient water for its reasonably foreseeable needs?
(3) Will the proposed development cause an unreasonable burden on an existing water supply when one is to be utilized?
(4) Will the proposed development cause unreasonable soil erosion or water retention of the land?
(5) Will the development result in unreasonable highway congestion and/or unsafe conditions?
(6) Will the development cause an unreasonable burden on the educational services of municipalities and its ability to provide them?
(7) Will the development place an unreasonable burden on the ability of the local government to provide governmental services?
(8) Will the proposed development have an undue adverse effect on scenic, natural beauty, aesthetics, historic sites, or rare or irreplaceable natural areas of the region?
(9) Does the proposal conform with the state-wide plan under Act 250?
(10) Does the proposal conform to a duly adopted local or regional plan?

The permit process in Vermont has been in effect for over half a decade. In the first 5 years of its existence, 2,030 permit cases were heard and 1,888 permits were granted, often with conditions. Only 57 applications were denied, while 85 were withdrawn. Sixty-five cases were appealed to the environmental board of Vermont.[43]

Coupled with the permit process has been the development of legislation affecting land sales designed to discourage land speculation.[44] The law is essentially a capital gains tax on land sales designed to prevent artificially high prices for land which have a tendency to impact local residents to the greatest extent because they are unable to afford the high land prices that outsiders from more urbanized states have been willing to pay. The tax must be paid on all gains from sale or exchange of land, but does not apply to the structures on the land. Capital gains on up to one acre of land on which a taxpayer makes his principal residence are exempted. Thus, gains on vacation home sites are taxable but ordinary dwelling lots are not. The tax is designed to tax the rate of increase and provides an incentive for owners to maintain their ownership rather than resell their property. Taxes range from 60% of the gain on lands which are held less than 1 year and are sold for over 200% of their original value, to 10% for lands which are held 5 years but less than 6 and sold for 200% or more of their original value. After 6 years, the tax rate is zero, so the typical farmer who keeps his land for a long period of time does not pay the capital gains tax, but developers, who must sell their property rapidly, provide a high rate of taxes to the state. In practice, this portion of Vermont's approach to controlling land use is debatable, but it does have the effect of providing tax dollars from property which is subdivided, while at the same time encouraging individuals to refrain from rapid turnover of property for speculative gain purposes.[45] Obviously, developers are very adamant in their opposition to the act, but the Vermont supreme court has ruled that the tax is lawful and it seems to be having some effect in preventing subdivision.

Vermont has made extraordinary strides toward state control of land, but the legislature remains unwilling to adopt the final portion of Act 250, which would provide de facto state zoning. Nonetheless, Vermont's 250 legislation represents a pioneering effort to control land use in America. Unlike Florida's legislation which concentrates on critical areas alone, the existing permit system in Vermont provides an effective way for controlling the type of development that takes place in larger subdivisions and in more rugged terrain. When coupled with the tax measures that apply a capital gains tax to sale of land, Vermont has produced legislation which seems effective in preventing the worst effects of rampant second home and recreational development.

CALIFORNIA: SAVING THE COAST FOR POSTERITY

California represents an environment different from those of the states discussed to this point. California has been a lodestone affecting migration in the United States for the past 100 years. In the post-World War II era particularly, California became the destination of the millions of Americans who were following Greeley's century old advice to go west. California is the largest state in the nation in terms of population, and between 1960 and 1970 the state experienced a 27%

population increase. The bulk of the population is urban, with over 91% residing in urban areas. More than one-half live in the Los Angeles/Long Beach and San Francisco/Oakland Standard Metropolitan Statistical Areas. The climate, life-style, and scenic attractions of California continue to attract numerous migrants to the state. Continued population growth creates problems of urban sprawl, pressure on sensitive lands, and destruction of the attributes which have attracted California's residents. Concern for the coastal area of California became especially acute in the late 1960s and early 1970s. Problems associated with denial of access to beaches fronted by private developments, dredging and filling of estuarine lands, and general access to valued beach areas resulted in a referendum in California entitled "The California Coastal Zone Conservation Act of 1972" (Proposition 20). Proposition 20 was initiated by the public through a petition process; the requisite percentage of the voters in the previous general election signed petitions to place Proposition 20 on the ballot. The leaders of this initiative stated that:[46]

> "the California coastal zone is a distinct and natural resource belonging to all the people and existing as a delicately balanced ecosystem; that the permanent protection of the remaining natural and scenic resources of the coastal zone is of paramount concern to present and future residents of the state and nation; that in order to promote the public safety, health, and welfare, and to protect public and private property, wildlife, marine fisheries, and other ocean resources, and the natural environment, it is necessary to preserve the ecological balance of the coastal zone and prevent its further deterioration and destruction; that it is the policy of the state to preserve the ecological balance of the coastal zone and to prevent its further deterioration and destruction; that it is the policy of the state to preserve, protect, and, where possible, to restore the resources of the coastal zone for the enjoyment of the current and succeeding generation."

Proposition 20 resulted from the increasing concern on the part of California citizens about access to the beach and associated coastal-zone problems. This concern had fostered bills in the state legislature in 1970, 1971, and 1972 to regulate coastal development, but none reached the floor of the senate. Consequently the California Coastal Alliance was formed in 1971, and through its efforts Proposition 20 emerged and was passed by a majority of voters in 1972. Proposition 20 is unlike other land laws in the United States for two reasons: First, it resulted from public initiative, and secondly, it was written entirely by environmentalists. Growing out of the Bay Area Conservation and Development Commission, which had been attempting to regulate San Francisco Bay since 1965, Proposition 20 proposed regulation of the coastal zone, defined as an area 1,000 yards from the shoreline.

The California Coastal Zone Conservation Act of 1972 required that a coastal zone commission be established to prepare a comprehensive plan for the orderly range conservation and management of the coastal zone. To prevent development from defeating the purpose of this act in the interim, the act established six regional coastal zone commissions to control land use in the coastal zone until such time as the California Coastal Zone Conservation Plan should be adopted. The regional coastal commissions consisted of 6 members of the public, who were not to hold any elected office nor to be guilty of conflict of interest, plus representatives from the counties affected to a total of 12 to 16 members. In addition, a state commission consisting of six public members appointed by the governor and six delegates representing each of the regional commissions served as an appeal body from the actions of the regional commissions.[47]

In practice, the commissions had the power to review all permit applications for any type of development within the 1,000 yard strip of land inland from the water's edge designated as the immediate coastal zone. Unlike other states where state regulations apply to only developments of a certain size, all developments in this contiguous zone were controlled by the coastal zone commissions. Activities relating to essentially all construction, filling, dredging, and discharge (except for maintenance dredging by the regulatory powers of the commission), as well as any proposed building, subdivision, or other development activity were subject to the commissions' approval. Permits for development in the 1,000-yard coastal zone were granted only when it was shown that development would have no substantial adverse environmental effect on the coastal zone and would be consistent with the maintenance, restoration, and enhancement of the overall quality of the coastal zone environment.

Control of the coastal zone under the Proposition 20 permit system required that permits should not be issued for any of the following without the affirmative vote of two-thirds of the total *membership* of the regional commission:[48]

(1) dredging or filling;
(2) developments which would reduce size of any beach or other area usable for public recreation;
(3) developments which would reduce or impose restrictions upon public access to the tidal and submerged lands, beaches, and the mean high tide line where there is no beach;
(4) developments interfering with or detracting from the view of the sea from the state highway nearest the coast;
(5) any development adversely affecting water quality.

From the beginning, the regional coastal zone commission and the state coastal zone commission were intended as temporary entities. The state coastal zone commission, in conjunction with the regional commissions, was to prepare a coastal plan to serve as the basis for all development within the coastal zone. Between February of 1973 and 1977, the commissions heard over 25,000 development applications, ranging from single family homes, to division of agricultural lands, to power plants and offshore petroleum development. The vast majority of the 25,000 permits were approved, but many were modified to protect the environment and to reduce densities.[49] In practice, the commissions tended to favor low density, more temporary types of uses in preference to land uses which would result in high densities and/or large-scale permanent developments.

In 1976, the California Coastal Plan was accepted. The California Coastal Plan requires that each city and county within a wide geographical strip called the Coastal Resource Management area submit a Local Implementation Program (LIP) to the state coastal commission and the appropriate regional coastal commission. When the LIP is found acceptable in terms of consistency with the coastal plan, it is certified by the regional and state coastal commissions. Once a local legislative unit has had its LIP certified, the local government becomes the exclusive permit authority for the portion of the coastal resource management area covered by its LIP.[50] Should a local government be unable to get its LIP certified, the state coastal agency would have permit jurisdiction in the area. When an approved LIP is not being followed, the state agency would also have the right to revoke certification. The six coastal commissions will go out of existence in mid-1979 unless legislation is passed to extend their existence. The LIP, which will be the basis of the coastal zone management after that time, will be implemented by some 68 local governments plus state and federal agencies operating in the coastal zone.

It is unclear at this point whether or not the coastal zone mangement plan, which emerged from the 1976 California legislature, is as strong as the petitioners had hoped in Proposition 20 of 1972. The present coastal plan is assailed by environmentalists as too weak, while development interests argue that it is too restrictive. Whichever view one adopts, it is apparent that the initiative of 1972 has had a profound effect on California's coastline. Much of the agricultural land in the coastal zone has been protected from subdivision into summer or exclusive residential homes, wildlife habitats have been protected, and beach access by the broader public has been enhanced. Although the favorable granting of permits to 90% of the applicants may seem high, it should be remembered that many of these permits were granted with the provision that modifications be made. These modifications ranged from height reduction to elimination of visual barriers caused by beach homes too close to one another, to dedication of public access across private lands. California's Coastal Zone Act of 1972 is the prime example of the impact which the citizenry can have on state land use. As a protective device for a critical area, it has shown that it is possible to overcome local interests where they detract from the broad benefits and interests which the public has in the land in its state.

STATE PLANNING: PERSUASION AND SUPPORT
—THE GENERAL RULE

Discussion of state regulations in Hawaii, Vermont, Oregon, and California has provided examples of some of the more effective land use control mechanizations adopted by states. Interest in state land use controls continues to grow, and by 1978 every state had created a planning office to coordinate the planning of existing agencies and to establish a state development strategy.[51] In those states where a state land use law was actually adopted, the emphasis is on cooperation with local governments, encouragement of local planning efforts through funding and technical expertise, and requirements for local planning entities to develop comprehensive plans and other planning related guidelines. For example, Colorado has a land use law that was most recently severely amended in 1974. Although the resultant law emphasizes state influence on local decisions related to land use, it allows the local governments to make most of the decisions. The law identifies numerous types of critical areas of statewide concern, but the local government designates and identifies the specific areas. The state has little power to impose statewide interests on local governments and is thus relegated to suggesting policies or proposals to local governments.[52]

Wyoming provides another example. The State Land Use Planning Act was passed in 1975, creating a permanent land use commission. The commission is involved in developing policies for state land use and development of a state land use plan. Of central importance to the plan is designation of areas of critical environmental concern and development of mechanisms for coordinating land use related activities at local, state, and federal levels. Local governments were initially given 18 months to develop land use plans consistent with state guidelines. The State Planning Division and Land Use Commission cooperate with local entities in developing their comprehensive plan, but it is the local people who are responsible. The actions of Wyoming are indicative of the types of controls envisioned by many states. Wyoming's Land Use Law of 1975 developed in an area of rapid urban growth in small towns impacted by energy related development. In 1973, of 82 towns in Wyoming, only 32 had any type of zoning, and only 8 of the state's 23 counties had any zoning.[53] Only 15 towns had a master plan, as had 8 of the counties. Faced with the problems of rapid growth, the state acted to provide financial and other support to allow cities and towns within its boundaries to have some type of control over the development they faced. The state does not mandate the form or content of a specific comprehensive plan, but provides research support, financial support, and review of completed plans to insure minimum standards.

Other states have taken related action. These actions are either in the form of provision of support services and funding to local planning agencies, or in development of a state land use law mandating development of local zoning and subdivision ordinances, or in development of legislation dealing with specific areas of land use. As of 1978, Delaware, Hawaii, and Maine employed a statewide classification of land which was legally enforceable. An additional 12 states were considering a statewide classification, and 8 more were in process of developing a statewide system of land classification. Of the 50 states, 39 have the primary thrust of planning authority at the local level while only 11 have the primary emphasis at the state level.[54]

CONCLUSION

Emergence of the so-called Quiet Revolution as a force in land use planning in the United States in the past decade has been of singular import, but still the fundamental land use decisions remain at the local level in most states. Nevertheless, all states are faced with the issues which create the need for state regulation; the only difference is the degree of immediacy of the problem. Arrayed against the issues which encourage state land use controls are the conventional problems associated with the question of non-local control of a highly local action. People are concerned with "big government," and are increasingly reluctant to allow greater exercise of the powers of states, particularly when it is perceived that decisions will be made by a faceless bureaucracy at the state capitol without consideration of local citizen interest.

The question of citizen involvement and participation is particularly critical in land use decisions. In addition to these personal interests, there is a real question about the economic impact of state regulation. At the very least, it may provide an additional layer of paperwork which will involve time and cost for developments within the state. At the very worst, state land use regulation may result in decisions and regulations which benefit the populace of the entire state at the expense of the local citizenry. A particular concern that has been used to argue against state regulation (and regulation in general) is that it increases land prices. Whether or not this in fact is the case, there is no doubt that it is a highly emotionally perceived issue. Landowners who have opted not to develop their property in the past argue that state land use regulations are often unfairly biased against them, since they are restrained from developing their property and are forced to maintain it as open space at great paper cost to themselves. These and other factors seem to indicate that future state land use regulation in the United States will tend to emphasize the following: (1) provision of support services for local planning agencies, (2) designation of certain specified critical regions for regulation by state agencies, (3) designation of specific land use types as coming under the jurisdiction of one or more state agencies.

It is doubtful whether many states will adopt statewide zoning (as Hawaii has). Simply because of the emotional issues involved, for the future it appears that the existing pattern of land use regulation through zoning and subdivision regulations of local government will continue to dominate land use in the United States. Nevertheless, state planning agencies can have a significant impact on land use decisions at the local level through:

(1) encouragement of cooperation between state, regional, and local organizations in the planning process;
(2) provision of information to local planning agencies which they may not have the manpower, expertise, or budget to acquire;
(3) provision of alternative scenarios to local planning entities, to insure that they take their actions in a climate of understanding of both the issues and the potential results.

When provided information on outcomes, nearly all people will act in their best interests. Perhaps in this area the states may have the greatest impact. In such a situation, it is entirely probable that the end result of local actions will be much less negative in terms of its impact on the entire state than the historical process of each local planning agency acting in its own interests without awareness of the broader implications of its actions.

It is too early to make a truly quantitative analysis of the effect of state regulations, such as those in Hawaii, Florida, and Vermont, but observers have suggested that state land use acts have caused attention to be focused on the problems, leading to enactment of state legislation. The regulations have prevented some people from making application for development when they felt their proposed project could not be approved, and at least some critical environmental areas have received a level of protection previously not available.

Even if central state legislation is overturned by the courts, as in the case of Florida, the court decisions provide guidelines necessary for passing acceptable legislation. The unfortunate side effect of state land use regulation has been the polarization of growth versus no- or slow-growth groups. Such pressures, of course, are not new, but simply represent the verbalization of the issues which fostered state land use regulation. It is doubtful whether opponents of state regulation can ever mandate a return to what they perceive as the halcyon period of limited or nonexistent land use regulation. The increasing population of the United States, with its high mobility and influence, mandates more, not less, regulation at the state level.

NOTES

[1] *State Growth Management*, Council of State Governments (Lexington, KY: Department of Housing and Urban Development, 1976), p. 26.

[2] *The California Land: Planning for People*, California Land Use Task Force (Los Altos, Calif.: William Kaufmann, Inc., 1975), pp. 16–22.

[3] Robert G. Healy, *Land Use and the States* (Washington, D.C.: John Hopkins Press for Resources for the Future, 1976), p. 6.

[4] Ibid., p. 14, footnote 13.

[5] Ibid., pp. 254–255.

[6] Fred Bosselman and David Callies, *The Quiet Revolution in Land Use Control* (Washington, D.C.: Council on Environment Quality, 1971).

[7] Ibid., p. 3.

[8] *Summary of State Land Use Planning Activity* (Washington, D.C.: American Institute of Planners, for the Department of Housing and Urban Development, 1976), p. 451.

[9] Thomas Creighton, *The Lands of Hawaii: Their Use and Misuse* (Honolulu: University of Hawaii, 1978), p. 103.

[10] Ibid., pp. 64–65.

[11] Ibid., . 68.

[12] See Creighton, op. cit., pp. 61–90 for a full discussion of the pressure affecting changes in the designation of the districts.

[13] *Summary of State Land Use Planning Activity*, op. cit., pp. 452–453.

[14] Creighton, op. cit., p. 68.

[15] Ibid., p. 70.

[16] Ibid., p. 230.

[17] Ibid., p. 270.

[18] Ibid., p. 271.

[19] Charles E. Little, *The New Oregon Trail* (Washington, D.C.: The Conservation Foundation, 1974), p. 13.

[20] Ibid., p. 13.

[21] Ibid., p. 12.

[22] Ibid.

[23] *Summary of State Land Use Planning Activity*, op. cit., p. 497.

[24] Oregon Department of Land Conservation and Development, telephone conservation, March 1980.

[25]Little, op. cit., p. 31. The concept of critical areas was suggested by the American Law Institute in *A Model Land Development Code* (Washington, D.C.: The American Law Institute, 1976), pp. 257–269.

[26]Robert G. Healy, op. cit., p. 105.

[27]Ernest R. Bartley, "Status and Effectiveness of Land Development Regulations in Florida Today," in *Environmental Conference on Land Use* (Miami: Environmental Land Management Study Committee, June 11–13, 1973), pp. 8–9.

[28]For an extensive discussion of the Florida State legislation see Luther J. Carter, *The Florida Experience* (Washington, D.C.: Resources for the Future, 1974), pp. 117–137.

[29]Carter, op. cit., p. 133; *Summary of State Land Use Planning Activity*, op. cit., p. 160.

[30]Healy, op. cit., p. 112.

[31]Ibid., p. 113.

[32]*Developments of Regional Impact: A Summary of the First Five Years* (Tallahassee, Florida: Division of State Planning, 1979), Appendix B, pp. 3–5.

[33]Ibid.

[34]Jon L. Mills, *Analysis of Laws Relating to Florida Coastal Zone Management* (Tallahassee, Florida: Florida Bureau of Coastal Zone Planning, 1976), p. 245.

[35]If the proposed development is in a designated area of critical concern, the developer must meet the regulations adopted by the state for that zone but does not have to go through the permit process. *Developments of Regional Impact*, op. cit., pp. 2–3.

[36]*Developments of Regional Impact*, op. cit., pp. 5–16.

[37]*Summary of State Land Use Planning Activity*, op. cit., p. 47.

[38]Ibid., p. 54.

[39]Ibid., p. 49.

[40]Healy, op. cit., p. 49.

[41]*Summary of State Land Use Planning Activity*, op. cit., p. 49.

[42]Healy, op. cit., p. 224.

[43]Ibid.

[44]Ruth Kreplick et al., *Setting a Statewide Land Use Policy* (Amherst: University of Massachusetts, 1973), p. 57.

[45]Healy, op. cit., pp. 57–59.

[46]*The California Coastal Plan, Report of the California Coastal Zone Conservation Commission* (December 1, 1975), p. 431. The entire California Coastal Zone Conservation Act of 1972 is quoted on pp. 431–434.

[47]Ibid., pp. 431–432.

[48]Ibid., p. 433.

[49]*Sierra: The Sierra Club Bulletin*, June 1978, p. 12.

[50]Eugene Bardach et al., *The California Coastal Plan: A Critique* (San Francisco: Institute for Contemporary Studies, 1976), p. 26.

[51]Carl Hainze, "Two Keys to Effective State Planning," *Practicing Planner*, June 1978, pp. 18–20.

[52]Keith M. Honey, "Land Use Planning," *Practicing Planner*, March 1978, pp. 15–17.

[53]*Cheyenne, Wyoming: A Land Use Inventory* (League of Women Voters of Wyoming, 1973), p. 120.

[54]Richard A. Mann and Mike Miles, "State Land Use Planning: The Current Status and Demographic Rationale," *Journal of the American Planning Association*, Vol. 45 (1979), pp. 48–61.

Chapter 5

Land Use:
A Community Dilemma

Introduction

The increasing interest in state land use regulation should not mask the fact that the vast bulk of land use decisions are still made by municipal and county governments. There are over 80,000 governing bodies in the United States making decisions, many of which affect planning; and it is this group which faces the most immediate and most persistent land use issues and problems.[1] The issues which are presented to local governing bodies by land use questions are diverse. For example, seemingly simple questions involving zoning changes can in reality involve the issue of exclusionary zoning, as maintenance of large lot-size effectively excludes lower income residents from a neighborhood. In similar fashion, the seemingly innocuous designation of a street as a "collector" for a city's highway system can profoundly change the character of the residences along it. The diverse nature of land use issues faced by cities is indicated in the list below. The list is designed to be indicative rather than exhaustive, but it is apparent from even a casual reading that diversity is the hallmark of urban-related land issues.

LAND USE ISSUES IN URBAN AMERICA

A. Urban renewal related issues
  1. Low income housing type and location.
  2. Exclusive residential developments.
  3. Decline in available housing stocks.

87

   B. Zoning related issues
      1. Zoning which is exclusive in its effect if not its intent.
      2. Zoning changes resulting in "windfalls" or "wipeouts."
      3. Down-zoning to protect neighborhood integrity.
   C. Transport related issues
      1. Routing and timing of transport arteries.
      2. Availability of public transport systems.
      3. Parking related questions in residential and commercial districts.
   D. Municipal services related issues
      1. Timing of development of services.
      2. Equitable distribution of costs for providing services.
   E. Growth related issues
      1. Impact taxes to recoup financial cost to community of development.
      2. Impact of growth on schools and other urban services.
      3. Growth regulation related issues.

In all of the above issues, as well as in a host of other land use related issues, the metropolitan areas of the United States are faced with the problem of making decisions and plans for their lands which will allow for the continued integrity of the community and its character. Changes in the population distribution, in social attitudes and expectations, and economic situations result in trends which further affect the land use issues of America's metropolitan areas. The problems facing America's cities are the result of a combination of all of these factors. They are further compounded by the multiplicity of agencies and governments involved in the land use decision process. If we consider only the Standard Metropolitan Statistical Areas (SMSAs) of the United States, there is an average of 91 governments within each. Chicago has over 1,100 local governments affecting land use decisions, and Philadelphia has some 870.[2] The decisions of each of these governing bodies affect not only their own jurisdiction, but impinges upon the land use and land use related decisions of contiguous areas.

TRADITIONAL APPROACHES TO LAND USE DECISIONS IN METROPOLITAN AREAS

Land use in America's large metropolitan areas reflects the impact of three centuries of growth and change. The major cities have their origins in the colonial era. Although a few (e.g., Philadelphia) were designed according to a plan, most simply developed over time through accretion of population and central place function. Consequently, control of land use in metropolitan America reflects the general history of land use regulation in the nation as a whole. The villages from which the cities of today grew normally had only limited regulation of land use, usually directed at the location of nuisance activities. The widespread adoption of zoning regulation in the early twentieth century represented the initial impetus for land use regulation, and the resultant zoning districts had the greatest effect on land use within the large cities. The resultant land use in metropolitan America is difficult to accurately quantify, because of varying definitions of "metropolitan." One definition for which data is available is that of the SMSAs. The SMSA is defined by the census bureau as a county or group of contiguous counties with at least one city of 50,000 inhabitants or more, or cities immediately adjacent to one another with a combined population of at least 50,000. In addition to the county or counties including such a city, contiguous counties are included in the SMSA if they are economically or socially connected to the central city according to certain criteria. As of mid-1977, the Bureau of the Census recognized 277 SMSAs in the United States.[3] The average land use in SMSAs is shown in Table 9.

It should be apparent from Table 9 that the majority of the land within an average SMSA is in fact not in urban-related land uses. Only 10% of the land is actually urbanized, and it appears that there is an abundance of land for expansion. This is partially misleading, however, since within the SMSAs there normally exists not only urban centers, but smaller communities, rural unincorporated land, and land managed by the federal government. This overstatement is compounded by the inclusion of SMSAs in the west which typically have very large counties. Nevertheless, SMSAs represent what is commonly viewed as metropolitan America. The range in size of SMSAs results in lumping such places as Lawrence, Kansas (population 64,229) with New York City (population 9,561,089). It is obvious that there will be major differences in type and degree of land use issues in urban places of such disparate size. In attempting to reconcile this great variation, this chapter will focus on only those SMSAs of over 500,000 population.

Although limiting our definitions to those urban areas with at least ten times the minimum population results in lumping such places as Orlando, Florida with New York, the majority of the cities in the grouping of the 72 largest urbanized areas have similar types of land use.

Table 9. Land Use in Metropolitan Areas: 1970[a]

Use	Acres
Total	1,044,000
Urbanized	104,000
Rural	940,000
Cropland	250,000
Pasture and range	198,000
Forest and woodland	336,000
Other	156,000

Source: The Changing Issues for National Growth (Washington, D.C.: Government Printing Office, 1976), p. 80.
[a]Average land use for SMSAs in 48 states.

Land Use in Metropolitan America

The uses of land in metropolitan America can be subdivided in numerous ways, but basically the land uses are, more or less, residential, industrial, commercial, roads and highways, public or quasi-public, and vacant lands. Figures on land use are misleading if presented for the entire SMSA, for reasons outlined earlier, but it is difficult to obtain reliable information on categories for the core city of the SMSA. The data in Table 10 does provide insight into the relative importance of the various types of land use for some of the larger American cities, however.

As evident from the table, residential-related land uses are normally the single largest land use type in metropolitan America. Approximately one-third of the land in the largest U.S. cities is devoted to residential use. (Cities such as Los Angeles, which are characterized by even greater sprawl, have much higher percentages.) Other land uses vary widely depending on the age, location, and economic activity of the city.[4] The use of land in metropolitan areas is changing slowly. Residential land increased an average of only 1½% in 22 cities examined in the 1950s and 1960s. Other land uses remained approximately the same during this time, with the exception of a small decline in the amount of vacant land reflecting the small increase in residential land.[5]

Zoning: Traditional Tool for Land Use Regulation in Metropolitan Areas

The traditional means by which these land uses have been controlled have been overwhelmingly oriented towards zoning regulations. Since the mass adoption of zoning in the 1920s, there has been sharpening and refinement of zoning as a tool for land use control, but there still remain valid criticisms of it as a primary means of land use control. Without commenting on the extent to which the criticisms are completely valid, it is obvious that the criticisms reflect an underlying sentiment which indicates that there are real problems with zoning as a tool

Table 10. Average Land Use in 22 Cities

Use	Percent of developed land
Residential	39.8
Industrial	10.4
Commercial	5.
Road and highway	25.4
Other public	19.3

Source: Urban Land Policies and Land-use Control Measures, Vol. VI, *Northern America*, (New York: United Nations, 1973) p. 136, table 26.

for managing land use in metropolitan areas. Although there are many complaints about the effectiveness of zoning, they seem to fall into several general categories.[6]

The first category of criticism concludes that zoning is unnecessary since the market will lead to a fair segregation of uses. That is, rarely can a commercial establishment afford the high land prices associated with moving into a high-class residential area. In addition, because people's perceptions of what constitutes good or bad zoning are restricted to the property closest to them, the existing broad zones do not realistically reflect the public's desires. Although a local household may not desire to have a convenience store adjacent to their property, they would be happy to have it in the next block where they could utilize it without the negative impact of traffic and congestion associated with it. In addition, land developers have an inherent interest in assuring that the lands which they develop will be used in a rational fashion. If they are to maximize their profits, they will insure that there is some mechanism for controlling the land use. Thus, before zoning became popular, developers used restrictive convenants to insure the land use on a property.

A second criticism involves social justice. Zoning is often criticized as a tool by which the poor are exploited by the middle and upper classes. Middle-class residents desire single-family zoning and are adamant in their efforts to maintain zoning to protect their property rights. Zoning arbitrarily limits the amount of land available in the city and thus forces property values higher and excludes the lower income families. As a consequence of the emphasis of the middle and upper class on single-family zoning, sprawl develops with all of its attendant problems of need for private transportation, increased costs of providing services to the dispersed homes, and increased municipal expenditure for schools, road repair and maintenance, and associated aspects of suburbia.

Zoning is sometimes criticized as being capricious, irregular, subject to graft, corruption, and favoritism. This is particularly true when variances or zone changes are requested. Because it is advantageous to the community to grant variances or zone changes which will result in increased property values, the system of zoning is not as suitable for maintaining neighborhood quality as many residents believe. Since land use controlled by zoning can be changed, an element of uncertainty has been introduced into land use which affects costs to the user.

Some observers have maintained that zoning can lead to premature use of resources, since the concern over zoning changes may encourage development of a use immediately lest future zone changes result in disallowance of that type of activity.

Zoning has been described as inflexible and overly committed to maintaining the status quo. As such, it is not only exclusionary in nature, but because of the legal interpretations of zoning, it is incapable of rectifying past poor land uses since zoning cannot be retroactive. Thus zoning tends to be a poor vehicle for promulgating change within the community.

Zoning is unequal in its effect and is used as a system of indirect taxation. Hence, a piece of property zoned for commercial uses within a residential area provides its owner with a windfall at the expense of neighboring residential owners who must bear the decline in property values associated with increased traffic, congestion, and noise.

The process by which the zoning game is carried out is suspect. Planning commissions, boards of adjustment, and zoning boards are not supervised by the courts, and consequently the actions of such boards and agencies may or may not result in wise land use planning.

Zoning has been criticized as resulting in poor utilization of site. Normally, the required setback, bulk, and uses associated with a zone are such that it is impossible to change them. Thus, even though a specific site may have attributes which would dictate zero setback or limited setback, in order to gain a building permit the owner must conform to the ordinance and its requirements.

Finally, zoning may have a negative effect on urban land because of the expectations of land owners. Due to the fact that some land uses result in a greater return to the owner than others, cities may overzone for certain categories of land. This is particularly important in older metropolitan areas in which the existing vacant land may be overwhelmingly concentrated in the areas of industrial or commercial uses, even though the demand is for low-income housing units. This latter issue is particularly important when the larger cities of the United States are considered. In Chicago, where slightly more than 9,000 acres were vacant in 1963, nearly 75% of the vacant land base was zoned for manufacturing, commercial, and business uses. It was estimated that the 25% zoned for residential land use could accommodate less than 26,000 housing units, which was inadequate for a community with over 215,000 substandard housing units in 1960 and a population which was growing at the rate of 40,000 new households per year in the 1960s.[7]

Los Angeles, with nearly 29% of its total area vacant in 1963, would seemingly have adequate land for additional residential development. But it is estimated that 80% or more of the vacant residential land will be zoned for single-family housing, and only 3% zoned for densities of seven or more units to the acre, a miniscule amount of land for low- and moderate-income family housing. If this problem is examined in terms of race and income, it becomes even more critical. Minority areas of Mexican and Black population comprise over 70% of the substandard housing in the city, further compounding the problem. Moreover, 99% of the vacant land in the city is located far from the areas of minority concentrations further damaging their attempts to obtain adequate housing.[8]

In the four counties of New Jersey which form the outer ring of the New York metropolitan area, 76% of the land is zoned for single-family uses (400,000 acres), industrial, commercial, and other nonresidential land covers 23% (124,000 acres). Only one-half of 1% of the available vacant land is zoned for multi-family development.[9]

Use of traditional zoning as a means of controlling land use in metropolitan areas was initially adopted as an extension of the nuisance doctrine. As such, it was effective in limiting noxious enterprises from locating in residential areas. By establishing zones for activities, metropolitan areas were attempting to manage their land use in a rational manner. However, since zoning is only as effective as the underlying comprehensive plan upon which it is based, and since it is further subject to considerable amount of change once enacted, it has been criticized as ineffective. Others argue that it is, in fact, a highly effective means for allowing local residents to determine at least part of the character of their neighborhood. Moreover, it is flexible, allowing change to occur through the process of zoning changes, variances, and special permits. In the New Jersey example cited above, for instance, such changes resulted in 40% of the building permits being issued for multi-family constructions between 1965 and 1972. One county issued permits for 17,200 apartment units when only 307 acres were zoned for multi-family dwellings, in essence expanding the area so zoned. Defenders of zoning maintain that its detractors fail to recognize that its widespread use and continued support result from broad public support. This support is based on acceptance of the idea that in spite of its weaknesses, zoning still is the single best method available to the public to control land use in communities. Whichever view one adopts in assessing zoning, it is obvious that its wholesale adoption and use during the past 50 years have, in large part, determined the existing land uses of metropolitan America.

METROPOLITAN PROBLEMS OF LAND USE

The problems of land use in metropolitan areas do not all stem from the zoning regulations, of course. But it is important to point out that zoning, present and past, does have a role in affecting the problems presently facing urban areas as far as their land is concerned. Urban land problems can be categorized as follows:

(1) Problems of obsolescence of buildings, homes, industries, and commercial activities;
(2) Problems of housing as housing stocks deteriorate and zoning and land costs prohibit replacement;
(3) Population loss as residents move to the suburbs and smaller micropolitan areas;
(4) Job loss associated with obsolescence of existing land uses;
(5) Transport-related problems as the decline of public transit and the increase of the automobile result in congestion, high transport costs because of time involved, and relative inaccessability of the metropolitan area;
(6) Racial and social problems related to land use resulting from the concentration of low-income and ethnic minorities in the central part of the community;
(7) Fiscal problems resulting from declining commercial and industrial activity and decreasing value of property for tax purposes.

The nature and extent of these problems are well known. In the past 20 years, for example, many of the central cities in the major SMSAs have lost population. Over the last two decades, 80% of the new jobs created in the nation's largest metropolitan areas have been located in the suburban areas around the central city. Many of these major metropolitan areas have experienced a net decline in the number of job opportunities. The situation then becomes one in which there is high unemployment in the central city low-income housing area, while industry and commercial establishments in suburban fringes are short of unskilled labor. This problem is compounded by the fact that the transportation system caters to the needs of the suburbanite who has historically commuted to the central city in private vehicles. The resident of the central city is either unable to find adequate public transportation to the suburbs, thus prevented from job opportunities available there, or the costs of commuting are so high that it is only marginally economical for him to engage in jobs in the suburban area. Many of the problems affecting land use in metropolitan America are either caused by, or exacerbated by, flight from the central city of both middle- and upper-income households and employment opportunities. In the decade of the '70s the problem has become even more serious. In the 1960s, the population loss was confined to the central cities of SMSAs, with only 1 of the 25 largest SMSAs having an absolute population loss from 1960 to 1970. By 1974, 10 of the 25 largest SMSAs were experiencing population loss.[10] An example of the nature of these problems is provided by an analysis of what has come to be known as megalopolis.

LAND USE RELATED PROBLEMS IN MEGALOPOLIS

Megalopolis is a term which has been applied to the urbanized region extending from Boston, Massachusetts to Washington, D.C. Within this area are found many of the major metropolitan areas of the United States, and concurrently many of the most severe land use related problems. An analysis of some of the metropolitan areas within megalopolis illustrates the nature of land use problems in metropolitan areas of the United States. Megalopolis is an area where the vast majority of the population reside in urban areas. Although it is difficult to determine the precise percentage of population in urban areas within megalopolis, an approximate figure is 80%, based on the 1970 census. An indication of the importance of the large urban centers in the northeast is given by the concentration of population in a few cities. Three-fifths of the total population of the northeastern United States is concentrated in the four largest metropolitan areas. Historically, these have been the areas of population increase in the United States, and the focus of land use issues relating to providing jobs and housing to the increasing population.

In the period ending in 1975, the urbanized northeastern megalopolis has undergone a significant change. Where historically this has been an area of population increase, it is now an area characterized by declining populations in the central urban cities, with the less densely settled communities and suburbs within the metropolitan region experiencing population growth. Ironically, this trend is occurring in a setting where a major characteristic has been the competition for space. Most of the metropolitan areas of the megalopolis have restricted city limits. This represents the historic development of these cities in which the original town that now constitutes the central city was platted and then surrounded by other towns. For example, Philadelphia has some 2 million people in a land area of 127 square miles, New York has nearly 8 million people in only 315 square miles, while Boston has over 600,000 people living in 48 square miles. Manhatten Island has an average density of 68,000 persons per square mile.[11]

The land use issues of megalopolis, as well as the industrialized and urbanized north central United States, are a function of their small areas and dense populations. Where the emerging metropolitan areas of western and southern United States have generally expanded to include their suburbs and suburban cities, which has allowed them to continue to grow in absolute numbers, the cities of megalopolis with their fixed boundaries have been unable to share in the growth taking place in the suburban fringe. Thus they are left with the older, obsolete housing, industry, and commercial areas. Examination of the 20 largest metropolitan areas in the United States reveals that from 1970 to 1974 there was an average loss of three tenths of 1% of their population annually. This translates to a loss of 1.2 million people from these 20 largest metropolitan areas in the 1970–74 period, while at the same time nonmetropolitan territories had a net in-migration of 1.5 million people.[12]

These figures are even more alarming when it is remembered that the population change represents the entire SMSA, which includes smaller towns that have in fact grown in population during the period. Within the city limits of major cities in megalopolis from 1970–1975, New York lost over 400,000 people, Boston lost over 4,000, and Philadelphia lost over 132,000. Thus, even though population has been growing in the suburban towns within the SMSA, the net loss to the metropolitan areas is significant. Examination of the population figures in Table 11 reveals that for many of the central cities in the northeast megalopolis region, the peak of population occurred between 20 and 30 years ago. The central city population of Baltimore in 1930 was 805,000, and by 1973 it was only 877,000, which was lower than it had been in 1960. In the same period, the population in the SMSA of Baltimore residing outside of the central city increased from 264,000 to 1,250,000.

New York City had a population in 1930 of nearly 7 million in the central city area. Forty-three years later, the population was 7,646,000, but this is lower than the peak in either 1960 or 1970. At the same time, the population in the New York SMSA had increased outside of the central city from only 1 million to nearly 4 million. A great growth in New York City proper occurred between 1900 and 1930 when the population nearly doubled. Post-1930 growth has been relatively small. The phenomenon of population loss in the central cities of metropolitan America is largely confined to the older northeast and northcentral United States. Cities of the south and west are, generally, experiencing population growth in their central cities and do not have a problem to such a great extent as do the cities of the northeastern megalopolis. This is the result of both population migration and the ability of western and southern cities to expand through annexation.

Land Use in Residential Areas in Megalopolis

The impact of the loss of population on metropolitan America is reflected in land use in the residential areas. New York City, for example, is the site of the largest residential rental stock in the United States. In 1970, in New York City, 2.2 million out of a total of 2.9 million housing units were rental units.[13] By 1975, there were only 2 million renter households in New York City.[14] These

Table 11. Population in Central Cities, 1900-1973
(in thousands)

Region and SMSA	1900	1930	1960	1970	1973
East					
Washington, D.C.	279	487	763	756	733
Baltimore	509	805	939	905	877
Boston	561	781	697	641	618
Worcester	118	195	186	176	170
Jersey City	206	317	276	260	255
Newark	246	442	405	382	367
Albany	186	296	278	256	250
Buffalo	352	573	532	462	425
New York	3437	6930	7781	7894	7646
Syracuse	108	209	216	197	184
Philadelphia	1294	1951	2002	1948	1861
Pittsburgh	452	670	604	520	479
Midwest					
Chicago	1699	3376	3550	3366	3172
Gary	22	220	347	330	328
Indianapolis	169	364	476	744	728
Detroit	286	1569	1670	1511	1386
Minneapolis	366	736	796	744	669
Kansas City	164	400	475	507	487
St. Louis	575	822	750	622	558
Cincinnati	326	451	502	452	426
Cleveland	382	900	876	750	678
Columbus	126	291	471	539	450
Dayton	85	201	262	243	214
Milwaukee	285	578	741	717	690
South					
Birmingham	38	260	340	300	295
Mobile	38	68	194	190	188
Miami	20	111	291	334	353
Atlanta	90	270	487	496	451
Louisville	205	308	390	361	335
New Orleans	287	459	627	593	573
Oklahoma City	10	185	324	366	373
Tulsa	0	141	261	331	335
Memphis	102	253	497	623	658
Nashville	81	154	170	448	427
Dallas	43	260	679	844	815
Forth Worth	27	163	356	393	359
Houston	45	292	938	1232	1296
Norfolk	64	1975	419	418	392
West					
Phoenix	6	48	439	581	631
Los Angeles	105	1380	2823	3174	3091
San Diego	18	148	573	698	757
San Francisco	410	918	1107	1077	1033
Denver	134	288	493	514	515
Honolulu	39	138	294	324	334
Albuquerque	6	27	201	243	273
Salt Lake City	54	140	189	175	169
Seattle	81	366	557	584	552

Source: Advisory Commission on Intergovernmental Affairs. *Trends in Metropolitan America* (Washington, D.C.: Government Printing Office, 1977), pp. 11-13, table 1.

units were primarily older, obsolete units with all the associated problems of such housing. In New York City, 12% of the housing had been built prior to 1901, and 45% of the rental units were built prior to 1929. Nearly 71% of the total rental stock was built prior to 1946, and only one in six was constructed in the post-1960 period.[15]

Land use problems presented to metropolitan America by the high proportion of older residential buildings are obvious. Although not all older residential buildings are, in fact, dilapidated and decrepit, the majority tend to be because of costs associated with changing or rehabilitating them. Consequently, these older buildings become areas with a high concentration of poor, minorities, and others who have little political or economic power to insure that they receive adequate housing. The oldest and least desirable part of the city, in essence, becomes a concentration camp for the poor, the aged, the Black, the Mexican-American, the Puerto Rican, and other ethnic groups. Ironically, this same area has high rents associated with it.[16]

Old, obsolete buildings are costly to maintain (in part, accounting for the relatively high rents), but zoning regulations which effectively confine the poor, the elderly, and the ethnic to the central city are also responsible. Exclusionary zoning regulations, by their nature, restrict the poor through such mechanisms as minimum requirements for lot size and/or home size, resulting in de facto elimination of the poor from the suburbs. With high land prices, it is impossible to build low-income housing in suburbs which require minimum lots ranging from 10,000 square feet to 5 acres. Limitations on floor space (1,500 square feet or more per unit) result in costs that make it impossible to produce housing the poor can afford. As a consequence, they are restricted to the existing older housing stock in the central cities with all of its attendant problems.

The transportation system is another land use problem of metropolitan areas, related to zoning, which forces the poor into the central city. Since the poor have the lowest incidence of automobile ownership, they are restricted to those locations with access to stores, jobs, medical care, schools, and other requirements for life. Although the bus and subway components of public transport partially provide access to the suburbs, the cost of housing and existing land use controls effectively prevent the poor from moving to them. Consequently, they remain concentrated in the central city.

Concentration of the poor in the central city is a direct function of past and present land use decisions. Neighborhoods in older metropolitan areas, such as New York City, Baltimore, Philadelphia, and Washington, were initially differentiated on the basis of income, race, nationality, and religion. Areas constructed for the working class in the pre-20th and early 20th century metropolitan areas were located in the most undesirable areas. Thus the tenements for the laboring class were found on interior streets, near railroads, and in the vicinity of manufacturing plants. The wealthy residential areas were located where there were views, in scenic or waterside locations, with wide streets and urban amenities. With the flight of middle- and upper-income urbanites to the suburbs, the higher-income housing was divided into individual rental units, but they still remained higher-class residences. In the past decade, as historic preservation has gained acceptance, it is these latter areas which are being renewed and once again becoming available for upper-income individuals. The poor remain concentrated in the neighborhoods originally designed for working class tenements. And it is in these areas that the greatest land use problems of obsolescence, deterioration, and abandonment occur.

A serious land use problem results when buildings are simply abandoned. The reasons for abandonment of residential units in the central cities are complex; they include rising taxes, higher interest costs, obsolescence, urban renewal, higher maintenance costs, absentee landlords, rising crime, racial tensions, zoning ordinances, housing code enforcement, and similar factors. Abandonment of commercial activity and loss of manufacturing jobs in the neighborhood also are involved in the cause of land abandonment in the central city. When stores become vacant, it signals to residents and property owners that economic decline is far advanced. As one residential unit is abandoned, it has a contagious influence on adjacent units, even those which are structurally sound. Thus the process of abandonment spreads from the deteriorated structures to the entire neighborhood.

The problems created for the central city by abandonment are obvious and have been often reiterated. Vacant buildings become attractive to arsonists and abandoned buildings have a disproportionate share of fires in metropolitan areas. Over 20% of all severe fires in Newark, New Jersey in 1971–72 were in vacant residential buildings, although such buildings constitute less than 5% of buildings in the city.[17] More importantly, as a building is abandoned, it signals to neighboring property owners that if they invest in maintenance on their sound buildings they may be unable to recoup their costs as abandonment spreads. This is further exacerbated as residences in the sound buildings are vacated by those who have the ability to move from the neighborhood. Residents witnessing the increased crime and related problems abandon the area if they have the wherewithal to leave. Residents of the city not living in the vicinity of abandoned structures are affected because the buildings do not return any tax revenue to the city, but become the focal points of increasing demands on the police, fire, and health departments because of the activities associated with them.

Where vacant buildings are razed, the problems presented by the initial abandonment are only partially alleviated. After an abandoned building is torn down, there is little incentive, for a number of reasons, for construction of a new residential building. Normally the abandoned building and resultant vacant land is in a deteriorating or blighted neighborhood with few site amenities to attract new construction. Investors are reluctant to build in such areas since they rightly perceive that the problems which led to the initial abandonment insure the questionableness of gaining an economic return on investments in a single new building in the neighborhood. The causes of the original abandonment would simple preclude renting to middle- or upper-income families, and the landlord would either be faced with a high vacancy rate or would need to rent to those who had participated in the original cause of abandonment. In addition, when buildings are razed, the resultant lots are often small, since the buildings were constructed either prior to or shortly after the turn of the century when lot sizes were uncontrolled or only

Fig. 9. Vacant lot in residential neighborhood in Philadelphia.

marginally regulated. The resultant vacant lot quickly becomes a receptable for trash, debris, and undesirable activities.

The number of abandoned buildings in the metropolitan areas of megalopolis is hard to determine. Although those which have been completely abandoned and consequently gutted by fire are easily recognizable, they represent the end product of an on-going process. The process of abandonment begins when the landlord decides that required improvements and maintenance will not be recouped in rents. At that point, the building begins to move in the direction of abandonment. As conditions become worse, those tenants who have an option will move and poorer residents, with fewer options, often will replace them. In many cases, the only ones who are poor enough to be forced to occupy the rapidly deteriorating structures are those on welfare. This is of particular importance, since studies indicate that the critical factors which lead to abandonment are not the size of the parcel upon which the building is located, the quality or type of construction, its location within an urban renewal area, or the prevalance of adjacent nuisances. Features which seem most closely related to potential abandonment are the quality of maintenance of the structure, the amount of neighborhood vacancy, the condition of neighboring housing units, and landlord dissatisfaction with tenants. The latter is especially important and seems to mirror the landlord's social and racial prejudices. In essence, when the landlord is forced to rent to minority groups and welfare recipients, he will rapidly abandon the building.[18]

The number of buildings which are actually abandoned, therefore, may be a highly inaccurate indicator of the potential abandonment facing a city. It has been estimated that 130,000 buildings were abandoned in New York City between 1966 and 1970. In 1974, there were an estimated 5,000 vacant buildings in Baltimore and 20,000 in Philadelphia.[19]

Land vacancy and residential abandonment of the central city area could conceivably be viewed as an indication of progress in providing housing. Under this accumption, proponents argue that the availability of housing in the suburbs and rising incomes are allowing inner city residents to move to higher quality housing beyond the confines of the central city region. Thus the existence of vacant structures, and vacant land in old residential districts of the central city, simply reflect the upward movement of families into better quality housing. Abandonment is simply a factor of surplus low-income housing. In fact, the opposite is the case. There is a shortage of low-cost, suitable housing in the central city areas. For example, in 1972, it was estimated that there was a need for over 100,000 new dwelling units in the Washington, D.C. area by 1982. But at the same time there were 1,500 residential structures that were abandoned in the city[20] and government urban renewal and rehabilitation efforts were resulting in destruction of housing units at a rate greater than that at which reconstruction and rehabilitation efforts were creating new homes. The owners whose homes were destroyed by these efforts were faced with difficult problems in finding suitable housing.

Solutions

A number of solutions to the problem of residential land use in metropolitan areas have been presented. One of the earliest of these was associated with the concept of urban renewal in which obsolescent housing was torn down and replaced by quality housing and commercial or government buildings. One of the major elements in this movement were the Housing Act of 1949, which authorized the federal government to pay a minimum of two-thirds of the cost of acquiring and clearing land in the city as compared to the price the land would bring if sold for a private development. The 1949 Act was built upon the earlier 1937 Housing Act, and has subsequently been amended and modified on several occasions, importantly in 1961, 1965, and 1968.[21] Urban renewal portions of the housing programs have resulted in new housing construction in a number of old central cities, notably Chicago, New York, Philadelphia, Baltimore, and Pittsburgh. The new housing has been criticized because it has been designed primarily as a warehouse for people rather than as a home for individual people. A classic example is the Pruitt-Igoe project of St. Louis. Built in the mid-1950s, it was hailed as a model of urban renewal and slum clearance. Covering several blocks, the multiple-story building became a nightmare for its residents, as it was designed in such a way that the interior courts became a haven for anti-social behavior and access to the individual floors from the elevator became a major risk. It was rehabilitated in the early 1970s in an attempt to overcome the problems which, in effect, led to its abandonment by the low-income sector it had been designed for. Rehabilitation was unsuccessful and in 1977 the Pruitt-Igoe project was destroyed (Fig. 10). Examples of other abandoned public housing projects or those suffering from high vacancies and all of the other problems of the older housing they replaced, can be found in most large cities of the United States. To make a broad statement about the success of the urban renewal projects, "the best available evidence is that residential renewal projects are in general not economically efficient."[22]

Another solution to the problem of residential housing in the central city is for the government to provide some type of subsidy for low-income families. This would allow them to pay higher rents and thus have a significant impact on land use in residential areas of the central city. There have been a variety of programs in the United States that have attempted to do this. The first of these was the concept of public housing provided by the government and set forth in the Housing Act of 1937. The program is designed to establish new and reha-bilitated rental units for low-income households at below market rents. This hous-ing is owned by local housing authorities who finance the projects through the sale of tax exempt bonds. The federal government gave a subsidy to the authority sufficient to insure that rents need only be high enough to cover operation ex-penses, repair and maintenance, and payments in lieu of taxes to the local govern-ment. Over one million such units have been constructed and occupied in the United States and they remain an important form of housing for the poorest sector of society. They have been criticized, however, because they are economi-cally inefficient and tend to limit the extent of assistance available.[23] Another program was enacted in 1965, entitled *The Rent Supplement Program*. Housing under this program is developed by private interests and the Federal Housing Administration supplies rent supplements to the landlord to cover the difference between a unit's rent and an amount equal to 25% of the occupant's adjusted income. Such housing is restricted to families and individuals who have an income at or below public housing income limits, and who are elderly, handicapped, dis-placed by government action, victims of disaster, or living in substandard housing.

In 1976, there were a total of 1,305,370 units in low income public housing. An additional 63,400 were under construction while 60,000 more were authorized but not under construction. Through 1974, the rent supplement program had produced an average of 16,000 units for occupancy per year.[24] Another program designed to help provide housing for the poor is the Section 235 Home Owner-ship program. This allows the individual to purchase a home with the government paying the difference in costs related to debt service, taxes, insurance, and mortgage insurance when those costs exceed 20% of the household's adjusted income. Be-tween 1968 and 1974, 400,000 units were produced under this program.

A number of other programs have been suggested to help resolve the problem of a central city. These include support for cooperative ownership of buildings that otherwise might be abandoned by their landlords, homesteading of vacant or abandoned buildings, and community efforts to maintain and repair deterio-rating buildings. Water, sewer, heat, and electricity are covered by an emergency repair program in New York City which is designed to insure or restore essential services to prevent abandonment of buildings not maintained by their owners. An analysis of the success of this program reveals, however, that essentially all

Fig. 10. Pruitt-Igoe Development in St. Louis: before and after.

buildings receiving such emergency services are subsequently abandoned. Thus, abandonment is delayed, but at high cost. Cooperative ownership has been of only minor success because of the lack of financial mechanisms allowing the poor to assume ownership and repair and maintain these structures.

Urban homesteading attracted the attention of many people in the 1970s as a possible alternative, but it has important weaknesses.[25] The concept of homesteading urban property is an extension of the homesteading system used to dispose of the vast areas of public domain in the 1800s. The increasing amount of housing abandonment in the metropolitan areas led to the development in the 1960s of the idea that properties which had been allowed to revert to private ownership because of lack of tax payments could be returned to private ownership through a modified homesteading program. Although the factors affecting property abandonment in the central city have been discussed above, it should be pointed out that the entrance of the federal government into the housing market in the late 1960s under Section 235 of the 1968 Housing Act apparently played a role in accelerating urban abandonment. By making it easy for low-income families to finance the purchase of homes, inner city property values were artificially inflated. Families who purchased older homes under this program often had insufficient experience and income; and faced with extensive repairs, they were unable to maintain their homes. Since the 235 Program resulted in limited equity in the homes purchased, and deterioration of the homes made them unattractive to buyers (especially at the inflated price associated with their original purchase), many 235 participants abandoned properties. Although the federal government has not officially acknowledged that the 235 Program in fact did cause greater property abandonment in the urban core, the federal government's Department of Housing and Urban Development (HUD) became the largest residential real estate owner and manager in the country as a result of property abandonment.

At the same time, HUD was acquiring responsibility for numerous properties, the problem of abandonment continued to expand, and local governments became owners through tax reversions. The problems caused to the city by abandoned property, coupled with a shortage of homes in a price range available to lower-income and low-middle-income families, led to the idea in the early 1970s that they could be transferred to the families through homesteading. Basically, the concept of urban homesteading involved the local government acquiring titles to abandoned properties and then providing these to individuals or families at a low or zero initial cost. The local government assisted in obtaining capital for improvement through loans, either guaranteed by city bonds or private institutions. The new owner's input was through the application of "sweat-equity" by the homesteader. As conceived, this would allow a person with minimum capital to acquire an abandoned property and then, using a minimum of cash and a maximum of personal labor, be able to rehabilitate the property.

The underlying theoretical basis for justification of homesteading was that just as the entry of low-income families into the neighborhood precipitates other residents to sell their properties, and the abandonment of one building leads to abandonment of others, so when an abandoned structure was rehabilitated and an owner/occupier in residence, it would spread to adjacent properties and reverse the trend of deterioration. Entry into a blighted neighborhood by owner/occupant families who were visibly revitalizing their homes and were supported by public and private organizations could change the perception of the neighborhood and reverse blight.[26] Several cities in the northeastern United States, including Philadelphia and Baltimore, began actual homesteading in 1973, with Wilmington, Delaware being the first.[27]

Some of the problems associated with urban homesteading reflected the nature of the abandoned buildings and the legal process of tax forfeiture. For example, in Wilmington there were 2,000 abandoned housing units in 1973, but only 150 were controlled by the city as a result of foreclosing on tax delinquent property. In addition, when the buildings are abandoned the market value and costs of rehabilitating often involve a greater investment than the building would be worth. Of the 150 housing units controlled by Wilmington, for example, only 50 units were considered marginally useful. The other 100 required rehabilitation in excess of $10,000 to meet local code specifications or were located in neighborhoods with so much abandoned housing that they were seen as unsuitable for homesteading.[28]

Associated with the dilapidated nature of abandoned buildings is the problem of transferring abandoned property to public ownership. In most states, there is a grace period in which a nonpaying property owner is able to pay his back taxes. This period may be as short as 1 year or as long as 5 years. But, in any event, the period between abandonment and the government obtaining title to the property is so great that considerably more vandalism and deterioration to abandoned buildings occurs. This further limits the number of units suitable for rehabilitation through homesteading. Another problem facing urban homesteading is selection of candidates for the program. Since it is impossible to successfully homestead an abandoned building without some financial resources and rehabilitative skills, the number of individuals who are qualified is limited. Most cities require minimum financial ability to undertake homesteading, which effectively restricts many low-income people. Associated with this problem is that of financing. It is difficult to obtain adequate financing for structures in neighborhoods which have a history and appearance of urban blight. Urban homesteading has succeeded where it has been associated with innovative financing programs.

One of the major problems associated with the homesteading phenomenon is that the initial underlying theory that rehabilitation could be largely accomplished through "sweat-equity" of the homesteader was overstated. Most of the properties available for homesteading have major repair problems, such as plumbing, heating, electrical, etc., which are normally beyond the abilities of the handyman and require trained personnel.

Another problem in urban homesteading, difficult to overcome, is the blight associated with areas of abandoned housing. Problems which originally led to abandonment of the structures remain, and properties which are being rehabilitated have been subject to vandalism, theft, and arson when located in areas of severe blight. Selection of properties for homesteading on a scattered basis, with only one property in a neighborhood and others scattered throughout the city, failed to make any contribution to the improvement of specific neighborhoods. Even in Baltimore, where 42 houses covering an entire block were homesteaded in an effort to change the neighborhood trends, it is unclear whether it will be able to affect the problems of the decaying neighborhood surrounding the block. Without special programs leading to revitalization and rehabilitation of the surrounding neighborhood, it is questionable whether homesteading can be any more than a holding action.

In spite of these problems (or as a result), the United States government became involved in homesteading in 1974 through HUD. Under a program entitled "Property Release Option Program" (PROP), 4,100 homes were offered to 43 cities for use in homesteading programs or other public purposes. Unfortunately, the administrative rules specified that homes supplied by HUD under the PROP program could not have any remaining market value. Thus, some cities either declined to accept any of the properties or demolished them and used the land for open space. To overcome this problem, legislation was proposed in 1973 allowing a department of HUD to transfer properties to the cities which were in much better condition than those being offered through the PROP program. As the largest owner and manager of housing in the United States, HUD had possession of homes which could be rehabilitated, and they also had programs for financing and neighborhood improvement which could be adapted to meet homesteading needs.

On August 22, 1974, the Housing and Community Development Act of 1974 was signed into law. Section 8-10 of that Act authorized transfer of one- to four-unit structures to entities of local government for use in urban homesteading. A total of 23 demonstration programs were chosen in 1976 to implement the urban homestead program for one year. The intent was to gain experience in developing effective processes for selecting appropriate properties, and homesteaders, and deciding what support programs needed to be provided to make the program successful. The experiences of the demonstration cities included a whole range of activities beyond simply providing housing. Such support activities ranged from provision of paint to residents willing to provide the labor to low-interest loans to homesteaders, to public improvement and provision of services, to a community-owned repair service for property owners with the cost based on the owner's income.

The Urban Homesteading Demonstration Program has revealed that in selected neighborhoods and with appropriate participants it is possible to transfer vacant homes owned by HUD to private ownership. Overall, however, the total numbers of units involved are small. As of May 1, 1977, only 1,045 properties had been conveyed from HUD to the 23 cities in the demonstration program. At the same time, only 581 of these homes were occupied by urban homesteaders.[29] The popularly conceived view of urban homesteading as a solution to land abandonment and residential housing shortage in metropolitan America is questionable. To date it has been effective in placing families in their own homes in only a small number of cases. Whether such a program would be successful if adopted on a broad scale remains to be seen. It is evident, however, that urban homesteading can form one of the approaches to revitalizing residential land use in urban areas. Nevertheless, it is not a panacea to overcome the problems of urban blight, land abandonment, and general deterioration of obsolete housing in America's central cities.

Table 12. Manufacturing Employment in Selected Cities, 1963 and 1972
(in thousands)

Region and SMSA	1963			1972			1972 as percent of 1963	
	SMSA	Central city	Outside central city	SMSA	Central city	Outside central city	Central city	Outside central city
East								
Washington, D.C.	50	22	28	55	19	36	86.3	128.5
Baltimore	191	104	87	180	91	89	87.5	102.2
Boston	293	88	210	273	59	214	71.0	101.9
Worcester	48	35	13	46	29	17	82.8	130.7
Jersey City	110	27	83	95	23	72	85.1	86.7
Newark	250	74	176	245	47	198	63.5	112.5
Buffalo	163	57	106	152	53	99	92.9	93.3
New York	1147	927	220	990	757	233	81.6	105.9
Philadelphia	536	265	271	498	203	295	76.6	108.8
Pittsburgh	272	82	190	262	63	199	76.8	104.7
Midwest								
Chicago	861	509	352	909	430	479	84.4	136.0
Gary	98	86	12	100	82	18	95.3	150.0
Indianapolis	116	70	46	123	93	30	132.8	65.2
Detroit	494	201	293	539	180	359	89.5	122.5
Minneapolis	111	62	40	120	57	63	91.9	128.5
St. Louis	260	129	131	256	98	158	75.9	120.6
Cincinnati	154	77	77	157	68	89	88.3	115.5
Cleveland	280	169	111	269	131	138	77.5	124.3
Columbus	80	66	14	89	62	27	93.9	192.8
Dayton	104	81	23	119	72	47	88.8	204.3
Milwaukee	194	119	75	200	106	94	89.0	125.3
South								
Birmingham	63	34	29	67	35	32	102.9	110.3
Mobile	19	34	5	24	14	10	100.0	200.0
Miami	43	19	24	86	26	60	136.8	250.0
Atlanta	96	52	44	116	48	68	92.3	154.5
Louisville	88	58	30	112	60	52	103.4	173.3
New Orleans	49	31	18	55	29	26	93.5	144.4
Oklahoma City	27	24	3	40	34	6	141.6	200.0
Tulsa	30	18	12	43	35	8	194.4	66.6
Memphis	47	43	4	60	54	6	125.5	150.0
Nashville	47	34	13	56	46	10	135.2	76.9
Dallas	110	86	24	153	107	46	124.4	191.6
Fort Worth	51	40	11	71	47	24	117.5	218.1
Houston	109	77	32	160	105	55	136.3	171.8
Norfolk	16	13	3	28	21	7	161.5	233.3
West								
Phoenix	41	29	12	72	52	20	179.3	166.6
Los Angeles	746	313	433	780	320	460	102.2	106.2
San Diego	60	49	11	65	45	20	91.8	181.8
San Francisco	196	92	104	181	69	112	75.0	107.6
Denver	70	38	32	95	42	53	110.5	165.6
Honolulu	18	16	2	20	17	3	106.2	150.0
Albuquerque	8	6	2	11	10	1	166.61	50.0
Salt Lake City	32	17	15	34	22	12	129.4	80.0
Seattle	122	84	38	109	48	61	57.1	160.5

Source: Trends in Metropolitan America (Washington, D.C.: Advisory Commission on Intergovernmental Relations, 1977), pp. 47–49, table 13.

INDUSTRIAL LAND USE IN METROPOLITAN AMERICA

Coupled with the problems of residential property abandonment, urban blight, and population loss in the central city of metropolitan America has been a loss of jobs in industry and commerce (Table 12). The reasons for this decline are many, but the same types of land use issues affect manufacturing and industry in the central city as affects the residential housing stock. Much of the industry in the older northeastern United States is housed in old and obsolete buildings. In addition, growth of SMSAs in the past 30 years has made accessibility to the industries in the central city more difficult. An indication of the importance of loss of jobs and resultant industrial land left vacant is found in New York City: There were a total of 3,458,300 jobs in New York City in 1974, making it the largest employer in the world; but between 1969 and 1974 New York City lost an average of more than 80,000 jobs per year. Over 43,000 jobs in manufacturing activities; over 30,000 jobs in private nonmanufacturing industry; nearly 7,500 jobs in finance, real estate, and insurance; and 2,200 jobs in federal government were lost yearly.[30]

The experience of Chicago parallels that of New York. From 1960 to 1970, Chicago proper lost 211,000 jobs. In the same period, the suburbs gained 548,000 jobs. Moreover, the rate of loss of employment was more than double that of population loss, 12% vs. 5%.[31]

The loss of manufacturing jobs and the movement of industry to the suburbs or to the southern sun belt result in idle manufacturing land. For instance, New York City has long been known as the center of the American garment industry, but the apparel industries lost jobs at an annual rate of 12,000 between 1970–1974. Although some of the resultant vacant loft area has been transformed to residential use or other activities, still a large area of the garment district is substantially desolated.[32]

The problems associated with industrial and manufacturing land use in metropolitan America is not uniformly distributed through the SMSA. The older central city areas are faced with the most severe problems, while the suburbs often become the home of new industries or corporate headquarters (Table 13). The majority of the central cities of the east and midwest suffered an absolute decline in numbers of jobs in the 5-year period. Only in the south and west where the central city proper covers a larger area and cities are younger did the majority of central cities increase in employment in the period. Even here the rate of employment growth in the central city was usually exceeded by the suburbs and satellite towns in the SMSA. The significance of this is indicated by New York City where, using an index of 100 for employment in 1965, by 1974 the index for the city had fallen to 96.7 and the suburban area of Nassau-Suffolk had increased to 104.6. During this same period, the entire United States increased to an index of 128.8.[33]

COMMERCIAL LAND USE IN METROPOLITAN AMERICA

Concomitant with the loss of manufacturing jobs in metropolitan America is the decline of commercial activities and employment in old residential neighborhoods

Table 13. Change in Employment by Place of Work, 1960–1970
(percent)

Region and SMSA	Central city	Outside central city	Change in central city acreage (percent)
East			
Washington, D.C.	8.2	96.2	0
Baltimore	-4.6	24.2	0
Boston	-4.0	24.0	0
Worcester	2.3	23.2	0
Jersey City	12.6	-4.1	0
Newark	-12.5	21.7	0
Buffalo	-15.8	29.2	0
New York	-1.9	31.1	0
Philadelphia	-4.1	22.5	0
Pittsburgh	6.1	-3.8	0
Midwest			
Chicago	-12.1	62.2	0
Gary	N.A.	N.A.	—
Indianapolis	-18.8	58.4	0
Detroit	N.A.	N.A.	—
Minneapolis	1.9	118.9	0
Kansas City	11.1	37.4	143
St. Louis	-14.2	49.9	0
Cincinnati	-3.8	36.5	1
Cleveland	-12.9	62.6	0
Columbus	20.5	45.8	55
Dayton	14.0	30.5	15
Milwaukee	-10.2	76.5	5
South			
Birmingham	5.7	23.9	6
Mobile	-3.8	5.5	-23
Miami	7.4	80.7	0
Louisville	15.1	57.6	5
New Orleans	0.0	78.6	0
Oklahoma City	38.5	21.1	97
Tulsa	35.4	-9.8	263
Memphis	22.4	18.5	37
Dallas	41.2	71.5	4
Fort Worth	9.5	126.9	46
Houston	51.4	58.1	23
West			
Phoenix	51.1	61.9	32
Los Angeles	5.4	35.3	2
San Diego	17.0	62.0	9
San Francisco	5.6	38.0	1
Denver	19.6	80.7	31
Honolulu	21.7	62.2	0
Albuquerque	25.8	5.5	46
Salt Lake City	16.5	70.9	51
Seattle	15.5	65.8	2

Source: Trends in Metropolitan America (Washington, D.C.: Advisory Commission on Intergovernmental Relations, 1977), pp. 44–46, table 12.

Fig. 11. Vacant stores in Philadelphia.

and central city areas (Fig. 11). This may take the form of large shopping centers moving into the suburban portions of metropolitan America; the movement of corporate headquarters and support authorities to less congested locales; or may reflect commercial establishments which were destroyed during riots in cities such as Newark, Detroit, or Chicago; or may be simply the closing of so-called "mom and pop stores" as their owners retire or give up their business in the face of rising crime, insurance costs, and loss of income. Between 1956 and 1974, New York City lost 30% of the corporate headquarters of those corporations listed in *Fortune Directories of 500 Largest Industrial Corporations*. In 1956, New York City was headquarters for 140 of the 500, but in 1974 only 98 remained. More significantly, as late as 1967, New York had 137 largest corporations headquarters.[34]

In Pittsburgh, the core area of the black ghetto, called the Hill district, suffered rioting in 1968. One hundred stores were looted or burned at that time and most were never rebuilt. In the Boston ghetto, from the south end into Roxbury, more than 50 stores were burned or damaged along Blue Hill Avenue during the 1967 riot and many of these remain closed. Chicago, it was reported in 1971, had a loss of as much as 50% of the businesses in the ghetto areas in the preceding 10 years. In some areas on the west side of Chicago, as few as

Table 14. Changes in Retail Sales in Major Metropolitan Areas, 1963–1972
(percent)

Region	SMSA	Central city	Outside central city	Central business district
East				
Washington, D.C.	117.9	27.0	180.1	15.4
Baltimore	99.1	38.3	174.9	18.8
Boston	78.8	36.4	98.0	7.3
Worcester	89.8	50.3	173.9	21.8
Jersey City	43.6	42.3	44.4	−18.6
Newark	59.2	−4.1	81.2	−15.3
Buffalo	65.2	21.2	96.7	3.2
New York	58.5	43.7	88.7	30.2
Philadelphia	83.2	43.0	113.2	15.2
Pittsburgh	69.3	14.9	97.2	13.0
Midwest				
Chicago	80.4	37.8	130.1	26.8
Gary	79.7	45.7	140.2	−5.0
Indianapolis	87.2	116.5	37.3	−23.5
Detroit	86.9	19.2	137.1	1.3
Minneapolis	101.6	32.8	206.6	8.0
Kansas City	93.6	48.2	148.0	−15.2
St. Louis	79.0	11.0	119.7	−5.1
Cincinnati	80.0	28.3	128.9	11.9
Cleveland	63.8	8.8	112.0	−8.8
Columbus	120.9	94.8	179.8	2.6
Dayton	87.6	19.3	147.8	−11.8
Milwaukee	76.1	32.0	146.7	10.1
South				
Birmingham	102.5	68.7	172.1	30.0
Mobile	85.4	87.8	80.3	45.0
Miami	135.2	80.3	171.9	28.7
Atlanta	179.0	78.3	343.5	5.9
Louisville	102.4	42.2	209.0	12.3
New Orleans	114.4	54.1	258.6	36.2
Oklahoma City	114.9	95.7	162.2	−32.3
Tulsa	105.7	125.7	51.2	13.6
Memphis	113.2	121.6	70.2	−8.5
Nashville	130.6	128.8	146.0	8.5
Dallas	123.1	97.1	181.2	−14.2
Fort Worth	118.0	65.7	255.9	−14.1
Houston	143.3	132.0	176.3	−30.5
Norfolk	115.4	71.8	287.5	6.6
West				
Phoenix	143.1	102.5	242.2	−45.3
Los Angeles	60.1	52.6	66.6	9.4
San Diego	133.5	107.3	167.1	−20.0
San Francisco	71.9	32.2	108.0	6.1
Denver	132.0	61.3	218.5	−10.7
Honolulu	145.7	131.3	209.9	18.1
Albuquerque	128.1	125.6	166.6	−64.0
Salt Lake City	106.5	53.8	190.1	41.1
Seattle	90.9	46.4	167.5	−10.6

Source: Trends in Metropolitan America (Washington, D.C.: Advisory Commission on Intergovernmental Relations, 1977), pp. 53–55, table 15.

one-third of the stores of 10 years ago remain in operation. A drive through the older ghetto areas of any major metropolitan area will reveal vacant residential, commercial, and industrial land. Buildings which once housed commercial activities in the lower stories and residential activities in the upper stories are now either boarded-up or burned-out ruins. Comparison of the rate of change in retail sales illustrates the problems associated with commercial land use in metropolitan America. While central business districts (CBDs) of major American metropolitan areas have been growing at a relatively slow rate or actually declining, suburban shopping areas doubled and tripled their sales (Table 14).

The stagnation and decline in the industrial and commercial land use sectors is particularly important to the cities because of their role in generating taxes and attracting employees and customers to the city. Unfortunately, some observers maintain that there is little hope for successful resolution of the problems presented to metropolitan areas by such changes in land use.[35]

OTHER LAND USE PROBLEMS IN METROPOLITAN AMERICA

Transportation

There are a number of important land use issues associated with transportation in metropolitan America. Some have argued that transportation is the key to metropolitan land use problems since the development of high speed transport systems have allowed middle-income residents to move to the suburbs and commute to their jobs in the central city. Others have argued that the intense competition of traffic to move into the downtown areas of New York City and other cities of megalopolis have caused businesses and corporations to move to the suburbs of metropolitan areas. In all probability, once the white flight to the suburbs was well under way, the executive level recognized that they could also have their jobs in the suburbs as well, rather than be forced to commute to the central city each day. Nevertheless, there remain numerous jobs in the central city area and problems relating to transport access remain a significant land use issue.

The problems associated with land use and highway transportation are of three types:

(1) congestion associated with the archaic street patterns of most of metropolitan America, particularly in megalopolis;
(2) parking problems in the high rent areas of central city America;
(3) expressway developments and their impact on existing neighborhoods, businesses, and other transport systems.

The archaic street patterns of America's old central cities are apparent to anyone who has visited areas such as Boston. Even in cities like Washington, which were laid out according to a formal plan, the problems of automobile transportation are immense. Since L'Enfant did not foresee the automobile when he laid out the plan for Washington, its grandiose system of circles and diagonals results in congestion during rush hours.

The development of expressway systems was intended to overcome some of the problems associated with archaic street systems. Fundamentally, they are designed to allow commuters to arrive at the location of their jobs by traversing the older sections of urban America at a rapid rate. Unfortunately, in allowing the rapid ingress and egress of the automobile to the central city, the problems of metropolitan America have been compounded. The flight to the suburbs increases as rapid transport links are completed. Moreover, neighborhoods which have developed over a long period of time can be destroyed by an expressway being placed across them. Increasingly there is recognition on the part of inner city residents that expressways tend to go through the low-income, Black, or other relatively powerless minority group sections. The resultant destruction of housing, urban inter-connections, and businesses may lead to a disastrous impact in terms of other land uses. Not only are commercial establishments and housing destroyed outright in the process of constructing a highway, but businesses which were located along the older routeways may be forced out of business because of loss of traffic volume. Because of a number of these problems, residents of many communities have banded together to prevent completion of some expressways.

While expressways are allowing additional flight from the urban center, they also cause a decline in alternative transport forms. The construction of an expressway for automobiles adjacent to or near existing commuter rail lines is an important causal agent in the decline of companies such as the Pennsylvania Railroad. As expressways cause people to abandon the railroad for what is perceived to be, or actually is, faster and more efficient transport by private auto, there is a permanent change in land use related to the railroads.

Ironically, while new expressways are destroying the mass transit of urban America, most central cities suffer from lack of adequate accessibility. The lack of sufficient high speed automobile expressways leads to additional movement of commerce and industry to the suburbs, where the population has moved. For example, in Washington, D.C. only three of the four bridges crossing the Potomac between the District of Columbia and Virginia are of major use for commuters coming into Washington. Consequently, much of the time involved in the journey to work in Washington is associated with delays on the limited access ways. In Baltimore, residents of suburban areas to the west and southeast of the city have poor access to the central city. In Manhattan's business district, some 750,000 automobiles enter and leave every working day. Most of the traffic coming to and from Manhattan suffers from the fact that there are only two tunnels and one bridge connecting Manhattan west with New Jersey, and there are inadequate expressways leading to the approaches to Manhattan.[36]

The planner of land use in metropolitan America is faced with the problem of not only determining the traffic needs of the downtown city, but minimizing the negative impacts of changes which result from improving the transport system. If additional jobs are to be prevented from leaving the central cities, then the middle- and upper-income workers who commute to those jobs must have a means to speedily and safely travel to the downtown area. Once there, there must be available parking at a reasonable fee. Where these situations do not exist, there is great pressure for the coporate headquarters or industry to move to the suburbs where they are more accessible. At the same time, provision of more rapid transit routes results in more flight to the suburbs and destroys existing residences.

Open Space

Another severe problem in metropolitan America is that of open space. The need for land for parks and recreation areas is obvious, but since the land use in urban areas reflects the development over hundreds of years in which private gain was the fundamental motivating force, there is little available. The cost involved in acquiring land for uses which do not yield a high economic rent is obvious. One proposed solution is to demolish abandoned and uninhabitable structures and replace them with parks. A difficulty with this approach is that the parks are often in undesirable neighborhoods and may well become a focal point for activities not accepted by residents of the city. Another solution common in urban America is that of vertical expansion of structures. Where lands which are desirable are limited in supply, as in Philadelphia, New York, Baltimore, Boston, Chicago, and other major metropolitan areas, the incentive to vertically expand has created the skyscraper phenomenon. This in turn creates problems of land use because it concentrates workers in relatively small areas and compounds the need for rapid transport and parking spaces.

It should be obvious that land use problems of the central cities of America are interconnected. The movement to the suburbs makes the central city area a repository for the poor, minority groups, those on welfare, and others with little political or economic power, or alternate opportunities. White residents of the central city portion of metropolitan America are moving at an alarming rate. Many of the older central cities lost one-third of their white population in the decade of the 1960s. The loss of middle-income families from central city residential areas prompts property owners to minimize maintenance of their buildings and thus begins the process of abandonment. A loss of manufacturing and commercial activities which follow the middle-income residents to the suburbs makes the city less able to support those people who remain. Faced with a declining tax base and rising costs to provide services, the central city is poorly equipped to deal with the land use problems it faces.

Although a number of solutions have been suggested and several programs have been funded by the federal government, including urban renewal, urban transport, public housing, rent supplements, and others designed to overcome the problems of the central cities which relate to land use, few have been successful. An alternative which has been utilized in the Twin City area of Minneapolis-St. Paul attempts to overcome some of the problems of the central city caused by the flight to the suburbs through tax base sharing.[37] Recognizing that the two basic problems of metropolitan America are the concentration of those who are least able to pay but most in need of assistance in the central city, and the fact that all of the metropolitan area is interrelated and decisions made in a suburb affect the central city, the Minnesota state legislature enacted a landmark statute in 1971. The basis for this act was acknowledgement that the tax base of the metropolitan area was tied to the high-income residents and industry of the city which was moving to the suburbs, while those who needed the greatest amount of urban services were left behind but did not have the ability to support their need. In addition, the actions of the independent local governments led to competition for the tax base rather than to rational cooperation by suburb and central city to overcome the problems common to all. The 1971 Minnesota act is designed to spread the financial benefits of nonresidential growth to all local governments of the metropolitan area and to provide an incentive for all of the local governments in a metropolitan area to cooperate. The Metropolitan Fiscal Disparities Act specifically set up a tax base sharing plan for the seven-county Twin Cities metropolitan area. Basically, the Minnesota act is designed to allow all of the communities within the metropolitan area to share in the growth in commercial-industrial assessed valuation. In theory, this will provide relief for the central city areas left with groups requiring increased services but low commercial-industrial property ratios caused by losses to the suburbs.

The plan consists of each local government in the metropolitan area calculating each year the difference in the assessed value of all commercial-industrial property within its boundaries as compared to the base year of 1971. Forty percent of the change in the assessed value of the commercial-industrial property is contributed to an area-wide tax base. Thus, only those communities actually having a growth in commercial-industrial property assessments will contribute to the tax base, but all communities will share. In effect, this has the goal of insuring that as industry, commerce, and middle-income families move from the central city, they will continue to help support the central city. The metropolitan areas of Minneapolis-St. Paul received an average per capita net gain in taxable base of $53 during the first 2 years of its implementation (1974–1975), while the suburbs were net contributors of tax base.[38] The act has had the effect of somewhat compensating for disparities and change in commercial-industrial land use. It is potentially a tool that will minimize movement of the industry and commerce to the suburbs as tax rates become more uniform throughout the area. Where it has little effect in so doing, it will provide at least a partial recompense to the central city in taxes for the loss of industry and commerce to the suburbs. Studies indicate that revenues from tax base sharing programs will be inadequate to completely alleviate the fiscal problems of large central cities.[39] But of greater importance, the Minnesota act in the Twin Cities metropolitan area holds promise of overcoming a major problem for wise land use in metropolitan areas: multiplicity of governing bodies and competition for land use activities. Existence of the act is indicative of the need to overcome the self-interest which motivates communities of metropolitan America at the present time. A primary need, in order for metropolitan America to overcome its land use problems, is to devise a system for true intergovernmental cooperation within the metropolitan region and adequate and efficient development of the land resources for all of the residents within its boundaries, whether they be residents of the central city, the white suburbs, or the satellite towns.

CONCLUSION

The irony of the land use issues facing the central city is that problems in the suburbs are related to those in the central city. Growth in the suburbs resulting from flight from the city generates increased demands for services. Although these demands may be for new services or simply upgrading and expansion of existing ones, the end result is increased tax rates and fiscal problems for the community. The central city faces the same problem but at a more intense level. Decline in the population of the central city is not paralleled by a proportional decline in demand for services. In fact, since it is the poor, elderly, and ethnic minorities who are unable to flee the city, there may be an actual increase in costs of services in a period of declining tax base. This helps explain the fiscal problem of cities such as New York, and emphasizes the interconnected nature of land use in city and suburb. Unless or until regional governments or tax systems like that in Minneapolis-St. Paul are adopted, the land use related problems of metropolitan America will continue to intensify.

NOTES

[1] *Urban Land Policies and Land Use Control Measures*, Vol. VI, *Northern America* (New York: United Nations, 1973), p. 23.

[2] Ibid.

[3] *Statistics for State and Metropolitan Areas*, U.S. Bureau of the Census (a preprint from the *County and City Data Book, 1977*; Washington, D.C.: Government Printing Office, 1977), p. ix.

[4] Cities used in developing the sample of 22 were: Boston, Buffalo, Chicago, Cincinnati, Cleveland, Dallas, Dayton, Detroit, Long Beach, Los Angeles, Miami, Minneapolis, New York, Newark, Oklahoma City, Pittsburgh, Portsmouth, Providence, St. Louis, San Antonio, San Francisco, and Seattle.

[5] *Urban Land Policies and Land Use Control Measures*, op. cit., p. 136, table 26.

[6] For a complete discussion of zoning-related problems, see Thomas E. Borcherding, "The California Coastal Plan as a Statewide Zoning Ordinance," in *The California Coastal Plan: A Critique* (San Francisco: Institute for Contemporary Studies, 1976), pp. 109–132. See also Donald A. Woolfe, "Zoning Is Doing Planning in," *Practicing Planner*, June 1976, pp. 10–13. A different view argues that zoning does not necessarily do what the experts anticipate, but is in fact an effective means of providing for change in which local interests control change in the local area. The fact that zoning is subject to pressure groups allows local people to retain control, or at least express outrage, if their wishes are not recognized. Constance Perin, *Everything in its Place* (Princeton, N.J.: Princeton University Press, 1977), pp. 180–183.

[7] *Urban Land Policies and Land Use Control Measures*, op. cit., p. 42.

[8] Ibid., pp. 41–42.

[9] Perin, op. cit., footnote 4, p. 181.

[10] Peter A. Morrison, "The Current Demographic Context of National Growth and Development," *Environmental Comment*, July 1976, p. 4.

[11] Lewis M. Alexander, *The Northeastern United States*, 2nd ed. (New York: D. Van Nostrand, 1976), pp. 21–22.

[12]George Sternlieb and James W. Hughes, *Current Population Trends in the United States* (New Brunswick, N.J.: Center for Urban Policy Research, 1978), pp. 69–70.

[13]George W. Carey, *New York, New Jersey: A Vignette of the Metropolitan Region* (Cambridge, Mass.: Ballinger Publishing Co., 1976), p. 29, table 2.

[14]George Sternlieb and James W. Hughes, *Housing and Economic Reality: New York City, 1976* (New Brunswick, N.J.: Rutgers, The State University of New Jersey, 1976), table 4:8, p. 80.

[15]Ibid., p. 68.

[16]Ibid., table 3–17, p. 66.

[17]George Sternlieb and Robert W. Burchell, *Residential Abandonment* (New Brunswick, N.J.: Center for Urban Policy Research, 1973), p. xxi.

[18]George Sternleib and David Listokin, *Housing, 1973–1974* (New York: AMS Press, 1976), pp. 193–194.

[19]William T. Nachbaum, "Empty Houses: Abandoned Residential Buildings in the Inner City," in George Sternlieb, *Housing, 1971–1972* (New York: AMS Press, 1975), pp. 193–194.

[20]Ibid.

[21]For a concise but thorough account of the federal role in housing, see *Housing in the Seventies*, Vol. I (Washington, D.C.: U.S. Department of Housing and Urban Development, 1974), pp. 82–144.

[22]Irving H. Welfeld et al., *Perspectives on Housing and Urban Renewal* (New York: Praeger Publishers, 1974), p. 268.

[23]Ibid., p. 15.

[24]Ibid., p. 19.

[25]For a more complete discussion of urban homesteading, see *The Urban Homesteading Catalogue* (Washington, D.C.: Department of Housing and Urban Development, 1977), 4 volumes; and James W. Hughes and Kenneth B. Bleakly, Jr., *Urban Homesteading* (New Brunswick, N.J.: Center for Urban Policy Research, 1975).

[26]See George Richard Meadows and Steven T. Call, "Combining Housing Market Trends and Resident Attitudes in Planning Urban Revitalization," *Journal of the American Institute of Planners*, Vol. 44, #3, July 1978, p. 299.

[27]James W. Hughes and Kenneth B. Bleakly, Jr., op. cit., pp. 157–170 discuss Wilmington's experience.

[28]*The Urban Homesteading Catalogue*, Vol. III, op. cit., p. 4.

[29]Ibid., table 11:4, p. 37.

[30]George Sternlieb and James W. Hughes, *Housing and Economic Reality, New York City*, op. cit., p. 204.

[31]John S. Adams, editor, *Contemporary Metropolitan America*, Vol. III, *Nineteenth Century Inland Centers and Ports* (Cambridge, Mass.: Ballinger Publishing Co., 1976), p. 214.

[32]Ibid., pp. 204–205.

[33]Ibid., pp. 196–197.

[34]Quante Wolfgange, *The Exodus of Corporate Headquarters from New York City* (New York: Praeger Publishers, 1976), pp. 43–45. There is evidence that the trend of the 60s and 70s for offices to move to the suburbs is slowing in New York City. As of 1979, seven new office towers were under construction, older skyscrapers such as the 792-foot high Woolworth Building are being renovated, and vacancy rates in office buildings are beginning to decline. (*Christian Science Monitor*, Feb. 23, 1979.)

[35]Jerry M. Flint, "Inner City Decay Causes Business Life to Wither," in Joseph Bansman and Arthur Vidich, *Metropolitan Communities: New Forms of Urban Sub-Communities* (New York: New Viewpoints, 1975), pp. 30–35.

[36]Lewis M. Alexander, op. cit., pp. 29–30.

[37]For additional information on tax base sharing and the experiences of communities utilizing it, see Katherine C. Lyall, "Tax-Base Sharing: A Fiscal Aid Toward More Rational Land Use Planning," *Journal of the American Institute of Planners*, Vol. 41, 1975, 2, pp. 90–100; and A. Reschovsky and E. Knaff, "Tax Base Sharing: An Assessment of the Minnesota Experience," *Journal of the American Institute of Planners*, Vol. 43, 1977, 4, pp. 361–369.

[38]Richard Dusansky and Lawrence P. Nordell, "City and Suburb: The Anatomy of Fiscal Dilemma," *Land Economics*, 1975, pp. 133–143.

[39]R. Bahl and D. Puryear, "Regional Tax Base Sharing: Possibilities and Implications," *National Tax Journal*, Vol. 29, September:328–335; as cited in Walter Vogt, "Tax Bas Sharing: Implications from San Diego County," *Journal of the American Planning Association*, Vol. 45, 1979, 2, p. 135.

Chapter 6

Land Use Problems and Micropolitan Areas

Introduction

At the opposite end of the spectrum from the metropolitan areas of the United States are the nonmetropolitan or micropolitan areas.[1] By census definition, the term micropolitan would include all counties that contain no city (or twin cities) of 50,000 or more population. The census definition is less than adequate, however, since many of the areas which they designate as metropolitan have characteristics which result in greater similarity to micropolitan places. It is absurd to assume that a town of 50,000 population has the same characteristics as New York or Los Angeles, yet the census bureau designates both metropolitan. Since the nature of their land use problems are more analogous to small town America than to New York, in this book the 50 smallest SMSAs in 1975 will be included in the definition of micropolitan. This is an arbitrary threshold which is not intended as an absolute value. The designation micropolitan refers to more than just small population and includes those characteristics normally associated with small town America. Since the change from small town problems to large city problems does not occur at a precise point, the discussion of land use problems of micropolitan America will refer to all places with the characteristics of small towns and cities, regardless of population.

RURAL AMERICA: CENTER OF SLOW GROWTH

Although there are numerous ways of categorizing the smaller urban centers, for the purposes of this book they will be divided into four general classes based on the nature of the land use problems they face:

    (1) slow-growing micropolitan and small metropolitan centers,
    (2) rapidly growing suburbs of metropolitan regions,
    (3) boom towns, and
    (4) retirement communities.

In the first category are the archtypical micropolitan areas. These are the towns of rural America which were characterized by slow, no, or negative population change in the decades from 1930 to 1970. Land use problems of these centers are associated with their stagnation or decline. As a group, they are concentrated in rural America. Mechanization of agriculture and concomitant industrialization in the north and east during the 40 years from 1930 to 1970 resulted in population loss or stagnation in most of these towns. The regional concentration of the category of micropolitan America is associated with the states of the Great Plains and the South. Many of the states in these two regions suffered absolute population declines during at least one of the four decades. In addition to this regional concentration, those states which did not have an absolute decline in population during the period had small towns and cities that lost population or grew only slightly when they were heavily reliant on rural areas.

During the 1970–1975 period, for example, of 135 places of 2,500 or more people in Alabama, 74 gained less than 6% in population, and 34 of these suffered an absolute loss of population. By comparison, in Florida, which has received retiree migrants and is overall less reliant on agriculture than Alabama, just 13 out of 311 towns suffered a loss of population during the first half of the 1970s. Only an additional nine Florida places showed population growth of 5% or less during the period.[2] Of 49 places with 2,500 or more inhabitants in Nebraska, 34 had either a population loss or an increase of less than 6% between 1970 and 1975.[3] Not all micropolitan areas have suffered a loss in population or slow rate of growth. Taken as a group, these areas which are classified micropolitan by the census actually grew at a rate higher than the national or metropolitan average if farm population is excluded. The nonfarm population of nonmetropolitan areas increased 19% between 1960 and 1970, while metropolitan population increased 16.6% and the nation's population grew 13%. This trend has increased in the 1970s. From 1970 to the end of 1976, areas in the census definition of nonmetropolitan increased by 6.6%, while the population of metropolitan (SMSA) areas grew by only 4.1%. Less than 10% of national growth was in nonmetropolitan areas in the 1960s, but 37% of growth in the 70s occurred there. More than one-half of rural growth in the 1970s has come from net immigration, amounting to 1.8 million people from 1970 to 1975. The increasing migration and high growth rates of rural areas seem to be the result of the following factors:[4]

    (1) Employment in agriculture and mining lost an average of 200,000 jobs per year in the 1950s and 1960s. In the 1970s, mining increased and agriculture decreased only 27,000 annually.
    (2) Other kinds of employment increased as a result of decentralization of manufacturing and related jobs in services, trades, and construction.

Nonfarm employment in nonmetropolitan areas increased 22% from 1970 to 1977, twice that of metropolitan areas.
(3) Retirement spurred growth in rural areas of Florida, the Southwest, the Ozarks, Texas, the upper Great Lakes, and coastal New England.
(4) Expansion of transport systems, particularly the Interstate System, makes it easier to live in rural areas and commute to jobs.

LAND USE PROBLEMS IN MICROPOLITAN AMERICA

The problems of land use related to the towns of rural America, whether they have been losing population, growing only slowly, or suddenly expanding, are related to the general categories of land use. Housing in micropolitan America tends to be of lower quality than that found in metropolitan areas. In 1970, there were 22.4 million housing units in micropolitan areas. The median value of owner-occupied units was $12,400, compared to $19,000 in metropolitan areas. Of the two-thirds of all housing units which are in metropolitan areas, only slightly more than 2% of these units lack complete plumbing. By comparison, over 10% (3 million) of the housing units in micropolitan areas have incomplete plumbing.[5] Regionally, the South has even greater problems of inadequate housing, with the 11 southern states (excluding Florida) ranging from 18 to 26% of housing with incomplete plumbing in their micropolitan areas. As in the central cities, housing of minority groups in micropolitan America tends to be even worse, with nearly 50% of the housing of southern Blacks having incomplete plumbing.[6]

Land use problems related to residential housing are not evenly distributed by size of town. The greatest problems tend to be in the smallest centers since, typically, they have seen the least growth or greatest declines. Established as service centers in the pre- or early automobile era, they have been superceded by larger centers in today's era of rapid automobile transport. Consequently, the small centers suffer stagnation. Idaho provides a classic example of this problem. With 44 counties, in 1960 Idaho had no town of over 35,000. By 1970, however, Boise had reached nearly 75,000 people, and the growth rate for larger towns (over 5,000 population) during the decade was 41.4%. By comparison, in the 32 counties with no town over 5,000 population, the growth rate for the decade was only 0.8%[7] Analysis of towns in the midwestern states for the 1960–1970 period reveals the same trend. Nearly half of all places with fewer than 500 inhabitants lost population, but less than 20% of places of 10,001 to 25,000 size declined.[8] The population of the declining or stagnated small towns is predominantly elderly, and normally the housing stock is also older and often obsolescent.

The problems of residential land use in communities of limited or no growth is exacerbated by lack of adequate services. Since there is a threshhold population below which it is uneconomic to provide specified types of services, the majority of residents of the towns of under 5,000 people either lack, or have inadequate, services of fire, police, sewage, garbage, water, health, recreation, and government.[9] This is particularly acute since the very services most needed by the elderly population of such towns (medical care, public transportation, access to shopping centers, adequate housing) are the items least likely to be found in the small centers.[10]

For the growing micropolitan centers of 5,000 to 50,000 size, the problems of services to residents may not be as severe, but they are still major land use issues. As a consequence of the National Environmental Policy Act and related acts, these towns are faced with the necessity of upgrading their waste-water treatment systems, with attendant costs to residents.

The problem of older housing is just as frequent in such centers, and the lack of adequate and sufficient rental units, particularly for lower-income and minority group families, becomes a severe land use issue. Vacant land within the corporate limits of slow growing centers compounds the cost of services since there are lots with water, sewer, roads, etc. adjacent to them which are unused. The capital investment has already been made by the municipality in this infrastructure, and the presence of vacant lots and houses increases the cost to other users.

Commercial Land Use in Micropolitan America

The existence of vacant housing in the slow growing or stagnated communities of rural America is often exceeded by vacancies in the commercial sector. A drive down the main street of small towns in rural America will nearly always reveal vacant lots and buildings which formerly provided important urban functions. The advent of the automobile freed residents of small towns from the necessity of relying on the limited services in their town. As more residents engage in shopping, banking, and allied activities in larger centers, the range of such services provided locally declines. This trend is compounded by the advent of chain stores, which have replaced the entrepreneur. Management of such stores look only at profitability and consequently do not locate in the smaller towns. Owners of locally owned businesses may persist in their activity even though the return is marginal, because of their ties to the community; but when they are abandoned through death, bankruptcy, or liquidation, they are not replaced. The result is a serious decline in the commercial sector. This decline is heightened by the decline in the American rural farm population which such centers have historically served. The rural farm population in 1930 and 30.5 million, or 24.9% of the nation's population. By 1970, this had declined to only 9.7 million, or 4.8% of the population. During the decade of the 1960s alone, the farm population declined by nearly 6 million (Table 15). Proposals and discussions over the need to rejuvenate small communities have limited potential for success in the face of such great population loss. Even the growth of the 1970s fails to rejuvenate the old commercial buildings, as new establishments tend to construct new buildings outside of the old commercial core of the town.

A land use problem of the commercial sector growing out of the declining population of the smallest towns is that of structural deterioration. Faced with reduced sales volume, lower profit, and potential closure, many of the commercial functions which do persist in the small towns are unable to adequately maintain their establishment. The structures in the commercial sector of the small town

Table 15. Distribution of American Population: 1790–1970
(in millions)

Year	Total U.S.	Urban		Rural		Nonfarm		Farm	
		Total	Percent of U.S.	Total	Percent of U.S.	Total	Percent of U.S.	Total	Percent of U.S.
1790	3.9	0.2	5.1	3.7	94.9	–	–	–	–
1820	9.6	0.7	7.2	8.9	92.8	–	–	–	–
1850	23.2	3.5	15.3	19.6	84.7	–	–	–	–
1880	50.2	14.1	28.2	36.0	71.8	–	–	–	–
1900	76.2	30.2	39.7	45.8	60.3	–	–	–	–
1910	92.2	42.0	45.7	50.0	54.3	–	–	–	–
1920	106.0	54.2	51.2	51.6	48.8	19.6	18.5	32.0	30.2
1930	123.2	69.0	56.2	53.8	43.8	23.3	19.0	30.5	24.9
1940	132.2	74.4	56.5	57.2	43.5	26.7	20.3	30.5	23.2
1950	151.3	96.8	64.0	54.5	36.0	31.4	20.8	23.0	15.2
1960	179.3	125.3	69.9	54.1	30.1	38.4	21.4	15.6	8.7
1970	203.2	149.3	73.5	53.9	26.5	44.2	21.7	9.7	4.8

Source: Fred K. Hines, David L. Brown, and John M. Zimmer, *Social and Economic Characteristics of the Population in Metro and Nonmetro Countries, 1970* (Washington, D.C.: U.S. Department of Agriculture, 1975), Ag. Econ. Report #272.

usually represent the capital investment of nearly a century ago. Although these were usually solidly constructed, their external appearances are often allowed to deteriorate. In the absence of the prospects for increased revenues, few small town entrepreneurs can afford to adequately maintain the structures their businesses occupy. The result is a commercial sector characterized by a sense of dilapidation. The extent of such physical deterioration ranges from faded paint and a general sense of genteel poverty, in the towns with limited growth, to general dilapidation and vacancy in those with severe population declines. The business district in towns hardest hit by loss in the commercial sector may become an area of general visual blight.

In the centers of 5,000 to 50,000 of rural America, the land use problems related to commercial land use are similar to those of the smallest centers, but with some important differences. In the first instance, these are places which are normally growing. Taken as a group, all places of less than 50,000 inhabitants grew 6.7% between 1960 and 1970. This growth rate masks important differences, with the communities at the larger end of the spectrum normally growing more rapidly as they become regional service centers and replace the commercial functions of the smallest centers.[11] In cities of 10,000 to 49,999, for example, the growth rate between 1950 and 1960 was 15%, while it declined through smaller size cities to only 1% for places of less than 500 population. In the 1960-1970 period, the same relationship exists, with cities of 10,000 to 49,999 growing 9% and cities of under 500 actually declining by 1%.[12] In the 1970s, the trend seems to be for increased growth in the nonmetropolitan areas. Of 3,097 counties in the U.S., some 2,500 in 1975 were not part of an SMSA and were classified as nonmetropolitan. Between 1970 and 1974, population in the 2,500 nonmetropolitan counties grew at an average annual rate of 1.27%, compared to .79% for metropolitan counties. This compares to a growth rate of .30% in 1950–1960, and .43% for 1960–1970 in these same nonmetropolitan counties.[13]

The larger micropolitan centers and the smaller cities designated as metropolitan by the government are not free from land use related problems in their commercial sectors. Such places are faced with three general types of problems:

(1)   those associated with the street pattern,
(2)   those associated with obsolescence, and
(3)   those associated with inadequate land use regulation.

In practice, these categories are highly interrelated, but it is useful to examine their impact separately.

Essentially all American cities classified as small metropolitan or large micropolitan centers have one or more core areas which were founded before the beginning of the 20th century. Historically, this has been the "downtown" or central business district (CBD). Designed in the pre-auto era, such CBDs commonly are plagued by narrow streets and inadequate parking. Consequently, even though the community may have less than 50,000 population, access to the downtown area is time consuming. With increasing dominance of the automobile in post World War II America, most of these communities have developed alternate traffic routes which bypass the CBD. In theory, this was to separate thru-traffic from that of the shoppers, but it has often resulted in re-location of CBD functions to these highways.

A visit to any smaller town will reveal that the CBD is faced with increasing competition from the dispersed stores and shopping centers. A drive through the downtowns of America's small cities will reveal that they are essentially deserted after 6 p.m. The businesses located along the highways, however, may remain open until 10 p.m. or even 24 hours a day. Such extended hours are not restricted to motels and gasoline stations, which cater to the ubiquitous automobile, but include grocery stores, shopping centers, drug stores, and other central place functions.

A primary cause of the development of shopping centers and other businesses along the so-called "through-routes" is the existing land use regulations in America's smaller cities. The majority of communities in this size class rely on traditional Euclidian zoning for control of land uses. When it becomes obvious that traffic flows favor a particular area for commercial purposes, which is not so zoned, an entrepreneur will almost invariably purchase it at a relatively low price and then request a zoning change. Although the professional planner for the city may recognize the long-term impact of granting such a change, the American system of separating the planner from the actual decision-making process means that the local governing body will make the final decision on the zoning request. More often than not, the local city council or commission making the final decision is composed primarily of businessmen or those allied with the business community. In addition, the perceived tax benefits from new commercial activity are highly attractive. The result is an overwhelmingly favorable approval rate for such zone changes. The impact of the multiplicity of zone changes granted by the city council of the typical small city is to allow commercial establishments to locate wherever an entrepreneur perceives a profitable site. The tremendous profits which accrue to speculators and developers make it almost impossible for the zoning ordinance of the smaller city to accomplish what it was designed to do. In fact, some observers maintain that as a result of vested interests and outright graft, development of commercial land in such growing centers proceeds in the same fashion as it would had there been no land use regulations at all.[14]

Due to the development of competing businesses along highways, the CBD of many smaller American cities exhibits some or all of the characteristics of the small towns and villages which have been losing population. New buildings in the CBD are rare, with the majority representing construction of 50 to 100 years ago. These buildings represent capital investment which has been amortized; consequently, land rents are relatively cheap compared to that in a new building along the highway. Low rents is an important factor affecting the continued existence of the CBD. Nonetheless, the CDBs of these cities increasingly reveal vacant lots, and general dilapidation. This is particularly true of the upper floors of the sturdy 2- to 5-story buildings which were constructed during the pre- and early automobile era when the CBD had no effective competition. Once the offices of dentists, lawyers, opticians, hairdressers, accountants, and other tertiary activities, they are now almost invariably vacant. A drive through the CBD of any of these cities will reveal the obsolescent commercial structures, many of which have had their effective space on the first floor changed through cosmetic rehabilitation. The painted, siding-covered, plasticized first story is normally in stark contrast to the deteriorating upper floors.

Attempts by planners, businesses, and government to overcome the problems of the CBD in these smaller cities are almost certainly doomed to fail. So long as land use regulations do not effectively prevent the emergence of competing centers in more accessible locations, any such actions can provide at best only a temporary respite. Nevertheless, because of the investment represented by the CBD, efforts to restore it will continue. Normally, these attempts focus on the following types of actions:

(1) construction of new government buildings,
(2) improvement of parking, and
(3) development of a unique quality in the CBD.

Government spending for municipal buildings, theatres, or museums is often resorted to in attempts to save the downtown. The rationale for this assumes that the investment by the government will stimulate private investment as well. Activities associated with the completed structures normally represent a service by the government which is essentially a monopoly, and it is not affected by additional development away from the CBD. Since there is no profit motive, such functions are located wherever the government determines and the users have no alternative source. Theoretically, the movement of government workers and those they serve to the CBD will lead to increased trade throughout the CBD.

Various schemes to improve parking in the small city CBD have been attempted. Commonly they take the form of demolition of obsolescent structures, changing the style of parking (i.e., from parallel to diagonal), or removal of parking meters. These and other efforts are designed to offset the free and abundant parking associated with the shopping centers located away from congested CBDs.

Another alternative to the parking problem is related to the attempt of communities to develop a unique CBD which will act as a magnet to shoppers. Many intermediate-sized communities have closed a section of their CBD to automobile traffic, creating a downtown pedestrian mall. In theory, the pedestrian mall becomes an attraction because of the variety of urban services available, and parking is provided on the perimeter through razing old structures, or use of alternate parking schemes. In other instances, communities capitalize on an existing unique aspect of their CBD, as Santa Fe, New Mexico, which emphasizes the Spanish origin of its central plaza area. Unfortunately, even where pedestrian malls, tourist attraction, or other CBD modification is made, rarely can it offset the locational advantages of the shopping center adjacent to the highway with its accessability, parking, and controlled internal environment.

Industrial Land Use in Slow Growing Areas

Industrial land use problems in micropolitan communities which are declining in population or growing only slowly are basically similar to those in the commercial sector. Many such towns are old company towns that have exhausted the local resources and diminished or abandoned their activities. Other towns have seen local industrial activity reliant on agricultural products decline as transportation advances have made it cost effective to centralize processing and manufacturing in fewer places. Still other small centers have lost industrial activity as local, small-scale industries are forced out of business as a result of obsolescence or competition. Examples of each of these problems are common in most parts of the west, south, and great plains states. In Utah, for example, the sugar beet industry was the primary industrial activity in 10 towns prior to the great depression. Consolidation after that time resulted in plants only in the north and central parts of the state, and after World War II it was centralized into only one plant in the north.

Loss of industry has been an important causal factor in towns actively losing population. Even when a town is growing, abandonment of industries results in large areas of land which are unused and may even present a hazard to the community. Such hazards range from danger to children playing on abandoned equipment, in abandoned structures, in flooded quarries or ponds formerly used in the manufacturing process, to environmental and health hazards from old dumps. In the western United States, communities in Utah and Colorado were the location of uranium processing plants during the boom of the 1950s. The radioactive tailings are a fine material used for fill under private and public structures. Dust from the sites has contaminated even larger areas. Residents of rural Toone, Tennessee have had their drinking water contaminated by a pesticide waste dump where chlorinated hydrocarbons were dumped in shallow trenches. In East Gay, Maine, the aquifers from which wells draw water have been contaminated by wastes from a company handling waste oils and solvents. In Love Canal in Niagara Falls, New York, poisonous chemical wastes buried in the 1950s began resurfacing in the schoolyards and yards of homes in 1978.[15]

For most of the slower growing communities, the primary problem related to industrial land is the need to attract new industry. In order to do so, many micropolitan centers and small metropolitan places utilize industrial development associations. From the planning standpoint, these associations attempt to combine the efforts of the city or county planning staff with the private sector. The land use issues center around location of industrial parks, provision of services to industrial parks or individual industrial sites, and attracting acceptable industry to the community. Those micropolitan places and small metropolitan areas that succeed in doing so are the ones to continue to grow. It should be mentioned, however, that such growth is not necessarily without cost. Analysis of the benefits and costs associated with new manufacturing establishments in micropolitan communities reveals that in many instances there is a net cost to the community associated with new industry, and where there is a net benefit it tends to be extremely small. Benefits from new industry overwhelmingly accrue to selected areas of the private sector, often at a cost to the balance of the community.[16]

LAND USE IN THE SUBURBS

Up to this point, we have nominally been discussing the land use issues faced by the micropolitan and small metropolitan places which are independent of the SMSAs of the U.S. As a group, they are represented by the towns of rural America. Another group of micropolitan and small metropolitan places which are the suburbs of large metropolitan regions can also be recognized. These are places which have been characterized by rapid growth as the automobile has facilitated the flight to suburbia (Table 16). Initially viewed as simple "bedroom" communities, they have emerged as centers in their own right competing with the major metropolitan areas they originally served.[17] Another group of smaller cities has been referred to as "exurbia."[18] These are towns and small cities farther removed from the metropolitan center. They are growing rapidly, as certain groups, primarily upper income, locate away from the immediate fringe of the metropolitan area. These towns include places like the towns of Connecticut which are becoming home to corporations fleeing New York City, or retirement centers in Florida, or the so-called "new towns" (e.g., Reston and Columbia). In any case, they share many of the land use issues faced by the suburbs (Fig. 12).

The land use problems as perceived by residents of suburbia reflect their history. The suburbs have always tended to be places where upper-income Americans

Table 16. Population Growth in Metropolitan and Suburban Areas, 1900–1970

Decade	Population growth rate of cities	Population growth rate of suburbs	Percent total SMSA growth in cities	Percent total SMSA growth in suburbs
1900–10	37.1	23.6	72.1	27.9
1910–20	27.7	20.0	71.6	28.4
1920–30	24.3	32.3	59.3	40.7
1930–40	5.6	14.6	41.0	59.0
1940–50	14.7	35.9	40.7	59.3
1950–60	10.7	48.5	23.8	76.2
1960–70	5.3	28.2	4.4	95.6

Source: Peter O. Muller, *The Outer City* (Washington, D.C.: Association of American Geographers, 1976), table 1, page 4. (Used by permission)

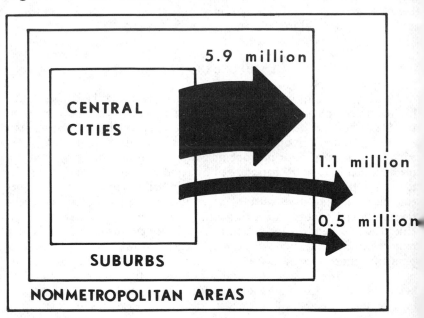

Migration from Central Cities   1970—75

5.9 million

CENTRAL CITIES

1.1 million

0.5 million

SUBURBS

NONMETROPOLITAN AREAS

Fig. 12. Population migration from central cities: 1970–1975.

sought refuge from contact with low-income migrants and ethnic groups. Once the electric street car provided rapid transport, upper-income Americans moved to the country where cheaper land allowed them to have the advantage of quasi-rural life on their estates. In the early decades of the 20th century, the suburbs of large American cities contained only about one-third of the population (Table 17). So long as this was the case, the suburbs tended to be homogenous communities composed of the upper-income groups. Development of the automobile and federal subsidy of highway construction made an even larger area around central cities accessible to commuters, and the percent of urban population increased dramatically. In 1940, only 37.8% of the residents of the 15 largest urban centers lived in the suburbs, but by 1970 nearly 60% had fled the central city. This tremendous shift of population to the suburbs represents the modern manifestation of the Jeffersonian ethic of the 18th century. The Jeffersonian ethic maintained that rural life was inherently better than urban life, and suburban land use issues of the late 1970s reflect this anti-urban bias.[19] The bias is borne out by public opinion polls showing that the majority of America's population prefers to live outside of the city. Only 18% of respondents in 1972 expressed a preference for living in the city, while 22% preferred the suburbs. Nineteen percent indicated a preference for life in a small town or village, and 38% preferred to live in a rural area.[20] With rural areas being perceived by the largest group as the preferred place of residence, it seems an anomaly that the suburbs contain the majority of American population. However, in another study in 1972, even though 74% of the respondents expressed a desire to reside in a small city, town, or rural area, only 19% wanted to live more than 30 miles from a central

Table 17. Percentage of Population in Suburbs for Selected SMSAs, 1900–1970

Metropolis	1900	1910	1920	1930	1940	1950	1960	1970
New York	32.2	32.4	33.8	36.2	36.1	38.9	47.3	51.2
Los Angeles	44.9	37.4	36.6	40.7	42.8	46.5	53.2	54.9
Chicago	18.9	19.1	20.4	24.1	25.7	30.1	42.9	51.8
Philadelphia	31.6	31.7	32.8	37.8	39.6	43.6	53.9	59.6
Detroit	33.1	24.1	23.9	28.0	31.7	38.7	55.6	64.0
San Francisco	24.5	26.7	28.4	31.9	35.9	45.7	58.2	65.4
Washington	26.4	25.7	23.5	27.6	31.5	46.8	63.2	73.6
Boston	57.7	58.1	60.0	64.0	65.1	66.8	73.1	76.7
St. Louis	30.4	33.4	33.7	40.7	44.3	51.2	64.4	73.7
Baltimore	26.2	27.5	18.7	22.4	24.6	34.8	47.9	56.3
Cleveland	17.2	15.1	18.0	27.6	30.7	40.3	54.1	63.6
Minneapolia-St. Paul	20.4	16.9	15.5	16.6	19.4	27.6	46.3	59.0
Mean for all SMSAs	37.9	35.4	34.0	35.4	37.3	41.4	48.6	54.2

Source: Peter O. Muller, *The Outer City* (Washington, D.C.: Association of American Geographers, 1976), table 2, page 4. (Used by permission)

city.[21] With the majority of the American population desiring to live outside of the central city, but within 30 miles of it, the suburbs have grown dramatically.

The rapid growth of the suburbs is the basis of the present land use issues which they face. Since nearly two-thirds of the population of the country resides in suburban places, out of necessity the land use issues here are of national significance. In general terms, land use issues in the suburbs can be categorized, from the viewpoint of the typical middle- or upper-income resident, in the following manner:

1. control of suburban sprawl,
2. protection of prime agricultural land,
3. maintainance of life-style in the face of growth,
4. control of growth,
5. provision of adequate services, and
6. maintenance of environmental quality and property values.

Exclusionary Zoning

From the viewpoint of the lower-income and minority group members, the critical land use issue centers around provision of adequate low-cost housing. The goals of the middle- and upper-income suburban resident which affect land use regulations are often in direct opposition to this goal of low-income Americans. The crux of the land issue in America's suburbs grows out of this dichotomy and is referred to as exclusionary zoning. Exclusionary zoning refers to all of the legal regulations adopted by suburban municipalities in their efforts to resolve the land use issues as preceived by their middle- and upper-income residents.[22]

By nature and design, Euclidian zoning is exclusionary. In his ruling in *Village of Euclid vs. Ambler Realty Co.* in 1926, Justice Westerhaver recognized that "the result to be accomplished [of zoning] is to classify the population and segregate them according to their income or situation in life." The assumption under Euclidian zoning, however, was that incompatible (i.e., nuisance type) activities would be excluded from residential zones. Expansion of this idea to exclusion of socioeconomic or ethnic groups was not necessarily intended, and it is these types of regulations to which the term exclusionary zoning is presently applied. Specifically, regulations requiring large lots (1/2 acre or more), three or more bedrooms, excessive floor space, or excluding multiple unit dwellings, high density development, or mobile homes, are all referred to as exclusionary because they serve to maintain high-cost housing. Another term for these regulations is *fiscal zoning*. Fiscal zoning is simply using zoning to attract activities which will return a high tax rate while excluding those which will not, but might demand a high rate of service.

The net effect of such land use regulations particularly discriminates against the black population with its lower average incomes and higher incidence of poverty. According to the 1970 census, 16.2% of the American black population resided in suburbia, but 58% of the white population lived there. For the blacks, this represented only a 1.1% increase over the 1960 results during a period of

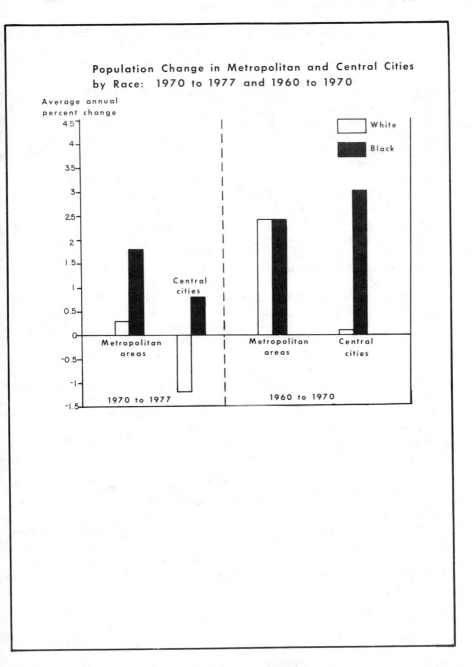

Fig. 13. Variation in population change by location and race: 1960–1970 and 1970–1977.

professed national effort to overcome segregation. During the same period, the proportion of the white population in the suburbs increased 5%. Even the great percent of whites in suburbia fails to show the almost total exclusion of the black population. In 1970, the proportion of blacks in the suburban population of America's SMSAs was 4.82%, representing only a fractional increase from the 4.78% in 1960.[23] The total black population in SMSA suburbs increased 800,000 in the decade, but during the same period the white population in these suburbs increased over 15.5 million[24] (Fig. 13).

There has been an increase in the rate of black migration to the suburbs in the 1970s (Table 18). Between 1970 and 1977, an estimated 1,184,000 blacks moved to the suburbs of the SMSAs, bring the total black population to 4,617,000 in the suburban portions of the SMSAs. During the same period, the black population in the central city increased by 828,000 to 13,737,000. The white population grew in the suburbs by 6,866,000 in 1970–1977. Although this represents a lower percent of growth, the total growth was six times as great as for blacks. Also, the white population in the central city declined by 4,031,000 in the period. In spite of the increasing numbers of blacks in the suburbs in the 1970s, they continue to be concentrated in the central city. Nearly 60% of the nation's black population in 1977 resided in the central cities of metropolitan areas, but less than 25% of the white population lived there. Bu comparison, the white population of the suburban areas of the SMSAs in 1977 represented over 90% of suburban population, but blacks had increased to only 5.57%.[25] This does represent a large increase in the total numbers of blacks in the suburbs and may suggest that government programs to insure economic and social equity are beginning to have effect. It may also represent only the movement of whites from older suburban housing in suburbia to newer suburban housing. It may well be that the growth of blacks in the suburbs in the 1970s simply results from obsolescence of housing and expansion of the black ghetto to similar portions of suburbia.[26]

Most white suburbanities are reluctant to acknowledge that their land use regulations are in fact racially motivated, instead maintaining that they are designed to benefit all suburban residents regardless of color. Defendants of exclusionary zoning argue that it prevents high density development which would overwhelm the communities' ability to provide services. By maintaining high-priced homes on large lots as compared to higher densities, the community effectively limits the number of automobiles on their streets, the number of children in their schools, and the number of users of libraries, hospitals, and other services. At the same time, by allowing only those with higher incomes to reside in the community, they maintain a population which is able to bear a high tax rate to insure that the community services which are required are of high quality. Other benefits perceived by the supporters of the exclusionary zoning techniques include maintainance of a sense of openness in suburbia through the low densities and prevention of sprawl by macro-lot (5 acres or more) requirements around the suburban community which nominally protect farmland from tract housing.[27] Implicit in all of these advantages of exclusionary zoning is the maintenance of the property values for suburban residents. The suburban home is touted by realtors as the best investment available, and the mounting price of single family

Table 18. Location in SMSA, Central City, Suburb, or Micropolitan Area
(in thousands)

Race and residence	1977	1970	Change, 1970 to 1977	Percent, 1970 to 1977	Change,[a] 1960 to 1970	Average percent, 1970 to 1977	Annual change, 1960 to 1970
ALL RACES	211,792	199,819	11,973	6.0	13.3	0.8	1.3
SMSAs	143,182	137,058	6,124	4.5	16.6	0.6	1.5
In central cities[a]	60,334	62,876	-2,543	-4.0	6.5	-0.6	2.4
Suburbs	82,848	74,182	8,666	11.7	26.7	1.6	0.7
WHITE	183,664	175,276	8,388	4.8	11.9	0.7	1.1
SMSAs	121,773	118,938	2,835	2.4	14.0	0.3	1.3
In central cities	44,878	48,909	-4,031	-8.2	0.1	-1.2	–
Suburbs	76,895	70,029	6,866	9.8	26.1	1.3	2.3
Micropolitan areas	61,890	56,338	5,552	9.9	7.8	1.3	0.8
BLACK	24,472	22,056	2,416	11.0	19.7	1.5	1.8
SMSAs	18,354	16,342	2,012	12.3	31.6	.7	2.7
In central cities	13,737	12,909	828	6.4	33.2	0.9	2.9
Suburbs	4,617	3,433	1,184	34.5	26.4	4.2	2.3
Micropolitan areas	6,118	5,714	404	7.1	-5.3	1.0	-0.5

[a]Refers to the corporate boundaries of the central city in 1970 for 1970 and 1977, and 1960 corporate boundaries for 1960.
Source: U.S. Department of Commerce, Bureau of the Census, *Population Characteristics*, Current Population Reports, Series P20, 1978, table 18, p. 32.

133

homes bears this out. The average price of a single family home in the United States at the end of the 1960s was less than $20,000. A decade later, the average cost of a new home exceeded $72,000.[28] For the suburban resident, protection of his investment is paramount, and he assumes that the way to do so is to exclude the poor, the black, and other groups who do not share the affluence and outlook of middle- and upper-class Americans.

The primary tool for doing so is the much maligned zoning ordinance. Numerous authors have criticized zoning, but it continues to be used as the chief means of land use control in suburbs even though other mechanisms, such as restrictive covenants, permits, control of nuisances, or a system of fines for noncompatible uses, could better serve the needs of Americans. The reason zoning continues to persist as the primary land use control is that it has some direct benefit for the residents of suburban (and other) communities, and is perceived as having even greater benefits than it actually does. Specifically, by limiting density of development, and consequently keeping demands for services low, the suburban resident effectively maintains a higher level of disposable income. Moreover, zoning allows residents of a community to regulate the density of development on other people's property without having to bear the cost of paying for development rights, or purchasing it either outright or as the result of condemnation through the power of eminent domain.[29] So long as local zoning regulations do not effectively prevent a landowner from using his land at all, courts have been willing to condone property restrictions associated with exclusionary zoning. Finally, zoning as practiced in suburbia allows the suburban resident to feel that he has a direct role in regulating use of land in his neighborhood.[30]

The end result of exclusionary zoning is that it artificially limits housing availability in the suburbs, inflates the value of suburban housing, and effectively maintains a homogeneous, white, middle-class population. Examples of this are numerous. In Sandy, Utah, a suburb of Salt Lake City, the 50,000 population is a typical example of the end result of such zoning. The population consists of young, middle-class families, with the typical income between $15,000 and $25,000 in 1977. The average age of the population is only 19.9 years, but adults in the community have a high level of education, 97.7% being high school graduates and over one-third having some post high school education. Only 6.4% of the families in the community are below the poverty level, as measured by family income; these primarily represent residents of the older part of town. A typical family consists of two parents, aged 30 to 40, with two or three small children. Homes are overwhelmingly single family, three and four bedroom, with a value of over $50,000 in 1977.[31] Total minority population is less than 1%.

The profile of Sandy could represent any of numerous suburban communities with only slight modifications. These are places which maintain their homogeneity through zoning restrictions accepted by their residents as a logical and fair means of making the community a better place in which to live. In some suburbs, however, the question of the legality of zoning regulations has been challenged. The resultant court decisions are important because they indicate both the tenacity with which middle-class white Americans strive to protect the character of their communities and the frustration of those who are excluded from them.

Challenges to Exclusionary Zoning

Arlington Heights is a middle- and upper-income suburb of Chicago. In 1970, it had a population of 64,884 of whom only 27 were black. The Metropolitan Housing Development Corporation (MHDC) of Chicago leased, with an option to buy, 15 acres of an 80-acre tract of land owned by a Catholic religious order in the early 1970s. The lease required MHDC to develop the property into low-income, subsidized housing. The MHDC proposed to Arlington Heights that they be allowed to construct the Lincoln Green project, a 190-unit town house complex. This was to be a project for low- and moderate-income residents subsidized under Section 236 of the National Housing Act of 1934. Since the 15 acres was zoned for single-family residents, the MHDC applied for re-zoning to multi-family. The planning commission of Arlington Heights refused to grant the zoning change on the basis of the community's comprehensive plan which specified that new multi-family construction would be allowed only as a buffer zone between single-family residential zones and industrial zones. Since the proposed complex was surrounded by single-family residences, they refused to grant the zoning change.

In response, the MHDC filed suit in district court, arguing that the rejection constituted racial discrimination because it prevented low-income minority groups who worked and wished to live in the area from obtaining housing in the community. The district court accepted the community's argument that the zoning change was rejected only because it departed from the comprehensive plan and denied the appeal of MHDC. MHDC appealed this decision to the Seventh Circuit Court of Appeals, arguing that since Arlington Heights was exclusively white and there existed no other plan to provide low-income housing, failure to grant the zoning charge would have the effect of perpetrating segregation. The appeals court agreed with the argument of MHDC and pointed out that the lack of lower priced housing was caused by the refusal of Arlington Heights to provide adequate zoning for such housing in the past. Consequently, the rejection of MHDC's request for a zoning change perpetrated racial discrimination.

Faced with the prospect of greater densities and more low-income residents, Arlington Heights appealed the case to the U.S. Supreme Court.[32] When the Arlington Heights case was accepted by the Supreme Court, it became the first zoning case based on racial discrimination to be heard by the court since 1917. The ruling of the Supreme Court in *Arlington Heights vs. MHDC* is highly significant. The court ruled that the decision of the planning commission to reject the proposed zoning change was a logical outgrowth of the community's comprehensive plan. The court found no evidence of intentional racial discrimination or inconsistency in the administration of the buffer zone concept for multiple housing which would indicate discrimination against MHDC.[33] In the opinion of the court, the comprehensive plan represented the desires of the citizens of Arlington Heights to maintain a community characterized by low-density, single-family housing. Even though the end result of the zoning which implemented the comprehensive plan was to prevent low-income minority groups from residing in the city, it was perfectly legal. In essence, the court states that the residents of a community have the right to determine the character of their town as long as it is based on a comprehensive plan and is not administered in a capricious or discriminatory fashion.

Numerous cases exemplify the importance of the suburban community having a comprehensive plan in order to justify existing zoning regulations. The courts seem to indicate that the land use issues related to maintaining the character and quality of life in the suburbs will be decided in favor of the affluent white majority even though it represents de facto segregation. Nevertheless, there is great disparity among state courts in their assessment of what constitutes illegal exclusion. The concept of "fair-share housing" has particularly been of importance in the states of megalopolis, especially New Jersey. New Jersey courts, as well as those of other states, struck down zoning regulations of some communities which prevented construction of high-density housing designed for lower-income families in the late 1960s and early 1970s.[34]

The most famous of these was the Mount Laurel case. Mount Laurel can be described as a somewhat typical suburban town with a large amount of open space. Located just east of Philadelphia, Mount Laurel is part of the Philadelphia SMSA. The problems affecting megalopolis resulted in movement of the affluent to such towns, and Mount Laurel, as most suburban communities, was engaging in exclusionary zoning. Since the black population was most uniformly excluded by such regulation, Southern Burlington County NAACP filed suit against the town. The significance of the case is that the New Jersey Supreme Court ruled, in 1975, that the Mount Laurel zoning ordinance was invalid because it failed to provide for its "fair share" of the housing needs of the broader region of which it was a part.

The court ruled specifically that each "developing community" must affirmatively plan and provide a reasonable opportunity for an appropriate variety and choice of housing "including low and moderate income housing by way of multi-family dwellings, town houses, mobile homes, small houses on small lots and the like to meet the needs, desires and resources of all classes of people who may desire to live within its boundaries."[35] The court opinion ruled that zoning of an entire developing community for single-family residences on large lots was unacceptable; that minimum floor space requirements could not be justified; bedroom restrictions in multi-family units (which eliminates families with school-age children) were arbitrary and that excessive zoning for industrial or commercial uses was arbitrary. Finally, the ruling required municipalities that zone land to attract industry and commerce for tax purposes must also zone to permit adequate housing for those who will be employed in such establishments.[36]

If uniformally adopted, the principles set forth in the Mount Laurel decision would help to eliminate exclusionary practices of land use regulation in suburbia, but it is doubtful whether such will occur. The ruling applied only specifically to "developing communities" facing development pressure and covering relatively large areas with abundant open space which could be zoned for moderate- and low-income housing. The decision in the Arlington Heights case seems to indicate that in a "developed" community with existing zones for low-income housing which is inadequate for the communities' "fair share" of regional housing needs, it is not mandatory that they re-zone vacant land for low income housing.

Furthermore, according to subsequent rulings by the New Jersey Supreme Court, "it is fundamental that zoning is a municipal legislative function beyond the purview of interference by the courts unless an ordinance is seen in whole or in application to any particular property to be clearly arbitrary, capricious or unreasonable, or plainly contrary to fundamental principles of zoning or the statute . . . ."[37] The court has refused to participate in determining what constitutes "fair share," or in "demarcating the region," and has restricted the application of the ruling to the "developing communities" whose zoning regulations are "exclusionary."[38] It is too soon to categorically state what the impact of the Mount Laurel decision will be on America's suburbs, but at least in New Jersey there has been some attempt to rectify the tradition of exclusionary zoning.

One of the most important attempts to adopt a regional policy of fair-share housing in the 1970s was in Fairfax County, Virginia. The county ordinance required that all new residential housing developments with 50 or more units (except single-family or high-rise apartments) reserve at least 15% of their units for low- and moderate-income housing. The Fairfax County Circuit Court declared the ordinance illegal in late 1971 on the grounds that it was not only not authorized by Virginia's zoning enabling act, but that even with adequate enabling authority the ordinance was arbitrary and capricious.[39] The court ruling apparently reflected concern with the establishment of quotas rather than the need for low-income housing, and exclusionary zoning remains a major suburban issue.

Control of Growth: Maintaining the Quality of Suburbia

Closely allied with suburban land use issues related to excluding lower income residents has been the concept of limiting growth to maintain the environmental quality and small town or country character of suburbs. The concept of growth control regulation is one of the most important land use issues in suburb and satellite towns alike in the 1970s. Attempts to regulate population size and growth rate have taken a number of alternative approaches, ranging from setting absolute limits on size (population caps) to limiting the number of building permits issued each year, to controlling location of growth through capital expenditure for services, to refusal to annex additional land, to large-lot zoning, to overzoning for commercial and industrial land. Boca Raton, Florida utilized a population cap (approved by its residents in the mid-1970s) to set an upper population limit. Petaluma, California set a quota on the number of building permits issued each year. Ramapo, New York developed a system of sequential timing for each area within its boundaries that specified the time when utilities would be provided to each. In each case, the justification for the program involved the desire of the residents to maintain community character or the inability of the community to provide services for increased growth. The action of Boca Raton was declared illegal, but Ramapo and Petaluma have served as models for other communities in the last half of the 1970s. Adoption of regulations patterned after these communities is but one manifestation of attempts by suburbs to deal with the land use issues of sprawl, community character, and environment. The importance of these issues to suburban residents is obvious. If communities are unable to successfully resolve these land use related issues, they face the prospect of seeing the very characteristics which foster the growth and sprawl destroyed or denigrated.

In addition to problems related to growth and maintenance of the perceived character of the suburb, suburban regions deal with all of the other forms of land use. Provision of and location of streets, schools, fire stations, libraries, and other urban services present issues which must be resolved. These are intricately related to the issues of growth and exclusion, since the number and socioeconomic characteristics of new residents greatly affect both the demand for services and the ability to be taxed to support same. In addition, use of zoning as the primary means of regulating land use in the rapidly growing suburbs presents opportunity for graft and collusion in making zone changes. Analysis of 372 zoning changes in Privatown Township, Suffolk County, New York, between 1968 and 1971, revealed most were in response to support by both the planning board and the town board. Thirty-two changes were granted by the Republican-dominated town board, but opposed by the planning board and the local citizens. The vast majority of these 32 changes directly benefitted business friends and partners of the local Republican party leader. Of eight changes to multi-family zoning from single-family designation, seven went to his active business partners. Of eight changes to commercial zones, three went to his partners and the remainder to Republican supporters. In 1968 alone, the Republic party leader realized over $1 million from re-zoning.[40]

Decisions concerning zoning changes, designation and location of major streets, location of shopping centers, multiple-unit housing, and other land use activities have the potential to change the character of a neighborhood and the associated land values. In these decisions, the land use issues in suburbia are very similar to those in any community.

BOOM TOWNS

Another group of micropolitan communities (sometimes labelled "boom towns") face related issues and problems relating to land use. Boom towns[41] are not identifiable by any single factor, but normally communities growing at rates of 10 to 15% per year are labelled "boom towns."[42] Using only the definition of growth rate would include many of the suburbs, as most experience such growth rates when they first become the focal point of suburban migration. For example, Sandy, Utah, a bedroom community to Salt Lake City, increased from 6,438 people in 1970 to 50,000 in 1977 as it experienced suburban expansion. America's large metropolitan centers also experienced rapid growth at one point or another in their history.

The land use issued faced by communities growing at such rates are broadly similar, but the suburban community undergoing such an experience normally has some infrastructure to support it. Boom towns, in this case, are the isolated villages and hamlets which become the center of rapid growth associated with some externality such as energy needs, fuel shortages, resource prices, or other factors that may create a sudden change in its population. In most cases, the rapid population growth is associated with extraction of a local resource through rapid expansion of an existing plant or location of a new plant or plants in or near the community, exemplified by the example of Sweetwater County, Wyoming. According to the 1970 census, the population of Sweetwater County was 18,391. Nearly 90% lived in Rock Springs (11,674 in 1970) and Green River (4,340 in 1970). No other town in the county exceeded 350 population in 1970, and no town within 100 miles exceeded 650. Between 1970 and 1974, the population of Sweetwater County doubled to 36,900. Employment increased from 7,230 to 15,205 as a result of construction of the Jim Bridger Power Plant and expansion of trona mining.[43] Population projections for the 1980s go as high as 89,000 for the county.[44]

The impacts of these rapid rates of growth include a variety of social, economical, and environmental issues, most involving some aspect of land use. The typical boom town area is, like Sweetwater County, characterized by rural communities with small populations. These communities typically have only a marginal infrastructure geared to provision of minimal services to their small population. Housing stocks are normally fully utilized regardless of quality, police and other governmental services are minimal, waste water treatment systems are inadequate, and the road system is designed for low density flows. Land use regulations are minimal, as many boom towns have no formal zoning regulations and very few have any professional planning staff to assist them in dealing with rapid growth. Faced with demands for housing, schools, police and fire protection, roads, water supplies, and sewage treatment, these communities are often overwhelmed. Their plight is exacerbated by the demand for housing and services before the community has the increased tax base associated with the resource extraction plant to rely on. The resultant unplanned development takes place in a fashion that often makes the town a worse place in which to live. As one observer concluded: "The energy boom town in the western United States is apt to be a bad place to live. It's apt to be a bad place to do business."[45]

The housing crisis is normally solved by use of mobile homes, often in unplanned, unlandscaped parks scattered over the landscape in poor locations. In Sweetwater County, by 1974, there was a deficit of 4,599 improved mobile home spaces and 1,397 permanent home sites.[46] Many of the mobile homes being used were located outside of the city limits where there were no waste water controls, since it was prohibitively expensive for their owners to make provisions for connections to sewer lines within the community. All of these land use problems and related social problems result from general lack of planning coupled with rapid growth.

The land use issues for boom town communities essentially focus on the needs of the original inhabitants versus those of the new arrivals. The increased population results in diminishing quality of city services to old residents; increased congestion on roads, in schools, etc.; increased crime, noise, and pollution; and potentially increased taxes to pay for upgrading services and providing planning. The new arrivals view their role as expanding business income in the town and influencing higher property values, and they feel the community should provide adequate housing and services through appropriate land use regulations.

Solutions to land use issues involved in boom towns have been suggested by many observers, and some states have adopted regulations to assist boom towns in overcoming their problems. Primarily, the solutions involve tax structures to recoup the costs of services from the company responsible for the growth, or provide income to state governments who can then provide technical assistance to help impacted communities. Analysis of the impact of coal development in the Northern Great Plains states of Wyoming, Montana, and North Dakota revealed that each have established coal severance taxes which return funds to the state based on the tonnage mined. The result is a large flow of capital into state governments, but this does not necessarily directly assist the local governments. In each instance, the local governments rely heavily on local property taxes and local sales tax. Unless a resource development happens to be within the corporate limits, the towns most heavily impacted receive insufficient new taxes to pay for the costs incurred in providing services to the new residents. Cities in the three states studied would receive an average of only one-third of their average per capita expenditures for services. The several states have state programs designed to help the impacted communities, with a fixed proportion of the coal severance tax revenus designated for projects in the impacted communities. The various towns must submit proposals for individual projects and the state agencies may grant funds if they believe they are justified. When an impacted community does not receive a grant or the grant is inadequate to cover costs, taxes increase or services decline in the boom towns.[47] The magnitude of costs to a community are illustrated in the town of Huntington in Emery County, Utah. Emery County is a rural county 150 miles southeast of Salt Lake City. Of 2.8 million acres in the county, 81% is federally owned and much of it has high quality coal resources. In 1970, there were 5,137 inhabitants in the county, nearly 20% fewer than in 1950. The largest town entirely in the county in 1970 was Huntington, with 857 residents. In 1972, Utah Power and Light Company began construction of a series of coal-powered generators to ultimately produce 830 megawatts of power and consume 2–4 million tons of coal per year. If all of the coal related developments proposed for the county are constructed, the population will exceed 30,000 people by 1985. Since Huntington was adjacent to the first units of Utah Power and Light, its population increased to nearly 5,000 by 1975. Community services were inadequate, the water delivery systems failed completely in the summer of 1975, and the community was faced with increasing demands for housing, sewage treatment, etc. Ironically, the county and county-wide school district have no financial problems, since the plant locations are outside of the city limits. Huntington, by contrast, has received only a minor share of the bonanza represented by the new plants. The community had a projected annual deficit of $340,000 out of a budget of $540,000 by 1977, and this deficit is projected to increase to $470,000 yearly by 1984.[48]

Some western states with boom towns have adopted alternate means to assist the impacted communities. Utah has devised a method for allowing impacted towns to develop special service districts which share bonding base and allows the industry causing growth to guarantee the districts' bonds, thus providing assistance to communities where the actual operation may be outisde of the city limits. In addition, a proportion of use and sales taxes from a new plant or mine may be paid in advance of construction to assist communities in providing services for the influx of population. Also, Utah and other states utilize part of the increased taxes accruing to the state government to assist local impacted communities with the planning process to help mitigate the adverse effects. Alternative programs for providing assistance to impacted communities have been suggested but not yet incorporated by legislation. One of the more promising of these proposes that the industry responsible for the "boom" town contract directly with the town to protect it from adverse effects of growth related to the industry's investment. This would involve negotiations between the investors and the local government to insure that the interests of the local citizens were protected. The results might include direct subsidy payments to the impacted community based on their additional costs, provision of some municipal services by the responsible industry, timetables of rates and dates of construction which would be followed to allow the community to respond to growth pressures, etc. Implicit in this approach is the concept that the industry causing the growth in a community be responsible for the costs of providing for it when increased revenues to the community from the growth are exceeded by costs of providing services.[49]

Whatever method is adopted by the various states and local governments affected by boom town growth, the issues will continue to be critical. Increasing demands for energy and other resources will severely strain the micropolitan communities impacted. The western states with their low population densities will apparently continue to be the site of most boom towns because of their energy and other mineral resources, as well as government regulations allowing operation of industries in the relatively pristine western environment not tolerated elsewhere. If the coal-fired electric generating plants proposed for the west are ultimately built, they will result in a host of new boom towns. Estimates indicate from 130 to 170 communities in the 6 western states in which most energy development is likely to occur (Colorado, the Dakotas, Montana, Wyoming, and Utah) will become boom towns. Of these, 38% presently have populations of less than 500, and another 37% have populations of from 500 to 2000. Only 11% have populations exceeding 5,000.[50] The land use issues created in such settings will remain a critical national concern for the foreseeable future as alternate energy sources continue to increase in cost. Resolution of land use issues to the satisfaction of both newcomer and long-time resident of impacted communities will continue to be a critical problem.

A problem of concern to the long-time residents of boom towns is the potential of a "bust." When the resource responsible for a boom is exhausted, the population can decrease as rapidly as it increased. The residents who are unable or unwilling to move are then left with a community infrastructure with excess capacity at the same time the property tax base is declining. Road systems, schools, water and sewer systems, are all usually financed through bonds. As the population declines, the remaining residents face even higher taxes to repay them.

RETIREMENT COMMUNITIES:
UNIQUE LAND USE ISSUES

While boom towns related to resource extraction wrestle with growth-related issues that span the spectrum of land use issues, retirement communities experiencing rapid growth face somewhat different problems. Retirement communities are usually planned in advance by their developers, and population growth usually occurs only as the community infrastructure is completed. Many of the lots in these communities are purchased by potential retirees long before they actually move to the community, so communities have the unique situation of having tax income without demand for services. Moreover, certain services provided by communities, particularly schools, are not required within retirement communities. The land use in retirement communities tends to be heavily concentrated in residential and recreational uses. Analysis of retirement communities in New Jersey found proportions of residential use of 55 to 95%, with recreation land use ranging from 5 to 45%. Commercial and industrial uses never exceed 5%.[51] These figures are similar to findings in California which showed that an average retirement community had 75% of its land in residential uses, 22% in recreation, and only 4% in commercial uses. Average land usage in nonretirement residential neighborhoods has over twice as much land in commercial use, about a fourth as much in recreation uses, but 11% devoted to schools.[52]

Most retirement communities tend to be either within an SMSA or within easy driving distance of shopping centers.[53] In essence, the communities are residential enclaves within existing communities, although some retirement communities in Florida and Arizona are an exception to this. But even the large retirement cities, such as Sun City, Arizona, still commonly rely on adjacent urban centers to provide many urban functions, thus limiting the land devoted to commercial use. In addition, since retirement communities are not reliant upon the local economy for economic support of their residents, industrial land usage is rare.

Land use issues in retirement communities involve the views of residents of such centers as opposed to those of the broader public. The primary issue emerging from retirees' views are restrictive regulations affecting prospective residents. Normally these take the form of restrictions on age, which prevents younger people or couples with families from residing within such centers. The age limits vary, but generally set a lower limit of 52 to 55 for residents. Nearly all retirement communities specifically exclude small children, but some will allow young adult dependents, with specified lower age limits of 16 to 18.[54] Issues affecting neighboring communities which serve retirement centers focus on such things as the impact of retirement communities on communtiy hospital services, influence of elderly on voting concerning bond issues for school or other community construction, and other concerns over the cost to the larger community to provide services. Analysis of spending behavior and revenues generated from retirement communities reveals that they provide a surplus of tax revenue and support commercial development outside of their boundaries. Financially, retirement centers seem to be a definite advantage to a community when compared to other residential developments. In terms of impact of retirees on land and other budget issues, the evidence indicates that their voting behavior is little different from that of the nonelderly voting population.[55]

A final land use issue related to retirement centers focuses on retirement communities developed on raw land in the so-called "sunbelt" states of Florida, Arizona, and California. These present issues related to local versus state regulation as they have sometimes been developed in unsuitable areas selected only because of the minimal land use regulations existing in the selected locality. These lands are then subdivided and sold on the basis of proposed development of the community. In some instances, the developments promised or implied by the development corporation have never been constructed. State and local governments are left with the problems associated with the subdivided land, perhaps including a few residents. In such cases, the demands for services may exceed the tax revenue generated. In Arizona, for example, there were 2,565 subdivisions in unincorporated areas. Not all were specifically for retirees, but most reflect the growth of the southwest as an area for future retirement. These subdivisions contained 742,829 lots covering 943,460 acres, of which 83% (786,555 acres) were subdivided between 1959 and 1973. In 1972 alone, 133,459 acres were subdivided. If fully occupied, it is estimated that these subdivisions will contain 2,220,700 people, more than the entire population of the state. The area of the subdivisions is 350,000 acres larger than the total land in all of Arizona's incorporated municipalities.[56]

CONCLUSION

The land use issues faced by micropolitan centers and small metropolitan cities are diverse, but common to all are the problems associated with growth. Even the smaller centers are experiencing a reversal of the trend of the 40 years from 1930 to 1970 and are growing at a rate (1.1%) greater than that of metropolitan areas (.8%) in the 1970s.[57] Attempts to regulate growth and associated sprawl have become one of the central issues of land regulation in the 1970s, as discussed in the succeeding chapter.

NOTES

[1] Luther Tweeten and George L. Brinkman, *Micropolitan Development* (Ames: Iowa State University Press, 1976), pp. 5-6.

[2] *County and City Datebook, 1977*, U.S. Bureau of the Census (Washington, D.C.: Government Printing Office, 1977), Appendexes F and G.

[3] Tweeten and Brinkman, op. cit., p. 23.

[4] *Environmental Quality, The Ninth Annual Report of the Council on Environmental Quality* (Washington, D.C.: Government Printing Office, 1978), pp. 220-224.

[5] Tweeten and Brinkman, op. cit., p. 15.

[6] Ibid., pp. 16-17.

[7] J. R. Hamilton et al., *Small Towns in a Rural Area: A Study of the Problems of Small Towns in Idaho*, Research Bulletin, No. 91 (Moscow: University of Idaho, 1976), pp. 1-2.

[8]Norman Walzer and David Schmidt, "Population Change and Retail Sales in Small Communities," *Growth and Change*, Vol. 8, 1977, table 1, p. 46.

[9]Joel R. Hamilton and Richard Reid, "Rural Communities: Diseconomies of Small Size and Costs of Migration," *Growth and Change*, Vol. 8, 1977, pp. 39–44.

[10]William R. Lassey, *Planning in Rural Environments* (New York: McGraw-Hill Book Co., 1977), p. 31.

[11]J. R. Hamilton, et al., op. cit., p. 2.

[12]Ibid., p. 3.

[13]*Environmental Quality-1976*, Council on Environmental Quality (Washington, D.C.: Government Printing Office, 1976), p. 287.

[14]Mark Gottdiener, *Planned Sprawl* (Beverly Hills: Sage Publications, 1977).

[15]"Tracking Toxics: A Tremendous Task," *Conservation News*, Vol. 44, No. 4, Jan. 1979, pp. 2–5.

[16]Gene F. Summers et al., *Industrial Invasions of Non-metropolitan America* (New York: Praeger Publishers, 1976), pp. 103–105.

[17]Scott Donaldson, *The Suburban Myth* (New York: Columbia University Press, 1969); Gottdiener, op. cit.: Philip C. Dolce, editor, *Suburbia, The American Dream and Dilemma* (New York: Anchor Books, 1976).

[18]Marion Clawson, *Suburban Land Conversion in the United States* (Baltimore: John Hopkins Press, 1971), p. 53.

[19]Peter O. Muller, *The Outer City* (Washington, D.C.: Association of American Geographers, 1976), p. 3.

[20]*Environmental Quality-1976*, op. cit., p. 297.

[21]Ibid., p. 299.

[22]Richard F. Babcock and Fred P. Bosselman, *Exclusionary Zoning: Land Use Regulation and Housing in the 1970s* (New York: Praeger Publishers, 1973).

[23]Muller, op. cit., p. 19.

[24]Ibid., footnote 18, p. 18.

[25]U.S. Bureau of the Census, *Current Population Reports*, Series P-20, No. 324, "Population Prophecy in the United States: 1977" (Washington, D.C.: Government Printing Office, 1978), table 18, p. 32.

[26]Muller, op. cit., p. 21.

[27]See Chapter 9 for a full discussion of techniques used to protect prime agricultural land from sprawl.

[28]*U.S. News and World Report*, May 21, 1979, p. 86.

[29]See Bernard H. Siegan, *Other People's Property* (Lexington, Mass.: Lexington Books, 1976).

[30]William A. Fischel, "A Property Rights Approach to Municipal Zoning," *Land Economics*, Vol. 54, 1978, pp. 64–81.

[31]*Desert News*, Salt Lake City, Utah, March 15, 1979.

[32]It can be argued that the town's motives were simply to prevent poor planning and insure that the comprehensive plan was maintained. In either case, the end result was to exclude the poor and minority groups.

[33]Carol R. Cohen, "The Equal Protection Clause and the Fair Housing Act: Judicial Alternatives for Exclusionary Zoning Challenges After Arlington Heights," *Environmental Affairs*, VI, 1978, pp. 63–77 (63–100 entirety).

[34]See Charles M. Haar and Demetrius S. Iatridies, *Housing the Poor in Suburbia* (Cambridge, Mass.: Ballinger, 1974); Daniel Lander, *Recent Cases in Exclusionary Zoning* (Chicago: American Society of Planning Officials, 1973); Edward M. Bergman, *Eliminating Exclusionary Zoning* (Cambridge, Mass.: Ballinger, 1974); David D. Furman, "Regional Housing Needs: Oakwood at Madison," in Randall W. Scott, editor, *Management and Control of Growth*,

Vol. I (Washington, D.C.: Urban Land Institute, 1975), pp. 449–506; Melvin R. Levin and Jerome G. Rose, "Suburban Land Use War: Skirmish in Washington Township," in Randall W. Scott, editor, *Management and Control of Growth*, Vol. I (Washington, D.C.: Urban Land Institute, 1975), pp. 507–513.

[35] Frederick W. Hall, "A Review of the Mount Laurel Decision," in Jerome G. Rose and Robert E. Rothman, editors, *After Mount Laurel: The New Suburban Zoning* (New Brunswick, N.J.: Center for Urban Policy Research, 1977), p. 41. Hall was an Associate Justice in the New Jersey Supreme Court and authored the unaminous decision.

[36] Ibid., p. 42.

[37] Ibid., *After Mount Laurel*, p. 242.

[38] Ibid., p. 252.

[39] Bergman, op. cit., pp. 24–25.

[40] Mark Gottdiener, op. cit., p. 79.

[41] Ronald L. Little, "Some Social Consequences of Boom Towns," *North Dakota Law Review*, Vol. 53, 1977, p. 402.

[42] Ronald G. Cummings and Arthur F. Mehr, "Investments for Urban Infrastructure in Boomtowns," *Natural Resources Journal*, Vol. 17, 1977, p. 223.

[43] Ibid.

[44] *The Growth Shapers* (Washington, D.C.: Council on Environmental Quality, 1976), p. 65.

[45] J. Gilmore, "Boom Towns May Hinder Energy Development," *Science*, Vol. 191, 1976, p. 191.

[46] Cummings and Mehr, op. cit., p. 224.

[47] Thomas F. Stinson and Stanley W. Voellser, *Coal Development in the Northern Great Plains: The Impact on Revenues of State and Local Governments*, Agricultural Economic Report No. 394 (Washington, D.C.: U.S. Department of Agriculture, 1978), pp. 8–19.

[48] J. S. Gilmore et al., *Analysis of Financing Problems in Coal and Oil Shale Boom Towns* (Washington, D.C.: U.S. Department of Commerce, 1976), p. 57.

[49] Allen Vander Mullen and Orman H. Paananen, "Selected Welfare Implications of Rapid Energy-Related Development Impact," *Natural Resources Journal*, Vol. 17, 1977, pp. 319.

[50] *Rocky Mountain Energy Resource Development: Status, Potential, and Socioeconomic Issues*, by the Comptroller General of the United States (Washington, D.C.: Government Printing Office, 1977), p. 37.

[51] Katherine McMillan Heintz, *Retirement Communities: For Adults Only* (New Brunswick, N.J.: Center for Urban Policy Research, 1976), pp. 10–14.

[52] Michael B. Barker, *California Retirement Communities* (Berkeley: Center for Real Estate and Urban Economics, 1966), p. 37.

[53] Heintz, op. cit., p. 18.

[54] Ibid., pp. 8–9; Rosabelle Price Walkley et al., *Retirement Housing in California* (Berkeley: Diablo Press, 1966), pp. 49–50.

[55] Heintz, op. cit., pp. 65–101, 144–148.

[56] David M. Hamernick and Beverly A. Brown, *Arizona's Remote Subdivisions* (Phoenix: Office of Economic Planning and Development, 1975).

[57] *Population Characteristics, 1978*, U.S. Bureau of the Census (Washington, D.C.: Government Printing Office, 1978), p. 32.

Chapter 7

Changing Methods of Controlling Land Use

Introduction

Ultimately, any regulation of land use has an impact on population growth of the area regulated. The earliest forms of land use regulations involved the control of nuisance activities, which effectively limited the growth of certain types of establishments in order to protect the rights of adjacent landowners or users. The establishment of traditional Euclidian zoning presupposed that it was essential to control the type of land use activity in an area through direct regulation. This effectively regulated control of types of growth in the sense that residential construction was discouraged in industrial zones, and industrial land use was prohibited in residentially zoned areas. Euclidian zoning, however, did not absolutely limit the population of a specific area; it only limited the growth of types of land use in a particular zone. In the 1960s and 1970s, there emerged a great concern over absolute population growth as it affects the quality of life, fiscal ability, and character of communities. There have been numerous attempts to initiate programs limiting growth in particular areas during the past decade and a half. Initially, attempts were oriented towards absolute limits of growth based on such things as population caps and numbers of building permits issues. More recently, control of growth has focused on limiting the negative impacts associated with growth through wise planning rather than the absolute limiting of population.

In attempting to limit the negative effects of growth, the various governmental bodies engaged in land use regulations responding to a set of perceived growth related impacts which vary from community to community. The rationale for regulating growth may be a legitimate one associated with insufficient community

147

infrastructure, or it may be a blatant effort to exclude low-income or racial minority groups. Concern for growth related problems is manifest by all levels of government involved in regulating land use, but it is primarily the local community level which has experimented with innovative management controls to regulate that growth. The growth management systems utilized vary from direct regulation through limits on infrastructure to indirect regulation of growth through zoning regulations. Some communities have restricted new building permits to those areas served by water, waste disposal, highways, or other services. Some communities have utilized moratoriums to accomplish the same result through providing a period when no new growth is allowed, during which time the community can undertake to overcome the deficiencies then existing. Other communities have utilized the concept of planned unit development (PUD) to improve design quality and insure special amenities by allowing greater flexibility in development of larger residential projects. Many communities are familiar with the wide range of available techniques related to land use regulation which limit growth, and incorporate one or more of them.[1] Over one-half of the communities surveyed in a recent study reported that they sought to influence the location, environmental impact, design quality, type, and fiscal impact of growth.[2] Although the general trend has been away from absolute population limits, 42% of those responding in this study revealed that they attempted to influence the total amount of growth in their area. The types of programs used for controlling growth are widespread and numerous (Table 19).

LAND: COMMODITY OR RESOURCE

The number and type of regulations presented in Table 19 is indicative of the changing attitude towards land use in the United States. Whether such regulations are explicitly designed to regulate growth or not, they reflect a growing awareness that land use affects more than the individual property owner. Historically, land in the United States has been viewed as a commodity, something which could be bought and sold to the highest bidder, and which was in essentially limitless supply. As such, land was defined in purely economic terms as a "factor of production." Thus, land was a focus of speculation, of construction for residential purposes, a part of the industrial process and the basis of the agricultural production of the country. Central to the view of land as a commodity is the idea that benefits and costs associated with the production and use of the commodity are associated solely with the individual or group who purchases and uses the property. The impact of a new subdivision on surrounding residents is not considered when land is viewed as a commodity, nor is there concern for the irreversible changes associated with certain types of land use.

In reality, of course, there are costs and benefits associated with land use that do not accrue to the private entrepreneur. Moreover, the increasing population of the United States, with its attendant penchant for suburban residence, has fostered an awareness of the weaknesses associated with viewing land as a commodity. It is obvious that the amount of land is finite. For all intents and purposes

Table 19. Techniques of Controlling Growth (Type of Regulation)

Public acquisition	Conventional subdivision regulations
Fee simple acquisition	Zoning/subdivision regulation/
Less than fee simple acquisition	building codes used for permanent
Land banking	population regulation
Compensable regulation	Exclusive nonresidential zones
Public improvements	Exclusion of specified types of
Location of facilities	housing (mobile home, multiple
Access to existing facilities	family, etc.)
Environmental controls	Minimum floor area or lot size
Floodplains, wetlands, slopes, etc.	Height restrictions
Critical areas	Zoning or other off-site regulations/
Developments of regional impact	exactions and other requirements
Pollution controls	Mandatory dedication of land or
Development rights transfer	capital
Restrictive covenants	Low-income housing requirements
Zoning techniques	Tax and fee systems
Conventional zoning	Urban and rural service areas
Conditional zoning	User and benefit fees
Contract zoning	Special assessment
Planned unit development	Preferential taxation
Flexible zoning	Development districts
Performance standards	Annexation
Bonus and incentive zoning	Timing of infrastructure development
Floating zones	(capital programming)
Special permit	Numerical limits and quotas
Variance	Total population goals
Miscellaneous management and planning	Annual limit on building permits
activities	Fair share allocations
Moratoriums and interim controls	
Administrative delays	
Analysis of benefits vs. costs, environ-	
mental impact, carrying capacity, etc.	

Source: After Michael E. Gleeson et al., *Urban Growth Management Systems* (Chicago: American Society of Planning Officials, 1975), pp. 8–9, and David P. Godchalk, *Constitutional Issues of Growth and Management* (Chicago: American Society of Planning Officials, 1977), pp. 12–13.

new land cannot be created, even when land has been transformed into uses which are no longer useful. Competition among land uses in recent years has heightened public awareness of the finite nature of the land resource. Loss of prime agricultural land to suburbia, destruction of unique and highly valued environments, and overcrowding of national parks and recreation areas have fostered the growth of the attitude that views land as a resource rather than a commodity. Viewed as a resource, the land base is recognized as a finite quantity whose heritage belongs to the entire public rather than to the highest bidder. The implications associated with this changing view are profound.

The most obvious result of viewing land as a resource is that the finite supply of land, like most natural resources, must be apportioned among the competing uses according to some measure of the value of the resources to the prospective users. Conventionally, we would distribute the finite resource in terms of willingness to pay for that resource, but since land uses result in benefits and cost to both the individual entrepreneur and to the broader public, the traditional market mechanism for allocating this resource is not always completely effective. Since any parcel of land may have a variety of potential uses, its allocation as a resource must reflect not only the reward and cost to the individual, but to the broader society as a whole. This becomes an important source of conflict in land use when a parcel of property is viewed by a developer as a potential source of revenue, but the same land is viewed by the broader society as a potential "open space" which would be reserved for recreation or aesthetic purposes. In this case, if the developer is allowed to construct homes on the land, the property is lost as far as the broader public use is concerned. If, however, the developer is restricted in his use of the land, he has lost the monetary benefits he would have received from the development, while the public is able to continue to enjoy the open space they may not have paid for. This dilemma of public vs. private costs and benefits, in terms of using the finite land resource, is difficult to resolve. Some unique lands, if allowed to be developed, are lost forever. Yet the private landowner should not be expected to bear the public costs associated with maintenance of lands in their pristine conditions. The mechanisms discussed in this chapter will focus on techniques that have been utilized or suggested for resolving this dilemma.

Fundamental to the concept of land as resource rather than commodity is the public interest in the use of the land. Recognition that land has uses and roles other than providing an economic return has resulted in efforts to regulate land for what are known as externalities. Externalities are the broader public benefits associated with land use. For example, a farmer living in an urban area provides not only the agricultural output from his land, but he provides open space for the urban resident. Moreover, the urban resident does not pay for this land as open space, but receives it gratis. The interest of the public in maintaining this land as open space is an externality which historically has not affected the sale and conversion of that land into subdivisions, but those who advocate land as a resource rather than as a commodity would maintain that the interest of the public be considered in determining the use of the land.

Areas where the concept of land as resource has been implemented vary in the goal they are attempting to accomplish. Hawaii implemented its state land use plan on the basis of conserving its agricultural land and maintaining the scenic beauty of the state. New Jersey is attempting to preserve portions of the Hackensack Meadows to insure that they are utilized wisely for both development and maintenance of open space. Puerto Rico and Florida have attempted to control areas of critical environmental concern, as has California through its coastal zone regulations. In each case, the justification was the public interest in the use of specific parcels of land.

It has been suggested that the dichotomy of land as either resource or commodity is itself in error. Land has both elements of a commodity and of a resource. The traditional right of any individual or group to buy or sell land freely in any area is a part of the American constitutional right to own land and to use it for economic benefit. To treat it as a resource in which those rights are restricted would eliminate a significant portion of our economy and result in chaos. On the other hand, those who speculate in land or otherwise view land only as a commodity ignore the fact that our land resource is a finite commodity and that it must be managed, at least partially, for the good of the public.[3] However land is defined, the problem of protecting the interests of the public while not infringing on the rights guaranteed the owner of the property remains.

TRANSFER OF DEVELOPMENT RIGHTS

The transfer of development rights (TDR) has emerged in the past decade as a major proposal for resolving some of the problems associated with regulating land use while resolving the dilemma of land as both resource and commodity. Historically, land in United States viewed as a commodity was bought and sold primarily for purposes of production, i.e., agricultural or development purposes. The normal way of so doing was to transfer the land in fee-simple as a bundle of rights associated with land ownership. TDRs (or purchase of less than fee-simple rights) attempt to disassemble the bundle of rights associated with property ownership and separate the commodity portion of the land from that of the resource portion. Specifically, TDRs recognize the value of land for development purposes and for its present use as agricultural, open space, environmental lands, or unique and historic sites. The concept behind the use of TDRs is to allow the owner of land to sell the development rights to that land separate from the land itself. Thus it would be possible to purchase rights to development from a farmer and these rights could then be transferred to land which had been designated as suitable for development, allowing greater density on the latter while maintaining the open nature of the former.[4]

The underlying justification for use of the TDR concept is that it overcomes some of the major criticisms of traditional Euclidian zoning. Under Euclidian zoning, when an individual's property was zoned for a specific use, he lost the development rights associated with other uses. If his land was zoned agricultural with minimum lot size of 50 acres, he lost the development rights associated with subdivision, commercial establishment, or industrial development. On the other hand, the individual who had land zoned for low density use, which was subsequently rezoned for high density uses, received an unearned benefit through the action of the local governing body. The former case is known as a wipeout, while the latter is referred to as a windfall. Use of TDRs would, in theory, eliminate both. The landowner whose land was zoned for low density uses would have the opportunity of selling the development rights from that property, while the individual who wanted to develop a high density land use would be forced to purchase those rights from other landowners.[5]

In principle, the TDR concept is similar to that used in Britain. Beginning in the 1930s and early 1940s, the British parliament funded several studies which made suggestions concerning land ownership and development. In 1947, the British parliament adopted the Town and Country Planning Act under which the government took over the development rights of all undeveloped land. Owners maintained all other rights, but if they wanted to develop the land they had to purchase the development rights from the government by paying a development charge. Subsequently, there have been several changes in the actual details of administration of the British system, but at the present time the development rights remain separated from the balance of the land title and are retained by the British government. However, the government has been unable to develop an effective system for controlling the marketability of the development rights so that they might be an effective land use regulation system.[6]

In the United States, the concept of transferable development rights had its origins in the concept of cluster subdivision. Under cluster subdivision, a specified parcel of land which could be subdivided into a given number of lots under traditional zoning could also be used to construct the same number of housing units, but clustering them in part of the land at greater densities, thus preserving the balance of the area as open space. This concept was ultimately refined into the planned unit development (PUD) concept. PUD is similar to cluster subdivision but concentrates all of its single family housing as town houses and/or apartments, with a resulting high density. The criticism of both PUDs and clustered subdivision is that the open space which is preserved is private space that is not available for use by the general public. Consequently, in 1961 Gerald D. Lloyd, a developer, recommended the concept of transferable densities for building purposes. It was not until the decade of the 1970, that there were serious attempts to utilize the concept of TDRs in this country.[7]

The most important principle in TDRs is the separation of development rights from other rights associated with property ownership. In practice, this would involve assigning a set number of development rights per unit of land, and then allowing these rights to be separated from the land itself, just as other water and mineral rights are severable from the land. In practice, the concept has been used in four general ways:[8]

1. preservation of agricultural, open space, or scenic lands;
2. preservation of historical sites and structures;
3. as a means of acquiring increased density, or floor area requirements; and
4. as an alternative to zoning.

Scenic Easements

One of the earliest experiences of TDR involves the United States Park Service in its attempts to develop national parks and trails and to acquire a less than fee simple interest in the land surrounding them. Basically, this involved acquisition of scenic or conservation rights from the landowners and consisted of purchasing from the property owner certain rights concerning cutting of timber, construction

Table 20. Examples of Public Purchase of Scenic or Conservation Rights

Location/*Agency*	Date of acquisition	Acreage	Type of right
Blue Ridge Parkway (Virginia, N. Carolina)	1930s	1,200	A, B
National Park Service	1940s		
Natchez Trace Parkway (Mississippi, Alabama), Tennessee)			
National Park Service	1930s	5,000	B
Adirondack Northway Interchanges (New York)			
New York Department of Environmental Conservation	1960s	1,000	B
Piscataway Park (Maryland)			
National Park Service	1960s	2,000	C
Sawtooth National Recreation Area (SNRA),			
Idaho U.S. Forest Service	1973–76	12,000	D
Wild and Scenic Rivers (Oregon, Idaho, Missouri)			
U.S. Forest Service	1974–75	5,000	E
Waterfowl Management Rights (North and South Dakota, Minnesota)			
U.S. Fish and Wildlife Service	1958 ff	500,000	F
Great River Road and other Roads (Wisconsin)			
State Division of Highways	1950	17,00	G
Farmland Preservation Program (New York)	1977 ff	3,252	H
Farmland Preservation Program (New Jersey)	1978 ff	study only	H

Type of restrictions indicated by following letters:

A. No construction.

B. No construction, except with permission, for farm and residential purposes, no tree cutting, no dumping, and no signs or billboards.

C. Development only with permission of park superintendent for residential purposes restricted to ½ to 1 acre in every 5 acres.

D. One homesite per 200 acres; building materials must meet S.N.R.A. guidelines; no commercial buildings.

E. Public access to river; no building within 20–30 feet of high watermark; limited residential use (2–3 houses per 50 acres).

F. No drainage of wetlands areas.

G. No new commercial development; minimum 5-acre lot or 300-foot frontage for residential construction; no dumping; no tree cutting; no signs or billboards.

H. Farming and related processing activities only.

Source: Personal communication with New Jersey, New York, and Sawtooth officials, and Robert E. Coughlin and Thomas Plaut, "The Use of Less-Than-Fee Acquisition for the Preservation of Open Space" (Regional Science Research Institute Discussion Paper No. 101, Philadelphia, 1977), table 3, p. 11.

of buildings, etc. These development rights have sometimes been referred to as scenic easements, which is misleading because easements have a specific and narrow interpretation. However they are described, these were and remain early examples of TDRs in the United States. A summary of the scenic rights transfers which had taken place in the United States through 1979 are shown in Table 20. In each case the agency or governing body involved acquires a less than fee-simple right from the property owner in return for payment of the value of that development right. In theory the property owner is then prevented from utilizing his property for those activities which would destroy or denigrate the rights which have been purchased.

The rationale behind the acquisition of the scenic rights, as with all development rights, is that it is cheaper to purchase only a portion of the rights associated with the property than to purchase the land outright. Figures on the cost of development rights are difficult to obtain and are variable depending on the development pressure applicable to a specific parcel. One study indicates that the cost of development rights in the New Jersey area averaged nearly $3,000 per acre in terms of the farmer's perception, but only $2,400 per acre was bid by the governing body. In the Suffolk County area of New York State (Long Island), initial studies indicated a cost of over $4,500 per acre to acquire development rights to farmland, but as a result of declining land pressures, by 1977 the average value was projected at $2,900–$3,200.[9]

In order for scenic development rights transfers to be successful, it appears that the following criteria must exist:[10]

1. local initiative by property owners;
2. education of property owners as to what rights are being transferred;
3. careful monitoring to insure that the agency who has the less than fee-simple rights is aware of any construction or changes which are not allowed in the easements;
4. flexibility to insure that variable situations will allow a changing of the TDRs;
5. adequate enforcement by the administrative body to insure that landowners do not subvert the intent of the easements;
6. TDRs must leave some form of economic use for the land sufficient to allow the landowner to adequately use the land to maintain his income.

Agricultural Development Rights Transfers

Another major use proposed for TDRs is in preserving farmland in the face of pressure to subdivide. Several states, including Maryland, Florida, Pennsylvania, Connecticut, Massachusetts, New Jersey, and New York, have either planned or implemented programs allowing the use of TDRs to preserve farmland. Two programs presently being implemented on a relatively large scale are in New Jersey and New York. A 1973 study of New Jersey's agricultural future recommended that the state purchase 1 million acres of prime farmland, and the state's TDR program grew out of this proposal. Initially, four townships in Burlington County some 25 miles from downtown Philadelphia were involved in a $5 million pilot study. Subsequently, a bond issue to raise $34 million to acquire additional easements was defeated in 1978 and no development rights have been purchased. A similar program in Suffolk County (on Long Island, New York) was designed to preserve 12–15,000 acres of prime farmland through a bond issue to pay the cost of purchasing the development rights on the land. The first phase, including a bond of $21 million, is now under way.[11]

In both of these programs, the difficulty lies in the fact that even though a less than fee-simple interest is being purchased, the large area involves tremendous sums of money. An alternative means for financing these TDRs is necessary to facilitate more widespread adoption. The most logical solution would be the sale of development rights to private individuals, but even though the theoretical basis for TDRs is sound, there has been little market for development rights, since it has been difficult to determine a fair price and to set up a marketing mechanism. There have been some sales of development rights associated with farmland in Pennsylvania; and programs in Florida for TDRs are nearing fruition. The use of private purchase of TDRs to preserve open space and farmland has largely been restricted to private organizations. In addition, development rights to lands are donated to conservancy groups.

A more limited use of TDRs to preserve agricultural land involves cluster zoning where the resultant open space is dedicated to agriculture; programs designed to involve private developers in TDR programs are being developed in Florida and Pennsylvania to preserve farmlands, but to date they have been largely used by governmental agencies. The use of TDRs as a major tool of land use is viewed by some as a solution to the problem of rising land prices, which make it prohibitively expensive for the younger generation to engage in farming and encourage transfer of agricultural land to urban functions. The fact that the concept of TDRs has not been widely adopted reflects the general public's ignorance of their utility and the fear of the unfamiliar.[12] Even if these two obstacles are overcome, however, TDRs do not represent a panacea. They do provide another tool for managing agricultural land, one which will be particularly valuable in suburban areas of rapid growth.

TDRs and Historic Preservation

Transferable development rights to preserve historic buildings was one of the first uses of the concept in the United States. Architecturally, aesthetically, or otherwise historically important structures are often demolished in urban centers as demand for space makes it economically attractive to replace them with structures such as high rise office buildings. In the U.S., the courts have ruled that regulations prohibiting demolition of historic structures constitutes an unreasonable "taking" of property rights. Since urban centers lack funds to purchase all important historic structures, the use of TDRs to protect them emerged in the 1970s. New York City initially promulgated zoning regulations which allowed the transfer of rights for building purposes between adjacent lots under the same ownership. The New York ordinance was based on the fact that land in urban centers is valued in terms of the intensity of development it will support. Older structures in areas having a high land rent often do not utilize all of the density allowable because of their smaller size. The New York plan initially allowed the owner of such a property to transfer his unused floor area rights (FAR) to a contiguous lot.[13] Once the surplus FAR had been transferred, there is no incentive to demolish the historic structure. Ultimately the New York law was extended so that the building rights could be transferred to other areas within the historic district not owned by the owner of the landmark structure, and more recently was amended to allow transfer of the surplus FAR outside of the preservation district.

Chicago developed a program in the early 1970s that provided that development rights could be transferred to any property within the same landmark preservation district. This included the right to transfer all of the floor area applicable to the site instead of only the surplus, and allowed special tax reductions and municipal subsidies where necessary to compensate the property owner for the cost of maintaining the historic structure. Washington, D.C. also enacted legislation in 1974 providing for landmark preservation through transfer of floor area ratios.[14]

An alternative to the New York City and Chicago programs is found in San Francisco. Under the San Francisco system, the downtown is divided into four districts, each with a prescribed floor area ratio. Instead of directly transferring the FAR from one lot to another, the city provides bonus densities for builders who provide certain public benefits, such as (1) improved accessibility, (2) improved pedestrian movement, (3) pedestrian amenities, (4) light and air for streets, or (5) view enhancement. The San Francisco plan is not a strict TDR in which rights are bought and sold by private parties, but it is similar to the TDR system in that the right to develop is separated from the other rights of ownership.[15] A number of other communities have and are experimenting with the concept of development rights transfers for preservation of open space, but the general impression is that they have been less than successful to date as a mechanism for effectively protecting historic structures.

Impact of TDRs

The TDR concept has been billed as one of the major innovative means of controlling land use in the 1974-1979 period. It has been experimented with in a number of communities, states, and by government agencies. With all of the publicity relating to it, and the advantages which it provides in a number of land use management decisions, it remains relatively minor in terms of actual implementation. Several suggestions have been made to explain this relative lack of widespread adoption of TDRs, e.g., that the primary problem facing development rights transfer is lack of public understanding of the concept. Not only does the public not understand TDRs, they do not understand the present system of land use regulation and place too much faith in the zoning process presently used. The broad assumption is that zoning protects them and that something different might not. Consequently, the public is unwilling or reluctant to accept new ideas. Against this major disadvantage are a series of advantages which many authors argue would seem to indicate that TDRs might well become the primary land use control of the future. The primary advantages of TDRs are as follows:[16]

1. TDRs remove the advantages associated with purchasing cheaper land away from the developing community, which has traditionally allowed speculators to reap higher profits. Use of TDRs eliminates this leapfrogging beyond community-provided urban or suburban services as it is no longer advantageous to the developer.
2. A TDR would eliminate the exclusionary nature of typical large lot zoning in suburbs. Low density would result from economics rather than zoning due to the fact that high density development could still occur, but only after the developer had assembled sufficient development rights. In addition, the government could subsidize such housing by distribution of development rights associated with government owned land.
3. TDRs would result in a greater tendency to effective comprehensive planning. Traditional zoning and comprehensive planning upon which it is based tend to be highly affected by developers and those individuals who would benefit directly from the plan as developed. The TDR would allow such individuals to still speculate in land through the TDRs themselves, but would lower the price of the land proper—allowing development of greenbelts, open spaces, and other land for the benefit of the community rather than resulting in an effort to develop each plot as intensely as possible. Moreover, those individuals who have land in activities which cannot withstand the competition for development purposes (i.e., agriculture or wetlands) would be able to gain the development value of their property while retaining the land in its open nature for the benefit of the public.
4. TDRs would have a favorable effect on taxation equity because the land would not be taxed for its development potential but for its actual use. Thus, only those areas in which urban services are provided would need to pay the higher taxes associated with them.
5. TDRs on public land could be sold to produce revenue that could be used by the community to upgrade community services, provide a subsidy for low income housing, or other community goals.
6. TDR use would facilitate provision of public facilities; it would not require development rights and land could be acquired at a lower price. The landowner would not suffer because he could sell the land to the government and keep the development rights (or sell them to someone else).
7. TDRs would result in preservation of farmland and open space for the reasons discussed above.
8. TDRs would have certain advantages for developments and developers since they eliminate the uncertainty and the potential financial losses caused by zoning changes by communities. The time and expense involved in obtaining zoning changes are voided; all the developer needs to do is purchase the requisite amount of land and the development rights necessary for the type of project he desires to construct.

Against these reputed advantages are arrayed public ignorance and American tradition, effectively preventing widespread adoption of TDRs. The whole American ethic of land as a private right and a source of speculative profit might well be challenged by TDR use. The use of TDRs in New York City has already been ruled unconstitutional in a situation where land owned by an individual was designated as suitable only for an urban park and he was given the option of selling the floor area ratio of the land to other property owners or transferring it to other property of his own. The court rules it was unconstitutional to deprive the individual of all development rights on the land itself.

TDR suffers from suspicion on the part of the public because of the general concern for government regulation. In addition, the land development industry is a significant component of the American economy and one in which great profits have been amassed. Those involved in development are often opposed to changes they are unfamiliar with, fearing they may challenge or threaten their livelihood.[17]

When used for preservation of space through government action in purchasing scenic easements, the value of the land for development is so high that only minimal values are assigned to the remaining rights, and it is often economically more feasible to simply purchase the land outright.

Given the inertia associated with the present system of land use regulation in the United States, it is highly doubtful that TDRs will be widely accepted as a mechanism for control in the short term. On the other hand, when the process of regulation of land is viewed in perspective, the 5-year period in which they have been seriously considered in the United States is too short to allow a strict conclusion concerning their future. In all probability TDRs will be adopted in the future on a wider basis, but their use and adoption will evolve over time just as other systems in land use control have done. Nevertheless, TDRs offer a very real alternative by providing advantages to both public and landowner not now available in traditional land use regulation.

TIMING OF DEVELOPMENT: PLANNING FOR ORDERLY GROWTH

The justification for traditional zoning is that it is necessary to insure the development of a community in an orderly, safe, and healthful fashion. Innovative land regulation mechanisms, such as TDR, also focus on the need for orderly growth, the same as traditional zoning regulations. The emphasis is upon controlling *where* the development takes place. Increasingly, communities are becoming aware that *when* growth occurs is equally as important as *where*. This concern has given rise to the concept of timing when growth or development occurs. The mechanism used to regulate when development will occur is typically associated with public utilities. A number of mechanisms affecting timing of development are being used in the United States today.

Timing with Regard to Public Expenditure for Public Facilities

One of the primary arguments used to regulate the timing of growth is that it is essential for a community to provide adequate infrastructure for its residents. Thus, growth occurring prior to construction of adequate water, waste water treatment facilities, schools, roads, and other public utilities, results in problems for the community and a deterioration of quality of life. Historically, provision of such services has often come after the fact, as developers are "rarely committed to the best interests of the entire community" and construct buildings and develop their land without proper regard for availability of services.[18]

Recognition of the problems caused by growth which exceed the ability of the public service base has prompted many communities to experiment with methods of timing growth or sequencing it to the construction of the necessary infrastructure. The concept of timing of development by the public was suggested in 1955 in an article that indicated five reasons for justifying municipal control of time of development:[19]

1. Planning for timing is essential to economize on the cost of municipal facilities and services.
2. Timing of development is necessary for the municipality to retain control over the eventual character of development.
3. Timing helps to maintain a desirable balance among various land use types.
4. Timing of development achieves greater detail and specificity in development regulation.
5. Without development timing it is difficult to maintain high quality community services and facilities.

The concept of development timing was first used on a broad community scale in the case of Ramapo Township in New York. Located some 25 miles north of New York City, Ramapo consists of several incorporated villages and one unincorporated village faced with the prospects of rapid growth in the late 1960s. The community adopted a plan to control growth based on the availability of public utilities. The community determined which portions of the township would be developed during each period of time, in 6-year increments, based on their budgeting cycle for capital expenditures. All land would be developed ultimately, but some land would not receive utilities for 18 years and the owners would be prevented from building in that area unless they provided utilities at their own expense.

The Ramapo case was taken to court and upheld in 1972 by New York State's highest court in *Golden v. the Planning Board of the Township of Ramapo*. The sequential growth plan used in Ramapo consisted of two critical elements: first, an orderly plan for providing public services to all areas of the township over an 18-year period, and secondly, a point system for determining whether a building permit would be granted to a specific site based on the proximity of the proposed development to the following public facilities and services.[20] By providing a timetable for implementation and construction of public facilities, Ramapo avoided the issue of taking property rights since the property owners would be able to develop their property. Only the time of development was affected. Since the Ramapo decision was issued in 1972 by the New York State Supreme Court, other cities have adopted regulation of growth based on a similar type of timing development.

Moratoria to Preserve Land and Time Development

Use of a moratorium to effectively control time growth through stopping development for a specified period of time is an old concept that has become increasingly important as growth management has become a significant issue. In essence, a moratorium stops development, or slows it, to a specified rate in a specified area or community, based on the lack of some public service. Most moratoria are justified on the grounds that the existing services would be overwhelmed if growth continued, or that the continuance of growth would damage the community health and safety. Normally, moratoria are implemented in order to allow the community time to develop other means of controlling the timing of growth. It has been suggested that moratoria serve three basic functions:

1. To permit planning and development of ordinances to proceed relatively free of development pressures. While the city or other governing body is in the process of developing ordinances a moratorium allows them to do so without fear that the area they are trying to regulate will be developed in the interim period in the absence of controls.
2. To prevent the establishment of uses that would not conform to subsequently adopted ordinances.
3. To provide the planning commission sufficient time for public discussion of the issues affecting growth.

Moratoria have been used by federal, state, and local governments and courts have upheld the rights of these entities to do so. Primarily, they are used by local governments, however, occasionally as a result of a public referendum. Moratoria are short-term solutions to timing of growth, as most are imposed for a set time of from 60 days to 1½ years. Although the length of time allowable for a moratorium has not been specifically indicated by courts, a 3½-year proposed moratorium in New Jersey was ruled too long by the courts.[21] In other communities, moratoria of 1 to 1½ years have been allowed, and have occasionally been extended to a 2-year period when the communities were able to show they were making satisfactory progress towards resolving the issues which fostered the moratoria. Moratoria, on specific aspects of public service, particularly sewer connections, have extended for over 2 years as a result of the time lag in constructing new waste water treatment facilities. In 1973, the Department of Housing and Urban Development, in a survey of area offices on the prevalence of sewer moratoria, found that 226 areas were using sewer moratoria. At that time, 28% had had a moratorium on sewer connections for less than 6 months, 40% for periods of 6 months to a year, 12% had been in existence for 1 to 2 years, and 15% had existed for more than 2 years.[22]

The type of moratoria actually applied in a community is highly variable, and usually involves more than one component of the development process. The 236 localities making use of moratoria in 1973 reported an average of nearly two restrictions each. The following general types of moratoria can be recognized as being used: building permits, extension of sewer and water lines, new sewer and water connections, zoning changes, new subdivisions, natural gas connections, building on environmentally sensitive lands, and a general ban on construction.[23] It should be noted that moratoria are often used without real justification as a method of excluding any growth. Unless landowners or others challenge such moratoria in court and prove that they are not justified by existing conditions, they can serve as an effective exclusionary zoning action.[24]

Land Banking to Time Development

Land banking provides another means of timing development. Land banking is the public acquisition and holding of undeveloped land in anticipation of future public use or resale to accomplish community goals. Historically, land banking has been used by communities to acquire sites for parks, schools, and other public facilities in advance of actual need. Land banking can also be used to influence the character and timing of future community growth. The community can acquire title to land and then make it available for private development through sale to the highest bidder at the time the community deems it proper for its development. The land may also be sold to private parties with attached deed restrictions to prevent certain types of uses, or it might simply be leased to a private individual for certain uses.

Some advantages of land banking are that it is said to minimize or eliminate urban sprawl, to serve as a method to redevelop the inner city, to curb public land speculation, and to provide for public uses. Through actual ownership of the property by the public, the land bank provides advantages not provided by traditional planning devices. By giving public officials a more direct interest in the property and its regulation, it encourages conformance to the comprehensive plan. It also allows for more restrictive comprehensive planning since private property rights are not being taken away. A drawback of the land banking concept is the large amount of funding required to adequately finance it. It has been estimated that in order for a land bank to control the growth of a metropolitan area with a population of 2½ million, it would need to be able to invest $250 million.[25]

Large Lot Zoning as a Development Timing Device

An alternative to land banking, which involves little additional cost and attains broadly analogous results, is large lot zoning. By using their zoning power, communities zone land for very low densities, and effectively limit the amount of development. Communities normally apply this technique to fringe areas that are underdeveloped or just beginning to be developed. When used in this fashion, large lot zoning allows a community to prevent too rapid development in areas inadequately served by public utilities. It also may serve as an interim device to prevent development while the community develops a permanent zoning ordinance, thus having the same affect as a moratorium. Large lot zoning can also be used to permanently establish low density uses in agricultural or environmentally sensitive areas. For example, many county zoning ordinances in agriculturally productive regions may have as much as 50-acre minimum requirements to qualify for a building permit.

It is important to distinguish between large lot zoning to affect the time of development, or to preserve agricultural land, and large lot zoning designed to exclude certain socioeconomic groups. When large lot zoning is used to time or phase development, it serves as a type of holding zone. High density residential development is not entirely prohibited in the zone, but is postponed until the community can develop the services to accommodate it. By slowing the rate of growth on the margins of the community, temporary large lot zoning also encourages construction in the central and developed portion of the community and maximizes use of the existing infrastructure.

REGULATIONS FOR PERMANENT POPULATION CONTROL

The types of regulations used in the devices for controlling land use, discussed up to this point, anticipate either a temporary control of development to insure the timing of development or allow development through transfer of development rights. There are a number of other zoning regulations resulting in permanent population control (Table 19). One method of maintaining permanent control over population densities through conventional zoning is to zone for exclusive agricultural or nonresidential use. Such single use zones exclude residential use, thus protecting the agricultural land while limiting number of households and population. The need to protect farmland from demand for commercial and residential use is evident, and will be discussed at length in a subsequent chapter. Factors which encourage scattering of residential construction through farmland are associated with the lower cost of construction on virgin land near the city and the desire of many people to have a quasi-rural life-style. The cost to the community is in the loss of the agricultural land and in the increased cost of services to the scattered residences.

A municipality cannot simply designate land as agricultural as a means of preventing development unless it is actually being used for agriculture. When it is used for agriculture and is designated as solely for agricultural use, the courts have upheld the right of the community to zone it for exclusive agricultural use in order to protect the health, welfare, and public safety of the community.

In similar fashion, communities have attempted to limit population densities by excluding mobile homes or multipe family housing. The rationale for so doing is that they result in increased density, higher costs of service, and a degradation in the quality of the community. Courts are reluctant to uphold this type of exclusionary zoning but it is used in many areas until it is challenged in court.[26] Closely related to this exclusionary device is the use of minimum floor area requirements in standard zoning ordinances. It was originally used as a means of insuring adequate space and to prevent unhealthy and unsanitary crowded conditions. In more recent times, the primary use of minimum floor area requirements is to maintain the tax base of the community while minimizing the number of children who require schooling, and the number of homes which require municipal services. Insofar as the minimum floor standards are actually used to protect the health of the community through preventing overcrowded conditions, they are justifiable, but courts have been reluctant to uphold them when it can be shown that they are exclusionary and designed to eliminate lower income families from the community.[27]

NEW ATTEMPTS TO CONTROL LAND USE THROUGH ZONING

There have been a number of attempts to control growth and regulate land use through modifications of conventional zoning techniques (Table 19). One of these has been designated *conditional* or *contract zoning*. Although these are separate techniques, they have not been used precisely nor defined precisely and hence are normally lumped as if they were the same. Under contract zoning, the landowner contracts with the municipality to subject his property to certain restrictions that are written into the deed and exchanged for a desired zoning change. His property is consequently zoned differently than surrounding property in the same zone. Conditional zoning arises when the governmental unit persuades the property owner to make certain promises regarding the location of structures on this property, dedication of property to the city, or similar activities. Unlike contract zoning, in conditional zoning the municipality has not made any reciprocal agreements. The advantage of contract and conditional zoning lies in providing flexibility to traditional zoning techniques. Thus, a parcel of land in a specific zone may not have been usable under the limitations affecting the zone it is assigned to, but it becomes suitable for development through this mechanism. The weakness of both conditional and contract zoning is that they may, in fact, constitute spot zoning, which is illegal. Nevertheless, the courts have been increasingly willing to accept them as tools of land use regulation when they do not result in a complete change in the character of the zone.

Planned unit development (PUD) represents another means of modifying existing zoning regulations to allow the development of large-scale developments planned and built as a unit with flexible design. PUDs involve planning for a larger plot of land as a unit, and eliminate the conventional lot by lot approval requirement. Normally, the builder is allowed greater densities on a portion of his property in return for providing open space or other urban amenities on the balance. PUD provisions are normally permitted when the proposed development exceeds a minimum size, such as greater than 5 acres, or exceeds a minimum number of housing units, such as 20. PUDs are normally included in the zoning ordinance but are not assigned to a specific mapped district. PUD is allowed in the residential districts but normally must meet the basic requirements of that district, with the exception that greater densities are allowable. It should be mentioned that not all PUDs resort to the use of greater density coupled with open space provisions (a concept known as clustering), as PUD may simply be used to design and gain approval for a large subdivision which is outwardly little different from those based on lot by lot approval and development.

Cluster zoning is a tool that specifically calls for maintenance of open space. This allows the developer to cluster the units which are allowable on a parcel of property while maintaining the balance in open space. As such, it operates on the principle of average density. Clustering is particularly suitable for steeper slopes or other areas where a portion of a plot would be better utilized by being retained as open space.

Another type of zoning adjustment is *performance standards*. Performance standards set levels for nuisance or side effects (externalities) of a development rather than specifying acceptable uses. They have been used to regulate such things as noise, smoke, and other externalities associated with industrial activity. More recently, they have been applied to demands for public services, such as sewage, transportation, etc. They have also been used to specify impact on the environment through devices like specifying the amount of runoff which would be allowed from a new development, the impact on wildlife, and similar performance standards. An advantage of performance standards is that they free the community from the need to specify an individual site for an activity, but allow activities to locate in those places where they can do so in an acceptable fashion.

Still another zoning adjustment is referred to as *bonus* or *incentive zoning*. As the name implies, this means provides the developer certain incentives in return for the provision of some type of amenity or benefit to the community by the developer. The builder is thus allowed an exception from the zoning ordinance to construct in a way that is otherwise not accepted in that zone. For example, the builder might be allowed to exceed the height restrictions if he provided an excess of open space around his structure. In New York City, a builder who rents the lower floors of his buildings for retail shops at reasonable rents is given a bonus, i.e., he is allowed to erect a larger building with more rentable floor space. Alternatively, a community might allow a landowner to build at a higher density than permitted in the zone if he would agree to sequence the development in conjunction with the community's provision of schools and other services, thus minimizing the economic impact on the community.[28]

Floating zones are another strategem used in conventional zoning ordinances to control the location of activities. In essence, the zoning ordinance provides for a type of activity but does not specify the location. A particular activity, e.g., a small shopping mall, may be desired in a given area but it is impossible to specify precisely where until after development of residential use. If a property owner can meet the conditions required in the zoning ordinance for the floating zone, he is allowed to construct it. In essence, the floating zone can be visualized as hovering over the city and descending to a specific site only when needed and when the site meets the requirements of the ordinance. At that time, for all intents and purposes, that particular size is rezoned to that activity.

Special permits are a means for conventional zoning to regulate certain desirable activities. The special permit, also known as *conditional use permit*, is used to regulate those activities recognized as desirable but requiring special control. The zoning ordinance then specifies all of the conditions necessary in order for a property owner to qualify for a special permit, in the same fashion as used for floating zones. For example, some municipalities use lack of adequate services as the basis for denying permission to develop property. In such an instance, the right to develop becomes a special use according to the ordinance. In order for a developer to utilize the land, the services necessary must be either in place or provided by the developer. The Ramapo residential development requirement is a special permit system, and the issuance of the permit depends on the availability of the level of essential municipal services. Other communities have used the special permit process through zoning areas for large lots, allowing more dense development through a special permit process when community services were available.

Floor Area Requirements

A final change associated with traditional Euclidian zoning has to do with the height and bulk requirements. Certain areas have height restrictions, to insure that low density development occurs, and others may use minimum lot size to insure the same thing. Increasingly there is a movement towards the use of "floor area ratio" as a substitute for height and area restrictions. The FAR allows the developer to choose whether to put a tall building on a small portion of the lot or a low building covering more of the lot. As such, the FAR technique is another in the general move toward attempting to modify conventional zoning to allow more flexibility without needing to change completely, as in the transfer of development right proposal.

EXACTION FROM DEVELOPERS

A type of land use control becoming increasingly important is that associated with requiring the developer to make a substantial input to the community in order to obtain permission to develop his property. This may take the form of mandatory dedication of a certain portion of land for parks, schools, or similar public facilities; or it may be in the form of requiring the developer to install roads, sewer and water lines, and to then dedicate them to the public. The rationale behind these measures is that the cost of development should be borne by the developer who benefits rather than by the community as a whole.

As a variant of the dedication of land, a community may allow a developer to pay cash in lieu of land or capital facilities. This achieves the same result but allows flexibility. Thus a developer may have a relatively small parcel of property and dedication of land for a road might seriously handicap successful completion of the project, or none of the land might be suitable for a park, or if land were dedicated for a park it might be too small to be feasibly used by the community. In such instances, payment of cash fees in lieu of dedication of the land provides both the developer and the community obvious benefits.

RESTRICTIVE COVENANTS

Controlling land use through restrictive covenants places restrictions on the use of property recorded with the deed. Hence, restrictive covenants are agreements between private parties in the transfer of land ownership. Restrictive covenants are often enforced by public laws in terms of length of time it will be enforced (in Houston, for example), but normally they would not be enforced unless the original owner or adjacent owners challenge them in court. Several areas use restrictive covenants on a broad basis, notably Houston, Texas, where covenants instead of Euclidian zoning are relied upon. The advantage of restrictive covenants is that they allow regulations to be tailored to a specific parcel of property. The disadvantage is that they may not adequately protect the broader neighborhood in the absence of other regulations.

TAXATION AND FEE REQUIREMENTS

A broad group of land use control mechanisms are associated with taxation policies and fees charged in conjunction with development. The use of fees is justifiable on the grounds that development ultimately must cost the community in that it allows new users to request services from the community. One form of fee tried in communities facing rapid growth is the so-called *impact fee* or tax. Construction of new homes or other development results in increased costs to the community in providing police and fire protection, schools, and other public services. The demand for services begins immediately upon occupancy of a new development, but the city receives no property tax revenue until the end of the taxation year. In order to help defray the additional costs, communities have turned to the impact tax (also known as the bedroom tax, the new construction tax, or the business license tax). In most instances such a tax is a direct charge to each new unit, sometimes based on the number of bedrooms, or the square footage involved. In some cases, the impact tax is utilized because state law will not allow a community to require a developer to provide sites for schools, fire stations, parks, or other public facilities. More importantly, rarely does a community have the option of requiring a developer to dedicate land to defray the cost of new sewer treatment plants or other facilities which are not actually on the site of his development. The impact tax provides the mechanism for doing so. The impact tax has been used in Florida, in California, in Utah, and many other states. In some instances, state courts have ruled that the impact tax is illegal (e.g., in Florida and Utah). Where such a tax has been ruled invalid, the general rationale has been that the resident who ultimately purchases the property is being subject to double taxation, since he must pay the impact tax plus the property tax. Nevertheless, the impact tax is being used successfully in California and in Virginia. Based on state laws, and as a device for imposing the cost of new development on the development itself rather than on the community, it may serve a valid purpose. Without the impact tax it is difficult for other residents of an existing community to escape from subsidizing new developments.[29]

Closely related to impact taxes are charges referred to as *user* and *benefit fees.* These are not taxes; they are the charges made by a municipality to offset the additional cost of providing certain services. Traditionally, these have taken the form of fees for connecting to the water and sewer systems. Although historically they have been used primarily to raise revenue, they are increasingly being utilized as a means of controlling and guiding growth. This may be done by using marginal cost pricing wherein a community determines the additional cost a new user would pay based on the location of his home. A new user in an isolated location costs the community more to service because of the cost of transport associated with either water or waste water. Such fees control growth by encouraging development in areas contiguous to the community's infrastructure. By charging prices which reflect the cost to construct new facilities a community may effectively limit all growth. For example, Alpine, Utah is a small farming community with a stable population of some 500 people during the 20th century. In the late 1960s and 1970s, it became the focus of subdivision pressure as commuters from the Salt Lake

City and Provo-Orem areas viewed it as a site for enjoying quasi-rural life-styles. The population increased dramatically and by 1977 the community was faced with overcrowded schools, inadequate water and sewage systems, inadequate fire and police protection, and inadequate highways. Because of the need to provide these services, the community enacted an impact tax to help recoup the costs. This was declared illegal by the Utah courts in 1979, and the city adopted a moratorium on all new development while raising the user fees for those developments which had been approved. The fee for connecting to the sewer system was raised to $1,500 per residence, and the cost to connect to the water system to $2,100. The community leaders maintained that such high fees are essential to pay the costs of providing the services, but they serve as a de facto regulator of growth, and in fact are an example of exclusionary regulations.

Another means of recouping the costs associated with providing services is via a *special assessment*. This is a taxation method by which the cost of a facility such as a road, sidewalk, sewer, or water system is assigned to the adjacent benefiting property. Special assessment programs allocate the cost of providing the service according to the benefits received, unlike general taxation which spreads the cost to all whether they are benefited or not.

Yet another form of regulation of growth that has become extremely popular is the use of *preferential assessment* or *preferential taxation*. This is a system for encouraging certain types of activities through various tax schedules for different parcels of property. It has been widely used in attempts to preserve farmland. The system consists of assessing a parcel of property at a value lower than its market value for development purposes so long as the individual owner maintains the land in farming-related activities. Such methods of controlling land use require special legislation, which normally take one of three forms. The primary focus is to assess the actual value of the land in terms of its agricultural productivity through:

1. Preferential assessments—property is taxed on the basis of the use at the present time.
2. Deferred taxation—the value of the property for development purposes is not taxed until the actual time of development; until that time only the productive use for farming is taxed.
3. Restricted use—the land must be subject to land use restrictions to insure that it remains in agricultural or other desired activities for a specified time in order to qualify for use value assessment.

ABSOLUTE CONTROL

Finally, a method of regulating population growth, utilized in the decade of the 1970s, is that of absolutely limiting the population through one of two means. The first of these consists of setting a total population limit on the community in either absolute numbers or number of households. The city of Boca Raton, Florida attempted to set an absolute limit of some 100,000 by limiting the number of residential units to 40,000 in the early 1970s, but this action was declared unconstitutional in 1975, and absolute population caps have generally become invalidated as a means of regulating population.

The second means of absolutely limiting population growth is through limiting the number of permits issued each year. Such means are used in several places in the United States—most notably in Petaluma, California—but they are used in such diverse places as Pinellas County, Florida; Lindon, Utah; and Boulder, Colorado. Basically, communities restrict the number of new building permits to those which can be accepted by the community and still maintain the quality of services and quality of life. The United States Supreme Court recognized the right of communities to do this so long as the community's program provides housing for all social economic groups.

CONCLUSION

All of the changes affecting land use regulation in the United States discussed in this chapter are part of an ongoing process which is resulting in some major changes in traditional Euclidian zoning. It should be obvious that in general terms, while new items are being grafted onto it, traditional zoning is only being transformed. Zoning is in the process of moving towards ever greater public control of private property. The changes reflect increasing acceptance of the concept that the public has an interest in how private property is used. The costs to a community which accompany land development, and the benefits to landowners from community actions, are increasingly viewed as being regulated partially for the benefit of the broader public. All of the plans and modifications discussed in this chapter are designed to insure that the public does not suffer from the actions of private landowners. The adoption of phased or timed growth regulations in order to minimize the impacts of unplanned sprawl on the community is but one example. The concept of development rights transfers as a means of protecting both public interest and private property values is another facet of the ongoing search for means to harmonize the interests of the public with those of the private landowner. There are many legal questions concerning regulations of land use and development, and the tools which are being used are in a state of flux as a consequence. Nevertheless, the latter half of the decade of the 1970s has seen the development of increasingly severe regulations affecting private landowners as the public attempts to insure that development will not cause negative impacts to the balance of the community.

NOTES

[1] David P. Godchalk, *Constitutional Issues of Growth and Management* (Chicago: The American Society of Planning Officials, 1977), pp. 9–11.

[2] Ibid., p. 11.

[3] Fred Bosselman and David Callies, *The Quiet Revolution in Land Use Control* (Washington, D.C.: Council on Environmental Quality, 1971), pp. 314–316.

[4]Jerome G. Rose, editor, *Transfer of Development Rights: A New Technique of Land Use Regulation* (New Brunswick, N.J.: Center for Urban Policy Research, 1975), pp. 1–3.

[5]Frank Schnidman, "TDR: A Tool for More Equitable Land Management?" in *Management and Control of Growth*, Vol. IV (Washington, D.C.: Urban Land Institute, 1978), pp. 52–53.

[6]Melvin R. Levin et al., *New Approaches to State Land Use Policies* (Lexington, Mass.: D. C. Heath, 1974), pp. 55–57.

[7]Schnidman, op. cit., p. 53.

[8]Ibid., pp. 53–54; Levin et al., op. cit., pp. 57–63.

[9]Robert E. Loughlin and Thomas Plaut, "Less than Fee Acquisition for the Preservation of Open Space: Does It Work?", *Journal of the American Institute of Planners*, Vol. 44, 1978, p. 456.

[10]Ibid., pp. 459–460.

[11]Ibid., pp. 455–456.

[12]Hershel J. Richman and Lane H. Kendig, "Transferable Development Rights—A Pragmatic View," *Environmental Comment*, April, 1978, p. 7.

[13]David E. Ervin et al., *Land Use Control* (Cambridge, Mass.: Ballinger, 1977), p. 132.

[14]Ibid.; Levin et al., op. cit., pp. 60–61.

[15]Jerome G. Rose, op. cit., p. 87.

[16]Ibid., pp. 337–341.

[17]John C. Keene, "Transferable Development Rights: An Evaluation," in *Land Use: Tough Choices in Today's World* (Washington, D.C.: Soil Conservation Society of America, 1977), p. 257.

[18]David J. Brower et al., *Urban Growth Management Through Development Timing* (New York: Praeger Publishers, 1976), p. 42.

[19]Ibid., p. 41.

[20]Manuel S. Emanuel, "Ramapo's Managed Growth Program," *Planners Notebook*, 1974, pp. 4–5.

[21]Brower et al., op. cit., p. 58.

[22]Rivken-Carson Inc., *The Sewer Moratoria as a Technique of Growth and Control and Environmental Protection* (Washington, D.C.: Department of Housing and Urban Development, 1973), pp. 15–18.

[23]Brower et al., op. cit., pp. 60–61.

[24]See John T. Hazel, Jr., "Growth Management Through Litigation: A Case Study of Fairfax County, Virginia," *Urban Land*, November 1976, pp. 6–14, for a discussion of how one county used moratoria and other devices to control growth when they were not justified according to subsequent court decisions.

[25]Michael E. Gleeson et al., *Urban Growth Management Systems: An Evaluation of Policy-Related Research* (Chicago: American Society of Planning Officials, 1975), pp. 35–36.

[26]Ibid., p. 41.

[27]Ibid., pp. 41–42.

[28]Ibid., p. 40.

[29]Frederick A. Jacobsen and Jeffrey Redding, "Impact Taxes," in Frank Schnidman et al., *Management and Control of Growth*, Vol. IV (Washington, D.C.: Urban Land Institute, 1978), pp. 216–221.

Chapter 8

Farmland Preservation: Necessity or Misperception

Introduction

One of the land use issues which has become noteworthy in the 1970s is that of loss of prime agricultural land. As the population of the United States has become increasingly urbanized, and the suburbs have sprawled ever farther from the center of the city, there has been a growing perception that we are losing an unacceptable amount of our prime agricultural land. Coupled with this fear have been statistics showing the decline of the farm population from nearly 9% of the total population in 1960 to only 3.6% of the total population in 1977.[1]

Although the decline in farm population and concomitant suburbanization of the metropolitan regions has prompted a feeling on the part of some that we are running out of prime agricultural land, only 3% of the total land area of the United States is in urban and built-up uses, according to the U.S. Department of Agriculture. The vast majority of the one billion acres of the United States remain in agricultural or other extensive uses. Nevertheless, the perception that loss of prime agricultural land is a severe problem has prompted adoption of special land use measures to preserve the agricultural land in 46 of the nation's states.[2] Regardless of the severity of the actual problem, the general attitude has been that it is a national crisis.

THE NATURE OF THE PROBLEM

The basis for the public view that loss of prime agricultural land is a crisis is related to facts emphasizing the magnitude of the loss. York County, Pennsylvania,

171

for example, lost an average of 5,000 acres of farmland every year from 1954–1974, while the number of farms declined from 5,549 in 1954 to only 2,390 in 1974. In Orange County, California, over 100,000 acres of farmland were lost between 1950 and 1975 as a result of population increase. Some 172,000 acres of farmland in Illinois have been "disturbed" by strip mining, while an additional 2½ million acres of Illinois land has strippable coal reserves of sufficient quality to justify further disruption of farming.[3] In Wisconsin, nearly 150,000 acres of productive farmland are converted each year to nonfarm uses.[4] Between 1950 and 1970, New York State lost 5.8 million acres of farmland, or about 290,000 acres a year.[5] In the 22 years from 1950 to 1972, 2 states lost more than 50%, 5 states more than 40%, 9 states more than 30%, and 17 states more than 20% of their taxable farmland.[6] In gross terms, there are some 1.2 to 2 million acres of rural cropland being converted to urban uses each year, while another 1 million acres are converted to lakes, ponds, and reservoirs.[7] Those who argue that loss of agricultural land is not an immediate problem point out that more farmland (some 2,700,000 acres) is "abandoned" each year in marginal farming areas of the country, and that 1,300,000 acres of new farmland are created each year through irrigation, drainage, and reclamation projects in general.[8] In 1976, the Soil Conservation Service reported that 24 million acres of prime farmland were idle or in pasture or other uses which could be converted to agriculture simply by beginning to till the land. On a per capita basis, the United States has 5 acres of agricultural land for every man, woman, and child in the country, while in Egypt there is less than ¼ acre per person, in India ½, and in France—with a relatively abundant agricultural base—only 1.6 acres.[9] Those pursuing this line of argument further point out that the rate of population growth in the United States is declining and hence there will be less demand for suburban expansion, further minimizing the extent of the loss of agricultural land.

Those who argue that there is, in fact, a serious problem facing the United States in terms of the agricultural resource base use a variety of arguments to justify their position. The basic arguments can be summarized as those relating to the following: (1) urban shadow affects, (2) quality of cropland converted, (3) location of prime cropland loss, and (4) costs of farmland conversion.

Farmers living in the vicinity of cities face certain problems resulting in either lowered yields or land not farmed, even though the land is not actually converted to urban uses. This is referred to as the urban shadow effect. As the suburban fringe advances, farmers residing in areas subject to present or short-term future development pressure begin to devote less capital to farm improvement and maintenance. The productivity of the land begins to decline. Other land is purchased by developers who do not maintain it as agriculturally productive land, but allow it to lie idle until such time as the advancing suburbs justify transforming it into suburban areas. Farmers opting to maintain their farming enterprise at the pre-suburban pressure scale face several diseconomies. Industries may locate nearby, which cause pollutants that minimize crop yields; suburban neighbors may engage in vandalism or outright theft of crops and animals; and finally, suburban residents may force the farmer to sell the land for development because the farm and associated animals create a nuisance activity in the suburban setting (Fig. 14). Tax rates

Fig. 14. Farmland surrounded by subdivisions: Utah County, Utah, 1979.

increase as the land becomes more desirable for subdivision and other urban developments, either forcing the farmer to sell a part or all of his land for development, or forcing his survivors to sell the land to pay the estate taxes upon the farmer's death. The net effect of these forces is to cause a much greater loss of land to urban uses than the figures normally given for land transferred to urban uses indicate. It is estimated that for each acre of land actually transferred into an urban related land use, from 1 to 2 acres of additional land is lost from agricultural use.[10]

The second factor affecting the impact of the loss of land from agricultural activities each year is related to the quality of the land. Not all land is equally suitable for farming purposes, and that which is most desirable is in limited supply. It is estimated that the prime farmland constitutes some 25% of land in private ownership in the United States, which is flat, well drained, adequately watered, and fertile land makes the best farmland, but these same characteristics also make it prime development land. The relationship of land converted from agricultural uses to prime agricultural land is shown in Table 21. Prime farmland is defined in this table as those lands occupying the Class I and II Land Capability classification of the Soil Conservation Service. These lands have no limitations for cultivation. Lands in Classes III-IV can be utilized for cultivation on a permanent basis, with varying levels of management practices necessary to overcome their physical

Table 21. Urban Related Land Conversion in the United States, 1967–1975

	Converted to urban areas	Converted to water areas	Total converted	
			Areas	Percent
Prime farmland (Capability Classes I–II)	6,200,000	1,191,000	7,391,000	32
Land in Capability Classes III–IV (not prime land)	6,128,000	1,862,000	7,990,000	34.5
Land in Capability Classes Classes V–VIII	4,044,000	3,637,000	7,681,000	33.5
Totals	16,372,000	6,682,000	23,055,000	100.0

Source: Linda K. Lee "A Perspective on Cropland Availability," Agricultural Economic Report No. 406 (Washington, D.C.: U.S. Department of Agriculture, 1978), pp. 14, 15; tables 8, 9.

limitations. If the lands in Classes III–IV are included, over 75% of land converted to urban uses in the 1967–1975 period is found in these classifications.[11] The fact that 32% of the land converted to urban uses was prime land, when only 25% of all land in the nation is prime land, is indicative of the disproportionate concentration of development on prime agricultural land. The significance of this is obvious. Lands in Class I yield a higher return for the same inputs of labor and capital. These are the lands which are of primary importance in maintaining our agricultural productivity. Although it can be argued that the availability of other prime cropland not now cultivated negates the loss of 8 million acres of prime land between 1967 and 1975, when viewed over the next 50 to 100 years, the persistence of such a rate of loss will become an alarming problem.

An additional problem that magnifies the actual number of acres lost to urban uses is the location of cropland being converted. Loss of agricultural land in states like Illinois or Iowa, where the majority of the land area of the state is arable, is less significant than loss of prime agriculture land in California, Oregon, Colorado, or other western states with only limited quantities of prime land. Loss of prime agricultural land is particularly critical in states such as New York, New Jersey, or Rhode Island where a disproportionally high percentage of the land is already in urban uses. As indicated in Table 22, the regions of the corn belt and northern plains states and southern plains states have large reserves of prime farmland, while their losses have not been overly great. In the mountain states and northeastern area, the reserves are less than the amount lost between 1967 and 1975. Loss of these lands is critical, particularly when it is noted that even though the major metropolitan regions of the United States occupy only a small percentage of the land area, 52% of the land designated as Class I or II quality is found near urban centers.[12] The pressure for conversion of these prime lands

Table 22. Distribution and Changes in Use of Prime Farmland,
1967–1975
(thousands of acres)

Agricultural region	Cropped 1975	Lost		Total	Potential reserve
		Urban	Water		
Appalachian	13,187	600	30	26,449	4,237
Corn Belt	61,217	1,120	260	76,896	3,089
Delta States	15,198	460	40	29,650	1,699
Great Lake States	30,444	440	10	38,361	852
Mountain	15,736	100	1	18,142	230
Northeast	8,948	970	90	17,885	392
Northern Plains	58,154	440	70	72,004	3,839
Pacific	8,919	460	0	13,813	834
Southeast	8,954	1,150	230	23,632	2,864
Southern Plains	29,240	390	460	67,175	6,034
43 State total	249,997	6,200	1,191	384,007	24,070

Source: Linda K. Lee, "A Perspective on Cropland Availability," Agricultural Economic Report No. 406, (Washington, D.C.: U.S. Department of Agriculture, 1978), p. 10 (table 6); p. 12 (table 7); p. 17 (table 10).

is even greater, since they are near the most intensive transport network, energy supply systems, and other public utilities. Thus the pressure on at least one half of the prime lands of the United States is quite intense.

A final factor intensifying the problem of loss of prime agricultural land is associated with the cost of such land conversion. These costs are twofold, and are related to the actual cost of replacing the lost farmland, as well as to government programs that prompt suburbanization and encourage loss of farmland. When the prime farmland is lost, the value of the crop production is immediately foregone. The cost of replace that land is fairly substantial. Although more land is reclaimed each year than is lost to urban sprawl, this land normally comes through subsidy from the general public. Bureau of Reclamation projects provide irrigation water for new lands in the west, but at a high price. One estimate indicated that the cost to replace the prime agricultural land lost adjacent to expanding cities in southern California would be an additional $1,500 per acre. If this figure were correct for all prime agricultural land lost, the cost of the 8 million acres lost from 1967 to 1975 would have been $12 billion. It does not necessarily cost that much to replace prime agricultural land with other prime agricultural land, where there is uncropped prime land available, but in certain areas the costs for providing additional land are extremely high. In addition to the direct cost associated with the giant reclamation projects of the Bureau of Reclamation, there are a host of other federal subsidy programs designed to encourage farmers to undertake irrigation, drainage, or other modifications to reclaim land. All of these programs function, in part, because the loss of prime agricultural land makes them necessary.

A second cost associated with loss of prime agricultural land is in the suburbanization process itself. Bond issues to provide utilities to newly created suburban areas, federal programs designed to loan money for purchase of private housing, and income tax deductions for interest associated with mortgage payments are all costs directly associated with the expansion of suburbia into the prime agricultural land.[13]

Those who accept the argument that the combined impact of expansion of urban areas results in a critical land use issue maintain that we need to preserve the prime agricultural land. The justifications for preserving this land are as follows:

The first justification for preserving prime agricultural land, aside from the factors discussed above, is that associated with the necessity of maintaining adequate food supplies for the world. Demand for food continues to increase on a worldwide scale at a rate faster than food production increases for the world. As the world's largest net surplus producer of food, the United States will become increasingly important as a source of food supplies. Each lost acre of prime farmland is of significant importance because it is the most efficient, environmentally stable, and energy-conserving land now available for production of food. Even given the large quantity of potential land in the United States, continued losses of 1 to 2 million acres per year are intolerable in the long run.

A second issue that has been used to justify control of loss of prime agricultural land is urban sprawl. Without regulation to protect those areas adjacent to cities that are more suitable for development, the waste and cost associated with sprawl will continue.

A third factor justifying regulation of prime agricultural land is related to local, national, and international economics. Export of agricultural surplus constitutes an important method for offsetting balance of trade deficits associated with energy imports into the United States. At the local scale, the economies of many of America's towns are highly reliant upon their agricultural setting. Continued loss of these prime agricultural lands results in a loss of their economic base. Not only do the farms provide the actual farm product to the local economies, but they affect a number of urban services, such as stores, farm implement dealers, and agricultural processing facilities, as well as jobs and taxes which accrue to the benefit of the local economy. In addition, the availability of a reliable, high-quality, and relatively reasonably priced supply of farm produce is an important factor affecting the residents of communities.

A final argument, used to justify preservation of prime agricultural land, is that farmlands are necessary for maintaining open space and environmental quality. Farmlands can serve as buffer zones between urban areas and environmentally sensitive locations, such as wetlands or floodplains. Farmlands also absorb precipitation, minimize run-off, and assist in replenishment of ground water supplies. As a source of open space for urban residents, the farmlands surrounding our cities are of inestimable value.[14]

DEFINING PRIME AGRICULTURAL LANDS

In all of the arguments for farmland preservation, a critical issue is that focused on the so-called prime agricultural land. Prime agricultural land has traditionally been defined in terms of its suitability for agriculture. The Soil Conservation Service defines prime lands as those with an adequate and dependable moisture supply from either irrigation or natural precipitation, being warm enough and with a sufficiently long growing season to produce the crops adapted to the area, free of high water table or frequent flooding, free of acidity or alkalinity problems, lack of erosion susceptibility, and minimum stoniness. It has also been argued that "prime" relates to factors beyond immediate soil character in terms of location. The value of land for agriculture as reflected in the marketplace must also be considered in defining what constitutes prime agricultural land.[15] In addition, another class of land that may not be normally recognized as prime has been suggested by some observers as a prime candidate for preservation. These unique lands produce a crop that is restricted to a small geographical area. Thus the lands of California that were suited to avocado and citrus production were not necessarily prime agricultural lands from the standpoint of the Soil Conservation Service definition, but they are unique lands in that there is only a limited amount of land suitable for production of these crops.

According to the Soil Conservation Service, there is an estimated 384 million acres of prime farmland in the United States (Table 23). It should be remembered that any definition of prime land is at least partially arbitrary. Changing economic conditions may well make lands which have been classed as less than prime lands suitable for inclusion in this definition. Also, the location of some prime lands with respect to all weather roads may make utilization of them difficult and result in them being less utilized than inferior lands which have a better location. The figures given in Table 23 should be viewed as simply the general range of prime land rather than as an unchanging absolute.

Table 23. Total Prime Farmland in the United States, 1975

Land use	Prime farmland (millions of acres)	Prime farmland	
		% of total	% of non-cropped
Cropland	250	65	0
Pasture and range	76	20	58
Forest	43	11	31
Other land	15	4	11
Total	384	100	100

Source: Environmental Quality, 1977 (Washington, D.C.: Government Printing Office, 1977), p. 91.

REGULATION OF LAND USE IN AGRICULTURAL AREAS

The significance of prime lands, by whatever definition, is in the area of their regulation. Concern for regulation of prime agricultural lands raises all of the issues involved in other land use regulation programs. These issues are further compounded by the fact that agricultural land in the fringe areas of urban development represents not only an environmental resource, but the chief financial asset of the farmer who owns the land, and the source of much of the supply of buildable land in the adjacent urban area.[16]

Agricultural land is affected by a wide array of public and private actions. Legislation and specific regulations drawn up to preserve prime agricultural land are only a small fraction of the forces determining the ultimate use of the land. Changes in taxation procedures affecting state taxes; environmental regulations affecting the use of pesticides, herbicides and fertilizers; implementation of coastal zone management programs; or even the changing price of petroleum products and resultant availability—all affect agricultural land directly or indirectly. These effects may result in a direct impact on land use, as in the case of federal support of prices for wheat, or they may have an indirect effect through affecting the economy and thus impacting upon consumer purchasing power, resulting in changes in farm operations.

Even when a single issue concerning prime agricultural land is addressed, it is not always certain that the preservation of prime agricultural land is the motive of all parties involved. Many who advocate preservation of prime agricultural land are primarily concerned with minimizing urban sprawl or maintaining open space rather than the agricultural land per se. In the same fashion, those advocating programs to preserve prime agricultural land as a green belt around communities may be doing so for selfish purposes related to recreational potential, or in an effort to exclude low-income residents from their middle-class society. In similar fashion, attempts to minimize growth in urban fringe areas are as likely to be the result of efforts to minimize taxes as to maintain agricultural land to insure adequate food production.

Nevertheless, the situation in the United States between 1972 and 1980 has resulted in a growing awareness of the need to conserve prime agricultural land. Prior to 1972, America had a large portion of its land area set aside in land banking programs to prevent overwhelming our economy with crop surpluses. In the ensuing years, the agricultural economy moved to a near-full farm production in a rapid fashion. This rapid expansion raised fears of what would happen as population continued to increase and demand for food also went up.

The non-prime land issues of taxation, exclusion, or open space have historically resulted in regulations affecting only those areas of prime land in or adjacent to urban areas. The addition of the perception that we are running out of prime agricultural land has added another element to land use regulation. As a consequence of the two factors, there has developed in the past 5 years a host of land use regulations, at the state level, designed to encourage preservation of the best farmlands.[17] At the federal level, concern for prime agricultural land fostered development of a policy statement by the United States Department of Agriculture in 1976, entitled "Statement of Prime Farmland, Range, and Forestland." It indicated that the goal of the Department of Agriculture would be to minimize loss of prime agriculture land through encouraging all federal agencies to adopt a policy of taking prime agricultural land only when there was no suitable alternate site and when the need for the action was overwhelming.[18] Congressional concern for loss of prime land resulted in passage of the 1976 Land and Water Conservation Act. This requires the Secretary of Agriculture to prepare an inventory and assessment of the nation's land and water resources and to update it every 5 years.

LAND USE REGULATIONS TO PRESERVE PRIME AGRICULTURAL LAND

The general concern for agricultural land preservation has resulted in a variety of proposals for its protection. These range from direct controls such as zoning, to indirect incentives associated with public spending. One of the most common methods is that of zoning. Most states now have legislation allowing local governing bodies to enact zoning regulations that could be used to protect prime agricultural lands. Counties, if they so desire, may enact a zoning ordinance resulting in either exclusive agriculture zones or large minimum land areas designed to prevent the spread of urban uses into the rural areas. As with all zoning regulations, agricultural zoning must be carefully developed to ensure that it is not arbitrary nor capricious. The zoning regulations must reflect the actual importance of the land for farming and not be a tool to simply prevent growth or maintain exclusive zoning in a case where it is already in the process of transformation to urban uses. The basis for the zoning ordinance must reflect the public welfare and be justifiable in terms of the goals and policies of the governmental unit. The zoning ordinance must not exceed the statutory powers given the governing body in the state enabling act. The zoning ordinance must be valid and nondiscriminatory when applied to a specific parcel of land. If it discriminates unfairly against a particular parcel as compared to other parcels, it is questionable that it can be maintained. The agricultural zones developed must not result in a taking or confiscation of the property. This issue is one of critical importance in all zoning, and particularly so in an area of rapidly inflating land values resulting from urban pressure. The zoning must be based upon defensible criteria and be justifiable in terms of the public welfare, health, and general safety.

Agricultural zoning has been used in a variety of areas of the United States in an attempt to prevent the loss of prime agricultural lands. Notable examples of this are the Sacramento County, California ordinance, the Oregon State Land Use Zoning, and similar activities. Nevertheless, zoning has been criticized as being ineffective in preserving agricultural and other environmentally important land. The weaknesses of zoning are associated both with the principal of zoning ordinances themselves, as well as with poor administration by local government. Specific criticisms of zoning as a tool to preserve prime agricultural lands are as follows:

1 Most states do not make zoning of agricultural and other extensive land uses mandatory. Thus there is no uniform regulation to protect all prime lands in any individual state, let alone in the nation.

2. In areas where zoning ordinances have been enacted, too frequently they are permissive, artibrary, or not enforced. The elected officials who are faced with enforcement are reluctant to take actions that might cause voters to oppose them in the next election. In addition, in many rural areas, the strong heritage of individualism makes elected officials reluctant to impose any type of regulation or enforcement on private farmlands.

3. A critical problem with zoning as a regulatory device for prime lands is the lack of coordination between governmental units. Individual counties draft ordinances reflecting their perception of the problems and the resultant documents are often unrelated to community or regional plans and objectives. This effectively prevents preservation of prime agricultural lands on a national basis.

4. Zoning regulations as adopted in most rural governing units tend to be piecemeal and ad hoc. Normally they are enacted in a crisis situation and too often reflect inadequate research and understanding of either the problems or potential solutions.

5. Zoning as a method for regulating and preserving prime agricultural lands has the potential for confiscatory impact. The present zoning may result in a diminishment of value to the extent that it constitutes a de facto public confiscation of land without compensation.

6. Zoning as a tool is normally implemented in a simplistic fashion. Zones are drawn requiring minimum acreage standards, without the adoption of more recent innovative zoning techniques such as impact or performance zoning, incentive zoning, or even PUD zones.

Alternate Forms of Agricultural Zoning

In the absence of other controls, zoning provides a minimal type of regulation which, in part, preserves prime agricultural land. As a result of the weaknesses listed above, however, and because of the tendency of local governing units to rezone upon request of landowners, it has been suggested that until better alternatives are implemented, it will be impossible to maintain prime agricultural lands in the face of urban pressure.[19] To overcome these problems, several states have adopted zoning procedures designed to allow farmers to receive some of the benefit from inflated land values while maintaining zoning regulations. Some Minnesota counties have implemented agricultural zoning known as quarter/quarter zoning. This is based on the concept of a quarter of a quarter section in the 640-acre township, or 40 acres. A quarter/quarter is 1/16 of the 640-acre section. The ordinance sets a standard of one lot per 40 acres of farmland. Thus, a farmer owning a 640-acre section would be able to sell 16 lots. The ordinance also insures that the remaining land will be retained in agricultural use.[20] The advantages of the system are twofold: The farmer is able to recognize capital gains associated with inflated land prices, and can do so without selling minimum parcels of 10 or more acres as required by most agricultural zoning. In essence, the quarter/quarter system provides a one-time opportunity for a farmer with 40 acres to sell one lot. The remaining land has no more development potential under the ordinance, and hence will remain in agriculture so long as the ordinance is in effect. Quarter/quarter zoning presents an attractive alternative to conventional zoning, combining some of the net effect of development rights transfer with that of zoning. It is ineffective when land ownership is highly fragmented, since the landowner who first obtains the building permit for a quarter/quarter section is the only one who benefits when more than one landowner owns part of a 40-acre piece.

An alternative zoning regulation for preserving farmland, which overcomes this problem, is the sliding-scale method of zoning. This zoning technique assigns each landowner a certain number of lots based on size of holding, with greater density allowed for smaller parcels. For example, the owner of a 5-acre parcel may be entitled to create two building lots, but the owner of a 20-acre parcel only three, and a 100-acre parcel only four. Justification for this is that the larger landowner is more committed to agriculture and preservation of the large parcels in agricultural uses is necessary to protect the agricultural base of the economy. Sliding scales normally have minimum and maximum size range. Maximums of 2 acres are typical, thus preventing the land from being broken up into "ranchettes" unsuitable for agriculture.

Sometimes performance standards are added to sliding-scale zoning. These may require using only rough, steep, or other land marginal for agricultural for lots. In Peach Bottom Township, Pennsylvania, a farmer who has used the building lots assigned him on the sliding scale, but who has agriculturally useless land left, may receive additional building permits for lots on his land. Thus the performance standard is one of encouraging building on marginal agricultural land.[21] Advantages of the sliding scale relate to its benefits to both small and large landowners. Small landowners are not prohibited from capturing any of the profit associated with rising land prices, as in typical agricultural zoning with its large minimum lot requirements. Large landowners are able to receive some of the benefits of inflation while maintaining the bulk of their land in agricultural uses. The weakness is that of any zoning, it can be changed and does not guarantee that future zoning will not result in greater densities than are desirable.

Another form of zoning is to create exclusive districts where only agriculture is allowed. These programs specify those areas which are and should remain agricultural, and attempt to prevent nonagricultural activities from locating within their boundaries. For example, New York enacted a program in 1971 permiting owners of farmland to petition the county and state governments for creation of agricultural districts. The Agricultural District Act requires 500 or more contiguous acres to be reserved in agricultural use for a minimum of 8 years. Organization into such a district results in several benefits to landowners. Land is eligible to be assessed at agricultural rather than market value. Local governments may not enact ordinances which restrict or regulate farm structures and practices beyond that required for health and safety. The powers of public agencies to acquire land by eminent domain are minimized. The farmer is exempt from benefit assessments or other taxes on farmland for water, sewer, light, and similar urban infrastructure. Construction by public agencies (highway department, sewage districts, etc.) cannot be undertaken until after the state has considered its impact on farming.[22] Some 355 districts have been organized, representing more than one-half of the farmland in the state, but to date it has primarily been used by those farmers in nonmetropolitan areas with less development pressure.[23] In addition, the commissioner of environmental conservation has the authority to create agricultural districts of a minimum 2,000-acre size when the agricultural land is designated unique and irreplacable.[24]

California's program for preferential assessment also embodies the principle of an agricultural preserve. The California Assessment Act requires that agricultural preserves be a minimum of 100 acres, except in certain cases. Individuals or groups of landowners may request designation as an agricultural preserve and after the appropriate public hearings, the county may so designate the land involved. This then allows the county to zone or otherwise restrict activities in the agricultural preserve to agricultural, recreational, open space, or other compatible uses. Only those lands participating under the restrictive convenants of the California Assessment Act can be so designated.

Use of voluntary agricultural districts to encourage preservation of prime agricultural land has the same weaknesses associated with other mechanisms discussed above. So long as the farmer views the potential from conversion of his land as exceeding the values associated with agricultural retention, it is doubtful that he will enter his lands into such a program. In practice, preserves have tended to be located away from the urban rural fringe where the pressure for conversion is greatest. To offset the pressures on conversion of agricultural lands in the urban rural fringe, it has been suggested that restrictions be placed on state activities within agricultural areas.

The program associated with the Oregon State Land Use Law represents another example of exclusive districts for preserving prime and agricultural land. The 1973 Oregon Land Use Act requires that local jurisdictions implement comprehensive planning and zoning. Of particular importance to the preservation of prime agricultural land is the requirement that all towns and cities set urban growth boundaries beyond which they do not plan to extend. All prime agricultural land outside the boundaries of growth for the city will be zoned for exclusive agricultural use. The Oregon program is particularly strong because it requires that the local comprehensive plans be tied to the state comprehensive plans, and be approved by the state agencies. In order to meet state guidelines, the area restricted to exclusive agriculture zones must have local ordinances that do not restrict farming practices, that exempt farmers from assessments and costs associated with sewage and water districts, and allow for use-value assessment for both property tax and state inheritance taxes.[25]

ALTERNATIVE MEANS OF CONTROLLING AGRICULTURAL LAND

A number of alternatives to zoning exist to control agricultural land use. Though not comprehensive, the following indicate the general range of types of land use regulation available:[26] (1) compensable regulations, (2) development rights easements, (3) transferable development rights, (4) land banking, (5) preferential taxation, (6) restrictions on state activities in agricultural districts, (7) exclusive agricultural districts, and (8) federal regulations and agencies.

Compensable Regulations

Compensable regulations were suggested in the 1960s as a means of providing strict property regulation while preventing loss of value to property owners. The concept envisions that before any land is regulated it is assessed and a guaranteed value set. Upon imposition of regulations, if the regulations result in a lowered market value for the land, the landowner is compensated for the diminishment or diminution in value of the property. It should be noted that the compensation received is based only on the degree to which the regulation reduces the value of the land for those uses actually being carried on when the regulation was imposed. The difference in compensation and value for market purposes is not paid until and unless the landowner sells the property and receives less than the guaranteed value.

Compensable regulations have been little used for obvious reasons. It is an expensive mechanism for the governing bodies; it does not allow for inflation of land values and thus is opposed by property owners. With increasing acceptance of the need to regulate private property for the interest of the public, it may result in overcompensation for landowners for valid restrictions placed on land use in the public interest. Moreover, in the rural urban fringe, where pressure on prime lands is greatest, it may be as economical for the local government to purchase the land outright as to pay compensation for dimunition of value. The final argument against the widespread use of compensable regulations is that when and if it is administered by local governments, it has all of the inherent possibilities for misuse, graft, and favoritism presently built into existing zoning ordinances.[27] As a tool for regulating and preserving the prime agricultural lands of the United States, it is doubtful that compensable regulations will ever be widely adopted, although Oregon has proposed a system for compensating landowners when rezoning depreciates land values by more than 20%.

Transfer of Development Right

Transfer of development rights (TDR) for the purpose of preserving prime agricultural land is an attractive alternative. By selling the state a less than fee-simple interest in the land, both the farmer and the state benefit. By purchasing the development rights, the state effectively prevents the land from being transformed from agricultural uses. The farmer benefits because he receives the value of the land for development purposes and thus recaptures his equity and the inflated value of his property, while maintaining the agricultural rights. In addition, the farmer benefits through reduced real estate taxes, since the land is permanently designated as nondevelopment land. This is particularly important in those areas not utilizing some form of preferential taxation for agriculture, since it may allow the farmer to reduce his tax payments to a level which will allow him to maintain farming. At least five states have adopted legislation allowing development rights transfer (Maryland, New York, New Jersey, Massachusetts, and Connecticut). Other states have legislation which will allow development rights transfer for the general purpose of "conservation," and other states are considering legislation allowing its utilization.[28]

The major weaknesses of TDR as a means of limiting conversion of prime agricultural lands relate to legal problems, acquisition cost, financing, and loss of tax revenue. Although purchase of development rights for rural lands in remote areas results in a relative low cost means of preventing development, the rapid inflation in land values in the 1970s has forced these costs upward. In and near the urban areas, where there is the greatest impetus to preserve prime lands, the development pressure has forced the value of the lands to a point where obtaining large quantities of agricultural land development rights would be prohibitive. In the Suffolk County, New York experiment, 17,949 acres were offered for purchase of TDR at a price of $116.5 million. The bond issue to purchase these lands was only $21 million.[29] Even though land prices subsequently declined in the county, by mid-1979 the cost of development rights for 3,252 acres on 52 farms averaged over $3,000 per acre, for a total cost of $9,870,000.[30] The New Jersey experiment with TDR failed to result in the purchase of any development rights.

Another criticism of TDR has been associated with legal questions. These questions concern the legal power of a public agency to acquire less than fee-simple rights in land, and the technicalities associated with the specific types of development rights and their regulation. Another issue relating to the legal question is that of persistence of the loss of development rights for a specific parcel of property through time, and the administrative problems presented by split ownership. The question of whether or not the use of TDR purchase will be adequate to prevent the courts from ruling that the loss of development rights as a taking has yet to be resolved. Finally, since zoning must be equitably and uniformly applied, some have suggested that the restrictions associated with lands where development rights have been sold may constitute an uneven application of zoning regulations.[31]

One of the major drawbacks to the use of TDR or other types of preservation techniques which diminish development potential through actual sale of rights is that of tax loss. Public acquisition of a portion of the development rights associated with land will eliminate that value for tax purposes. Since local governments are highly reliant upon the property tax, they may be viewed as an intolerable cost. In part, it will be offset by the potential for greater taxes on those lands to which development rights are transfered should a market for such development rights be developed, but at the present it constitutes a legitimate concern. An alternative to state sale of development rights to concentrate development and increase the tax base in selected areas, would be for the state government to provide remuneration to local governments in those areas where development rights had been purchased. In summary, the problems of administering a broad based TDR program, particularly that associated with financing the cost of acquisition of the development rights, make its use as the primary tool for preserving prime agricultural land rather doubtful.

Land Banking

Land banking, unlike TDR, is the acquisition by a governing body or agency of title to property in fee-simple. This may be done through the power of eminent domain, or it may be a voluntary program under which the public has the first right of refusal when property becomes available for sale. Historically, this method has not been widely used to preserve agricultural land in the United States. Commonly, communities have purchased lands for urban facilities such as fire and police stations in advance of their need, but have not purchased large quantities to protect its agricultural potential. Some states, including Massachusetts, have legislation allowing towns to purchase lands for conservation purposes which are then leased back to farmers, but the primary purpose was not preservation of prime agricultural land.[32] Banking has also been used to assemble the land needed for a park, or for a new urban community. In theory, land banking offers several advantages: First, promotion and encouragement of orderly growth and development which is in harmony with the development plan for the community; second, minimizes the adverse effects of sprawl and unplanned growth; third, reduces the price of land by controlling the land market and eliminating speculation; and fourth, preserves the prime agricultural lands.

The weaknesses of land banking are similar to those of a TDR program. The cost of acquiring large quantities of land in advance of development would be staggering. Although nominally these costs could be recouped when the land was sold for development purposes, a large initial investment would have to be met. As with TDRs, public ownership of large areas of land would eliminate the property tax revenue they generate and affect the tax base of the local community. A third major issue is that of whether such a program would be compatible with the general American tradition of private land ownership and concomitant land speculation. A final weakness associated with land banking is that the general American concern for government control and corruption make it questionable whether a public agency could adequately administer such a large program and do so in an efficient manner. As a result of such real or perceived weaknesses, land banking has been relatively unimportant as a means of preserving prime agricultural land in the United States, although it has been used in Canada.

Preferential Assessment

The process of preferential assessment is one of taxing prime agricultural lands at a rate lower than their value for development. It is sometimes used synonymously with use-value assessment, which is a part of the broader preferential taxation program. Preferential taxation or assessment programs are designed to allow a farmer in an area facing urban growth to continue to cultivate his land even though it may have a high market value for development purposes. In 1957, Maryland enacted the first statute allowing for differential assessment with farmland receiving preferential treatment. Since that time, an additional 45 states have authorized some type of preferential assessment program for agricultural lands. As of 1979, only Kansas, Alabama, Mississippi, and Georgia had not passed such acts, and Kansas was in process of doing so. The justification for this preferential treatment is that in the absence of reduced taxes, it would be uneconomic for a farmer to continue farming activities in the urban fringe area. Secondly, since a farmer in the urban fringe is often surrounded by lands in process of being developed, and urban residents require more services, if he pays the higher or market value tax based assessments, he is effectively subsidizing his nonfarm neighbors because he does not demand the extent of services they do. As a secondary item, use of preferential taxation systems results in maintaining land in farming, thus preserving the prime agricultural land. In point of fact, most of the states that have adopted preferential assessment for farmland seem to have done so primarily to lower the tax structure of the farmers, with preservation of prime land as a secondary impact.[33]

Three general categories of preferential assessment have been recognized. The first type is defined as pure preferential assessment. In pure preferential assessment programs, all land is assessed at its market use value. Such systems require only that land be designated as agricultural land in terms of its present use in order to qualify for the lowered taxation. A total of 14 state programs provide pure preferential assessment.

A second type of preferential assessment is referred to as a deferred taxation program. Under such assessment programs, an individual can qualify for assessment on the basis of present land use, but when the land use is changed, there is some provision for recouping the taxes that were not paid under the preferential assessment. Typically, this program, known as a rollback tax, is for a specified period of years, ranging from as low as 2 to as high as 20 under certain conditions in Hawaii. This is the most commonly used form of preferential assessment, with 27 states having at least one program requiring deferred payments when the land use is changed to a more extensive use.

The final category of preferential assessment involves use of restrictive agreements to ensure compliance with the intent of the law. Although there are nine states with statutes requiring that farmers enter into a restrictive agreement preventing changing the land use for a specified number of years, in Hawaii, New York, Pennsylvania, and Washington the farmer can be released from that agreement simply by paying the rollback tax.

There are four major arguments used as criticisms of the preferential assessment program. The first and most critical is that the actual impact upon farmland use is negligible. The second points out that reduction of overall tax rates reduces the tax base and means that services must be cut or tax rates increased to have the necessary funding. Both of these arguments maintain that the majority of taxpayers suffer more from the effects of the reduced tax base than they benefit in the form of positive effects upon land use in preventing development. A third criticism is focused on the administrative problems associated with a preferential tax program as follows: (a) What is the basis for defining agricultural use? (b) What minimum standards need to be set in terms of acres in farm use, minimum income per acre, percent of income from farming, etc.? (c) Setting criteria which adequately determine use value. A fourth criticism of preferential assessment focuses on the undesirability of differential tax structures. This argument maintains that to tax some lands differently from others is inherently unfair, results in potential for exploitation by interest groups, and destroys confidence in the taxation program.[34]

The idea that the majority of the taxpayers receive insufficient benefit to justify preferential taxation for one sector is apparently not widely held by legislators, as indicated by the fact that nearly all of the states have adopted some form of preferential assessment for farmlands. The problems associated with making a fair assessment of the value of the property in its present use have received relatively little study. Two other criticisms have been the focus of varying attention by the different state legislatures; there are important, if subtle, differences between each state's individual assessment programs. In the area of administering the programs, the states differ widely. For example, the variation in what constitutes agricultural land is extreme. In some states, in order for farmland to qualify, it must not only meet minimum acreage requirements (typically at least 5) but also must have been owned by the same family for as long as 7 years (North Carolina, and Minnesota), and have been the property of a natural person (Texas). These and similar requirements regarding length of tenure are designed to exclude speculators from benefiting from preferential assessment programs. Requirements on proportion of income derived from the land, the amount of profit per acre, and similar restrictions are designed to ensure that only bona fide farmers utilize the advantages of the program, and differ markedly from state to state.

The variation in programs related to rollback taxes is equally as great. Typically, rollback requirements require the seller to pay the difference between the taxes that have been paid and what would have been due had the property been taxed at market value. The period for which rollback taxes is required varies from as little as 2 to as many as 10 years, and normally does not require any interest on the deferred taxes. States requiring interest penalities for the deferred taxes charge between 5 and 10%. In addition, in some states the longer the time period that land has been under the preferential assessment program, the less the rollback taxes are. During the first 2 or 3 years under this program, rollback taxes would be 100% of the difference between use-value assessment and market value assessment, and this would decrease until after a given number of years maintained in farming there would be no rollback taxes involved. Other states have some type of penalty if land is sold within a prescribed number of years. This is normally a specified percentage of either the sale price or market price at the time the land is converted. The great variety of administrative arrangements utilized in the various preferential assessment programs is indicative of the criticisms indicated above.

One of the more severe criticisms levelled against preferential assessment programs is that they have very little impact on preventing conversion of land to more intense uses, and their tendency to be used by developers as a convenient means of purchasing land in advance of use at lower prices and then holding it under the preferential assessment acts. The experience of California in this regard is illustrative of this problem.

California's program for preferential assessment is based on the California Land Conservation Act of 1965 (CLCA), also known as the Williamson Act. This program utilizes restrictive agreements to insure that participants maintain their land in agricultural uses. The minimum length of the restrictive agreement is 10 years, but it may be longer. In order to end the contract before the end of the minimum time length, both the state or other governing body and the landowner must agree, and the landowner must pay a penalty equal to 50% of the new assessed value of the property. In 1967–1968 fiscal year, only 200,000 acres in 6 of California's 58 counties participated in the CLCA. By 1975–1976, over 14 million acres, representing slightly more than 40% of California's land in farms, were participating in the program.[35] There is an estimated 12,621,700 acres of prime agricultural land in California, and only 30% of total land enrolled in the program is prime land. The prime land enrolled represents approximately one-third of the total prime land available in California. Analysis of the land being contracted into the assessment program reveals that the primary beneficiaries of the program are those lands farther from urban centers. Where agricultural land is located near expanding urban regions, farmers have been reluctant to enter into the restrictive agreements necessary to qualify for the California preferential assessment program. All evidence indicates that the decision to enter into the CLCA relates to the perception that there is no near-term potential for realizing large capital gains from conversion of the land to urban functions. Where there is such an opportunity, farmers tend to remain under the present existing taxation program in anticipation of converting their land.[36] Consequently, the California act has had little impact on preventing transfer of agricultural land to urban uses.

In other states where there is a deferred or rollback tax, farmers are willing to enter into the preferential assessment program with the realization that when land prices justify it they can sell their property and pay their rollback taxes. Analysis of the rollback penalty in Montana revealed that the economics involved are too small to prevent a farmer from shifting his land use from agriculture to urban. Land located within 5 miles of Billings, Montana with a market value of $2,000 per acre and an agricultural use value assessed at $75 per acre would need to pay only $111.36 per acre in rollback taxes if it were converted to nonagricultural uses. When it is recognized that developers typically anticipate receiving at least triple the value or cost which they paid upon completion of subdivision, the $111.36 per acre on the ultimate $6,000 sale price is inadequate to prevent transfer of land from agriculture.[37] Unless a state adopts restrictions on length of ownership of the property, or restricts the participation to natural persons, there is also a potential that speculators and large corporations will take advantage of preferential assessment and thus detract from the goals intended.

Wisconsin has adopted a program providing for direct state income tax credits rather than simply lowering property taxes. Under the Wisconsin State Farmland Preservation Act of 1977 as amended in 1978, farmers are able to receive a direct credit up to a maximum of $4,200 on their state income tax. Through September 30, 1982, all farmers who participate by contracting with the state, who meet the requirements of 35 or more acres of land with a minimum of $6,000 of income in the previous year, can qualify to receive the tax credit. Furthermore, farmers who terminate their contract or remove their land from an agricultural zone must repay their tax credits for the previous 20 years. The act is designed to benefit the middle- and low-income farmers since farmers earning $46,000 or more would be excluded from receiving tax credits. It also excludes speculators or others who have large nonfarm incomes.

The Wisconsin program is also unique in that it emphasizes planning as a feature of its tax credit system. After 1982, a farmer can continue in the tax credit program only if his county adopts a farmland preservation plan or exclusive agricultural zoning that includes his land. If the county does not do so, the farmers within its boundaries become ineligible for the tax credit. Urban counties are required to adopt exclusive agricultural zoning. These counties are defined as those having 75,000 people or lying adjacent to counties having over 400,000 population. Farmers in such exclusive agricultural zones are protected from state interests, including special tax assessments for sewer, water, or other urban public services.[38] Counties designated as urban can circumvent the requirement to zone their agricultural land for exclusive agricultural use only when the majority of the towns in those counties agree to veto the exclusive zoning. In such cases, the farmers in those counties lose all rights to participate in the tax credit program.

Although the Wisconsin program provides more direct incentive to a farmer to maintain his land in agricultural uses, and attempts to utilize both exclusive agricultural zoning and preferential taxation, it suffers from its emphasis on the low- and middle-income farmer. The owners of high-income farms have been stereotyped as being more likely to capitalize on the opportunity for speculative profits and thus are excluded from the credits. Since large farms must be preserved if agricultural land preservation is to be successful, the goals of the program may be negated. Nevertheless, the program seems to be quite successful as measured by numbers of farmers participating. In July of 1978, in the five counties that had certified zoning as of July 1977, 1,113 farmers had already received their 1977 tax credit. By October of 1978, a sixth county had received approval for its exclusive agricultural planning plan.[39]

Some observers have concluded that preferential assessment is not as effective as using exclusive agricultural zones to protect agricultural lands.[40] Studies of the effectiveness of preferential assessment in protecting prime agricultural land thus indicate that it is largely ineffective as a means of insuring long-term preservation. The primary results of preferential assessment programs are to delay the time at which land may be transformed and to provide the farmer with a lowered tax structure. Preferential taxation has primarily resulted in a loss of local government tax revenues with resultant increased taxes for other property owners. It is effective in preserving farmland only in those instances when a landowner is already committed to preserving his property in farming and the preferential assessment program allows him to indulge his preferences. When such individual commitment does not exist, the preferential taxation benefits speculators who utilize these programs as a form of tax shelter to allow them to withhold land from development until inflation allows them to reap even greater windfall profits.

It has been suggested that preferential assessment can be useful in preserving farmland if the following conditions are met:[41]

1. In order to prevent conversion to urban uses, there must be strict regulations preventing such conversions.

2. Instead of having preferential taxation apply to all farmlands, it should be directed at specific agricultural lands designated as worthy of preservation in the public interest. Thus, only the prime or unique farmlands would be eligible for differential assessment.
3. Some types of realistic capital gains taxes needs to be assessed when land conversion takes place to insure that the public has not simply been supporting a tax shelter. This is particularly important when development takes place as a result of public investment in roads, sewers, or other infrastructure.
4. Administration of the assessment program and control of conversion must occur at the state level. Too much opportunity exists for abusing the program when control is vested in the local level. Preferential assessment programs including these elements provide an alternative for protection of prime land if they are strictly enforced.

Restrictions on State Activities

The underlying assumption behind restricting state activities in agricultural areas is that much of the pressure for development in the urban-rural fringe comes as a result of public investment. State activities that result in expansion of the urban infrastructure produce greater potential for rural land conversion. Limiting state activity to only those types of programs which would foster agricultural pursuits would minimize the potential for such land use changes. By preventing investments in roads, sewage treatment plants, culinary water systems, fire or police stations, schools, and related activities, the farm sector would not receive the pressure for conversion. The weakness of such proposals is that the farmer is outvoted by suburbanities who demand greater services in the rural-urban fringe, and developers too often have actively and effectively lobbied for such improvements. Farmers in areas facing urban pressure rarely have the political power necessary to prevent government expenditures for urban infrastructure. Only when there is a clear and overriding concern for preserving agricultural lands can programs limiting state expenditures or other activity which hastens development be successful.

Federal Programs to Preserve Prime Agricultural Land

A number of federal programs affect agricultural land in the United States, but do not directly underwrite their preservation. The concern by the Department of Agriculture for agricultural land preservation is obvious. Other actions of the federal government having an effect upon land use in rural areas include the Clean Water Act as amended in 1977; this provides for expenditures that affect rural lands. Section 209 requires long-range regional resource management studies and planning for water and related lands for each river basin in the United States. Section 303 establishes a continuing planning process for each river basin. Section 208 requires that those areas which state governments designate as having significant water quality problems develop an area-wide water treatment management program. Amendments to these actions and actions of the EPA in 1975 affect rural areas against further degradation of their waters. Taken together, these mechanisms may assist in protecting environmental and prime agricultural areas from water pollution and, because of their requirements for water quality, may prevent development from occurring in rural areas having high water quality.

The Clean Air Act of 1970 and its subsequent amendments provide that areas having high quality air not be subjected to significant deterioration of the air quality, and that new industry or related activities meet the performance standards of the 1977 amendments to the act. Together, these can have an impact on prime agricultural lands by preventing industrialization from occurring in rural areas with high quality air standards.

Another indirect measure for preserving prime agricultural land from the federal level is the Tax Reform Act of 1976, included amendments to estate tax provisions. These provide that farm real estate inherited by a descendant of the owner may be valued for estate tax purposes on a use-value basis, and additionally, that there be a rollback assessment if this property is sold to nonfamily members or converted to nonfarm use within 15 years after the death of the original owner. This helps to reduce the pressure for lands to be converted to urban uses upon the death of the individual who had a strong commitment to farming. In addition, the amendments provided that the first $175,000 of an estate be exempt from estate taxes by 1981. This will allow smaller farms to be passed on free of estate tax liability. Taken together, the effect of the Tax Reform Act of 1976 may have a significant indirect effect on maintaining prime agricultural land.[42]

THE RURAL ETHIC IN RETROSPECT

The programs which have been suggested as methods of preserving prime agricultural lands do not seem to have been highly effective in so doing. The innovative programs involved with preferential assessment have resulted in only a portion of farmers enrolling their property for a number of reasons. Most important is the perception that they can gain more by leaving themselves the option of converting their land, or else there is no incentive since the agricultural land is already underassessed either as a result of preferential assessment laws or custom. As of 1975, in those states without preferential assessment, the overall assessment values for farmland was actually lower than in those with such legislation because of de facto underassessment of rural land.[43] Other programs have been equally ineffective in preventing the transformation of rural to urban-related uses. The reasons for these continued conversions go beyond that of mere land use regulations.

The continued increase in scale of farm operations means that the capital necessary to undertake agricultural activities as a career continued to increase. There is a steady decline in the number of people employed in agriculture resulting from this and the general decline in desirability of farming on the part of those who have historically been so involved. Regulations to preserve prime agricultural land which do not also make provisions for assembling the necessary capital to engage in profitable farming and provide other amenities to make farming an attractive alternative will probably have only minor impact on land conversions.

The concern for prime agricultural lands and the programs they have fostered largely ignore the areas where the pressure for conversion is greatest. Preferential assessment and other programs are effective in areas removed from urban pressure, but ineffective in the urban-rural fringe. It is in this area that the cost of preservation is highest and the alternative to farming most profitable.

The historic ethic of individualism and independence associated with American agriculture makes it difficult for a regulatory program to succeed. The use of prime agricultural land in the United States is closely tied to a number of other actions that historically have not been regulated. In the long run, the forces that may combine to preserve our agricultural land may be totally unrelated to land use regulatory measures. A declining population growth rate, coupled with increased energy costs affecting the desirability of suburban living, may result in an end to the pressure for conversion at the urban fringe. Additionally, the growing population in the world may result in food prices sufficiently high to allow farmers to successfully profit from their land without the need to convert them to urban uses. Government programs regarding subsidies and minimum price floors may also result in making farming more attractive and minimizing rural land conversions.

Preservation of prime agricultural land in order to insure maximum crop production is only one method of maintaining food supplies. Intensification of productivity on less land provides the same return. Japan, the Netherlands, and other countries have shown that it is not necessary to have such a large agricultural base per person. Thus the preservation of agricultural land may in fact be a contrived issue reflecting the traditional Jeffersonian ethic towards rural life in America.

If it is accepted that preservation of prime agricultural land is essential, a program involving all of the regulatory measures discussed is necessary. Until and unless a program is devised which is fair to both public and farmers, the process of conversion to urban uses will continue. It has been suggested that several changes in attitudes are necessary before a successful program to preserve America's farmland can be implemented. It is essential that taxpayers recognize the importance of preserving agricultural land and be willing to invest more tax monies in acquisition of development rights to insure continuance of farming. Farmers themselves will need to change their attitude and accept more governmental control over land use. Until farmers are willing to accept government regulations on land conversions, such conversion will persist in areas of rapid urbanization or suburbanization.

The whole issue of taking associated with regulation must be clarified to allow more strict agricultural zoning, land banking, and similar government intervention which may reduce the farmer's potential capital gains from his property. There is a need for more precise identification and delimitation of the lands which are necessary for the well-being of the nation in order that they may be adequately protected. Without such overall action, attempts to preserve farmland will remain piecemeal and ineffective. In addition, the concern for environment and environmental protection laws should be designed and administered to encourage farming.[44]

These changes are essential if America's prime agricultural lands are to be preserved. All of the programs discussed in this and other chapters suffer from the fact that they do not utilize the full complement of land use management tools available to preserve agricultural land. It is doubtful whether any state will adopt regulations that are truly effective in light of the general American tradition of speculative profits and individualism. Nevertheless the programs being adopted and the general trend towards recognition that there is a need to preserve prime agricultural land even when it means the loss of some individual freedoms are important beginnings. Programs such as Wisconsin's, which require a 20-year deferred taxation, Oregon's program to restrict urban growth and zone for exclusive agricultural activities, and the utilization of development rights transfer in New York are all indicative of the increasing trend towards regulation of agricultural lands. The value of these lands for not only agricultural but for open space and recreation and allied uses makes it essential that we take affirmative action to effectively control their use and conversion. Even though the loss of prime agricultural land will not result in a food crisis in the short term, the land resource base is finite and it is essential that we manage it wisely in order to maximize the benefit we receive from it and to ensure that future generations will be presented with the land necessary to provide them a meaningful range of alternative decisions.

NOTES

[1] *Farm Population of the United States: 1977*, U.S. Department of Commerce, Bureau of the Census, Nov. 1978, p. 1.

[2] R. Neil Sampson, "Development on Prime Farm Land," *Environmental Comment*, Jan. 1978, p. 5; "Preserving America's Farmland," *Current Focus*, 1978.

[3] William Toner, *Saving Farms and Farmland: A Community Guide* (Chicago: American Society of Planning Officials, 1978), p. 2.

[4] Peter W. Amato, "Wisconsin Hopes a New Law Will Preserve its Farms," *Planning*, Jan. 1979, p. 10.

[5] Peter Meyer, "Land Rush," *Harpers Magazine*, Jan. 1979, p. 53.

[6] Raymond I. Dideriksen and R. Neil Sampson, "Important Farmlands: The National View," *Journal of Soil and Water Conservation*, Sept.–Oct., 1976, p. 196.

[7] Ibid; Ingolf Vogeler, "The Necessity for Prime Farmland Preservation in Metropolitan Areas," *U.S. Today*, Sept. 1978, p. 51.

[8] Vogeler, ibid. "Abandoned" is a general term which actually refers to removal from crop use. The land is still owned, but is not cultivated.

[9] Meyer, op. cit., p. 54.

[10] Vogeler, op. cit., p. 52.

[11] Linda K. Lee, *A Perspective on Cropland Availability*, Agricultural Economic Report No. 406 (Washington, D.C.: U.S. Department of Agriculture, 1978), table 8, p. 14.

[12] Sampson, op. cit., p. 5.

[13] Vogeler, op. cit., pp. 52–53.

[14] "Preserving America's Farmland," op. cit., p. 2.

[15] Philip M. Raup, "What Is Prime Land?" *Journal of Soil and Water Conservation*, Sept.–Oct., 1976, pp. 180–181.

[16] Roberta M. Mundie, "Managing Conflicts in the Urban-Rural Fringe," *Environmental Comment*, Jan. 1978, pp. 6–7.

[17] See Richard D. Collins, "Agricultural Land Preservation in a Land Use Planning Perspective," *Journal of Soil and Water Conservation*, Sept.–Oct., 1976.

[18]John A. Knebel, Acting Secretary, U.S. Department of Agriculture, Secretary's Memorandum No. 1827, Supplement, "Statement On Prime Farmland, Range, and Forest Land," June 21, 1976.

[19]Charles E. Roe, "Innovative Techniques to Preserve Rural Land Resources," *Environmental Affairs*, Vol. 5, No. 3, 1976, pp. 422-423.

[20]William Toner, "Zoning Alone Won't Save Our Farmland," *Planning*, Jan. 1979, p. 13.

[21]William Toner, *Saving Farms and Farmland: A Community Guide* (Chicago: American Society of Planning Officials, 1978), pp. 15-17.

[22]"Farmland Owners Guide" (Riverhead, N.Y.: Cooperative Extension Association of Suffolk County), c. 1977.

[23]"Preserving America's Farmland," op. cit., p. 4.

[24]John C. Keene, "A Review of Governmental Policies and Techniques for Keeping Farmers Farming," *Natural Resources Journal*, Vol. 19, Jan. 1979, p. 132.

[25]"Preserving America's Farmland," op. cit., p. 5.

[26]See John C. Keene, op. cit., pp. 121-144; Charles E. Roe, op. cit., p. 420; *Land Use: Tough Choices in Today's World* (Ankeny, Iowa: Soil Conservation Society of America, 1977) Special Publication No. 22; David F. Newton and Molly Boast, "Preservation by Contract: Public Purchase of Development Rights in Farmland," *Columbia Journal of Environmental Law*, Vol. 4 (1978), pp. 189-220; David Berry and Thomas Plaut, "Retaining Agricultural Activities Under Urban Pressures: A Review of Land Use Conflicts and Policies," *Policy Sciences*, Vol. 9 (1978), pp. 153-178; and Werner Z. Hirsch, "The Efficiency of Restrictive Land Use Instruments," *Land Economics*, Vol. 53 (1977), pp. 145-156.

[27]Roe, op. cit., pp. 428-429.

[28]Keene, op. cit., p. 139.

[29]Ibid., p. 138.

[30]Personal communication William R. Lockwood, Deputy Commissioner, Department of Land Management, Suffolk County, New York, June 5, 1979.

[31]Roe, op. cit., p. 49.

[32]"Preserving America's Farmland," op. cit., p. 3.

[33]*Untaxing Open Space*, Council on Environmental Quality (Washington, D.C.: Government Printing Office, 1976), p. 22.

[34]International Association of Assessing Officers, "Use-Value Farmland Assessments," *Environmental Comment*, Vol. 21 (May, 1975), p. 4.

[35]Hoy F. Carman, "California Landowners' Adoption of a Use-Value Assessment Program," *Land Economics*, Vol. 53, No. 3 (1977), p. 275.

[36]Ibid., pp. 285-286.

[37]"Preservation of Agricultural Lands: Alternative Approaches," A Report to the 45th Montana Legislature, Dec., 1976, pp. 14-15.

[38]Peter W. Amato, op. cit., pp. 10-11.

[39]Ibid., p. 11.

[40]S. I. Schwartz, D. E. Hansen, and T. C. Forn, "Preferential Taxation and the Control of Urban Sprawl: An Analysis of the California Land Conservation Act," *Journal of Environmental Economics and Management*, Vol. 2 (Dec. 1975), pp. 120-134.

[41]Roe, op. cit., p. 425.

[42]Keene, op. cit., pp. 122-129.

[43]International Association of Assessing Officers, op. cit., p. 5.

[44]Keene, op. cit., pp. 143-144.

Chapter 9

Implementing the Control of Land Use

Introduction

The concern manifest for preserving prime agricultural land and the adoption of devices to insure its preservation is but one example of the increasing concern over land use issues. The attempts by cities to limit their growth, the increasing development of state and national actions and regulations which affect land use, and the problems associated with urban and rural communities resulting from changing population patterns and land use practices are all indicative of the central role land use plays in the life of American citizens. All suggest a need to regulate the land use resource, and the actions of state, federal, and local communities are designed to insure that land use actions of private and public alike contribute to the well-being of the American people. The problem which develops in attempting to regulate land use through existing programs, or in efforts to implement a new program or regulations, centers around the questions of:

1. What types of land use decisions need to be controlled?
2. For whom should land use regulations and plans be controlling the land?
3. For what time period should the land use plan and resultant regulations be formulated?
4. How should the control of land be implemented?

These questions are often only partially answerable. Where answers can be given, they are complex and difficult for the public and planner alike to fully comprehend. Moreover, many of the types of issues which these questions present are not

195

amenable to answers since they are value issues for which there may be several correct answers depending upon one's viewpoint. Nevertheless, communities and other entities involved in the planning process must make basic assumptions in order to insure that at least some minimal form of control over land use exists.

IMPLEMENTATION OF A PLANNING PROCEDURE

Formulation of Planning Policy

The first step in implementing a planning process to control the land use of a city, county, state, or the entire nation is the establishment of policies to guide the plans and controls that are developed. Historically in the United States, this step has been overlooked, and planning and the controls which implement that planning have too often been based on reaction to a perceived crisis or short-term problem. In essence, it has been a process of applying specific actions, such as zoning changes, without having a basic policy guideline upon which to base those regulatory actions.[1] The reason for a lack of general policy direction, of course, is that the formulation of policies is a time consuming and difficult task if properly done. It involves the reconciliation of varying groups within the area where land use control is being developed, as well as the assumption of fundamental principles to shape the community or region for a period of decades. The difficulty of providing policy statements acceptable to the entire community or region has meant that traditionally in the United States they have been bypassed completely. In the past decade there has been an increasing awareness of the need to formulate policies upon which plans and regulatory controls are based to insure that planning is more than simply the application of zoning or other regulatory mechanisms without a clear understanding of what the regulations and controls are hoping to accomplish in the long run.

In order to be successful, the policies which are adopted must have certain characteristics. They should be general in nature to insure that they will not quickly become outmoded by changing circumstances. That is, a goal might be to provide adequate low-income housing scattered throughout the community. The policies would not state the specific sites of these housing units, but simply provide a guide that would then be used by the planning commission, the community planners, and legislators as they make decisions concerning housing within the community.

The policies should reflect the desires of the citizens and their input. The need for simple, straightforward goals is also necessary in that they are understandable whereas specific details on requirements for setback, road foundation, and other features would neither interest nor be necessarily understandable by the lay public.

The policies need to be more than platitudes such as "to make the community a happy and prosperous place in which to live," although these can be a part of the policies. Normally, however, it is understood that the policies and resultant plan and regulatory devices are intended to make the community a good place in which to live. The policy statements need to include at least the broad outlines of the general policies to be undertaken to insure that this is the case. Examination of the policies of Boulder's comprehensive plan adopted in 1978 illustrates how the policy's statement provides the unifying framework for decisions affecting the control of the land resource. It provides goals relating to population growth, location of population, a policy regarding expansion of urban services, policies concerning the location of specific urban functions, and a policy concerned with obtaining open space and recreation lands. Without policy statements of this type, a statement of goals, objectives, and policies is meaningless.

At the very least, a statement of policies should include goals or policies concerning physical, economic, and population growth; provisions of housing, transportation, and other community services; policies concerning timing of development, capital expenditures, and legislation affecting these goals. It should be obvious that in developing such a framework of policies, there will be a series of simple overall goals supported by a number of somewhat more specific goals to insure that the broad goals are met. For example, Petaluma, California decided that a fundamental policy of their land use regulations would be to limit the rate of growth. This represents the first level of policies or goals, the general statement. This is then followed by a series of increasingly specific goals or objectives designed to bring about this overriding goal. In the case of Petaluma, a secondary policy would be to limit the number of housing permits to 500 per year. A third level of goals would be to distribute the housing permits on a regional basis within the community to insure uniform development. Policies or goals for other elements of land use in the community are similarly structured. It is essential that the general policy be formulated first, rather than the supporting policies. If this is not the case, the result is to effectively curtail certain alternative actions. When a community takes actions without the guidance of overall goals and policies, this is often the case. For example, a community may decide to limit multiple housing starts in the face of public opposition, without considering the ramification of such actions on providing adequate housing for all social economic groups. If there is a goal or policy to provide adequate housing for all, it tends to eliminate arbitrary actions which would effectively defeat such a policy. Only when a community has adequately developed policies or goals and objectives to guide its land use control actions will it be able to insure that it maximizes the potential for making the particular area planned for a desirable place in which to live.

THE COMPREHENSIVE PLAN

Once a community has determined its policies, goals, or objectives, these serve as the basis for development of a comprehensive plan of development. Before the comprehensive plan can be advanced, however, it is necessary to develop base studies upon which the comprehensive plan is based. These studies must include development of accurate base maps for the community, development of existing land use maps, the economic base of the community, the present and projected populaiton, community services, and the existing and needed transportation network. This element of the planning process is imperative since the plan is only as good as the information upon which it is based. These and other basic studies need to be carried out accurately and be mapped so that the patterns of deficiencies are readily visible. The basic studies serve as the standard against which the communities' problems, needs, and even crises can be examined.

The critical elements of the comprehensive plan are, first, that it is truly comprehensive. It must include the entire community rather than just portions of it. In addition, all of the functional parts of the community which affect its development should be included in the comprehensive plan. Secondly, the comprehensive plan is somewhat general in nature. It indicates the broad areas where activities will take place in order to facilitate reaching the goals, objectives, and policies upon which it is based, but it does not normally specify the location of individual activities to a specific site. Finally, a comprehensive plan is a long-range document.

The comprehensive plan is designed to provide guidance for a 10- to 30-year period, rather than concentrating on the immediate events and problems. The comprehensive plan is necessary for successful accomplishment of the community's goals, but it should not be viewed as a blueprint. The plan is designed to give guidance for day-to-day decisions which affect land use in the community, but itself is subject to change. In order for a comprehensive plan to be truly effective, it needs to be updated periodically to reflect the changing circumstances within the community or other planning regions. Normally, a plan update would take place at least once every 5 years, although there is wide variation in actual practice. The comprehensive plan indicates how development should occur, and the actual specific implementation policies should reflect the guidelines provided by the comprehensive plan. Only when the comprehensive plan is the basis for decisions made by the legislative bodies on a day-to-day and week-to-week basis is it effective in leading to the end results envisioned in the policy statements. Requests for zoning changes, subdivision approval, extension of water, sewage or other services, should all be made in light of the guidelines of the comprehensive plan. Although historically the comprehensive plan has been viewed as a nonbinding document in that it is only for guidance, recent court decisions (such as the case of Milwaukie, Oregon) indicates that the comprehensive plan is coming to be viewed by the courts as the legal basis for all subsequent actions of the legislative bodies of a community or region. Thus the importance of the comprehensive plan cannot be overstated.

THE TOOLS OF IMPLEMENTING GUIDELINES OF A COMPREHENSIVE PLAN

Once a comprehensive plan has been developed and approved by the local governing body, it becomes the basis for decisions affecting the physical, social, and economic development of the community. The tools for implementing the guidelines of the comprehensive plan are as follows:

1. zoning ordinances;

2. the public purse (including taxation policies);
3. subdivision regulation;
4. annexations;
5. provision of streets, water, and other urban services;
6. health codes, fire codes, and similar regulations;
7. building codes;
8. applicable state and national legislation or regulations.

Zoning Ordinances

Zoning ordinances have traditionally been the most widely used tool for implementing the policies, goals, and objectives of the comprehensive plan. Although there has been repeated criticism of zoning ordinances, they remain the dominant form of land use control in most urban areas of the United States, as well as rural areas where effective land use control exists. A zoning ordinance must be designed on the basis of the comprehensive plan if it is to be successful in insuring that the quality and character of life in a community is maintained. Zoning ordinances contain three basic elements. The first is a section relating to the purpose of the ordinance, its enactment into law, and definitions of terms. The second provision defines the specific districts or zones and the regulations affecting each, plus those which related to land in the city in general. The final part consists of the format or procedure by which the zoning ordinance is enforced, appeals are made, building permits are granted, etc.[2]

In drafting a zoning ordinance for a community or rural area without existing zoning, or in updating an existing ordinance, it is important to remember exactly what a zoning ordinance can and cannot do. If a zoning ordinance is not designed to insure the public health, safety, and welfare, it is impossible to justify. All acts of zoning should be based on the necessity to accomplish these goals for the good of the general public. In order for a zoning ordinance to withstand challenge in court, it must meet the following requirements:

1. It must be based on the state enabling act requirements and constitutional guarantees of the nation.
2. Zoning requirements must be uniform throughout a district and have a reasonable basis for being classified as different from surrounding areas.
3. The entire city or region must be zoned, not simply portions of the community. Regulations must be reasonable as pertains to an individual parcel or lot to insure that the owner has not suffered the taking of his property rights.

Zoning is basically oriented to bulk, area, and height requirements for individual areas. A typical zoning ordinance will set specific standards for activities allowable in each district in terms of these three variables. Thus, in a residential single-family zone, the area might have a minimum of 10,000 square feet for a lot to qualify for a building permit, the height of buildings be restricted to no more than 20 feet to the square, and implementation of side, front, and back setbacks would effectively limit the bulk of the structure. Zoning does not usually designate the manner of contruction of the buildings, as this and the building materials used are normally covered in the building code. Zoning ordinances do not normally set minimum costs of buildings nor the external appearance of buildings, as these are covered by restrictive contents. When an area is designed as a historic preservation district, however, the appearance and type of architecture are sometimes regulated by zoning ordinances. Increasingly, this issue of aesthetic appearance is becoming acceptable as a zoning regulation. Zoning does not control the specific design of streets, although it sets width standards. The actual construction of the streets and the installation of utilities are covered in the subdivision regulations.

Residential Uses

Typically, a zoning ordinance will designate the bulk of the land in the area to which it applies for residential uses. Within the residential districts designated by the zoning map, there may be differences reflecting varying intensities for different zones. Thus, a typical city would have R-1 zones for single-family residences on individual lots. These would set minimum standards for front, side, and rear setbacks, height, and size of lot. These then progress through R2, 3, 4, 5 and so forth in increasing intensity reflecting the character and need of the community as expressed in the comprehensive plan. The zones with higher densities may eliminate side setback, reduce the lot size, allow greater coverage of the lot by the structure, allow taller structures, allow multiple residences in the same building, or similar actions designed to increase the density.

Business Zones

The second general category of zone is related to business and retail activity. Again, there may be a variety of retail and wholesale trade zones, ranging from a small community or rural areas' single zone for general business, to large urban centers' specific designations for districts for neighborhood retail (small stores or shopping centers), financial districts, wholesale trade, etc. Restrictions within the business zones will vary depending upon the type of activity, and may include regulations on setback, amount of lot coverage, minimum lot size, height of structures, etc. The critical element in zoning for a business is to insure that both the private owner of a business and the community at large are served by such zoning regulations. As the fundamental purpose of zoning is to prevent land uses which are antagonistic to one another, business districts are normally separated from residential areas. An exception to this is the neighborhood retail district designed to cater to the increasing suburbanization of the nation. In designating the zones for location of businesses, the critical factors to consider are accessibility, demand, and existing patterns. Thus the existing business district would be zoned for business purposes, and if there is sufficient projected need for additional growth in the central business district, adjacent lands might be zoned to permit their conversion to business uses. In addition, where rapid suburban growth is taking place, key intersections of major transport links might be designated as business zones even though they are not presently so used. The important feature of zoning the business districts is to insure that it is harmonious with the policies of the comprehensive plan.

Regulation of land use in business zones is accomplished by one of three methods. In the conventional method, a list of permitted uses is established similar to that used for residential zones. An alternative to this is to indicate those types of activities which are not allowable in a business district, but this method has a weakness in that it is difficult to foresee all possible activities which would not be allowable. A third method of regulating businesses is to require a special permit for business use and use a process of negotiation to determine whether a specific activity would be allowable within the business district.

Industrial Zones

The third general category of land use is traditionally classified as industrial land use. Historically, the industrial zone has been viewed as the least restrictive area and originally was one in which any of the uses in the other zones was allowable. Most zoning ordinances today, however, are exclusive in nature and restrict the types of allowable activities in industrial areas to those which are industrial in nature. The key elements in determining industrial zones are: location with respect to residential areas to insure that they do not negatively affect them, location with respect to transportation for raw materials and finished goods, provision of adequate space for expansion, and potential for noisome fumes or other undesirable side effects of industry. Where the size of the industrial base of a city warrants, it may be necessary to designate several industrial districts, ranging from the so-called light industry with its general lack of undesirable fumes, noise, or similar negative externalities, to the so-called heavy industries which require large land area, and are sometimes associated with undesirable side effects. Some communities may need or feel the need to designate a number of industrial districts ranging from the small-scale assembly of electric components to that of a large steel mill or similar industry. Criteria for designating what activities are permissible in each industrial district should not necessarily be based only on type of manufacturing or product. The principle consideration should be the degree to which an industry fits with its neighbors.

Other Zones

In addition to the traditional three categories of zoning districts, many communities may adopt a number of specific districts for one purpose or another. Increasingly, historic preservation districts are being utilized to protect the architectural heritage of communities. Typically, these may occupy older sections of the city with a distinctive architecture or historic importance. Such historic districts are found in most major communities in the United States and have requirements regarding maintenance of existing historic structures, including regulations on additions or changes thereto, as well as requirements concerning new construction and/or activity permissible within the historic zone in order that the character of the historic zone may be preserved.

Another increasingly important zone is the critical environmental zone. These are areas designed as of importance to the community or region because of certain environmental characteristics. Such zones may encompass floodplain zoning, designed to minimize the impact of floods by restricting the activities on the floodplain to farming, recreation, or industrial activities which would suffer little damage as a result of flooding. Coastal zones represent another environmental setting which has been the focus of zoning restrictions, particularly in the last decade. Another environmental zone is often that associated with steep slopes. Such locations have unique requirements in terms of development, and designation of them as specific zones allows the application of regulations designed to insure that their development will not result in damage to either the community or to those who utilize the lands. A third category of environmental districts could include recreational zones. Often designation as a recreational zone is used in conjunction with protecting hillsides, floodplains, forests, or other environmental settings perceived to be desirable.

Some counties and even some cities are designating exclusive districts for agricultural purposes. As discussed in the previous chapter, these are designed to protect the agricultural resource and to prevent unnecessary sprawl of the urban area.

Other specific zoning districts are sometimes designated to meet peculiar local needs. In the western United States, mining and grazing zones are sometimes designated by counties to recognize that although the land is primarily suitable only for grazing, the existence of certain mineral deposits allows this activity to occur since it is localized in space.

In addition to these conventional types of districts, many communities resort to what is known floating zones, or similar devices such as contract zoning, which allow a community to encourage desired types of activities without zoning a large area for their exclusive use. This is not particularly new since for all intents and purposes many types of urban activities have always been assigned a location through the process of floating zones. For example, schools, hospitals, fire stations, churches, and similar types of activities have rarely been assigned a specific zone of their own. In essence, they have been subject to a type of floating zone in which they are located in a specific area if it can be shown that they serve a need and do not result in unnecessary congestion or other problems. Historically, airports have often been located through use of floating zones, but essentially all states now have legislation allowing communities to zone airports to control the height of structures and density of buildings located nearby.

THE POWER OF THE PURSE:
PUBLIC SPENDING AS A LAND USE REGULATION

The power of the public purse in regulating land use cannot be overstated. Investment in utilities, schools, roads, airports, public buildings, and related actions have a direct impact upon land use in a specific area.[3] Decisions concerning extension of main waste water trunk lines, culinary water lines, or similar urban services, directly affect the potential for development of a given site. Location of major highways and their intersections is often the signal for increased development of retail or industrial features. It is imperative, therefore, that the comprehensive plan address the issue of capital expenditures by the particular governing unit involved. Without guidance for location and distribution of capital expenditures, the public spending tends to come in reaction to growth rather than as a guide for growth. The comprehensive plan adopted in 1978 by Boulder, Colorado and Boulder County, Colorado is indicative of how public spending may be guided by the policies of the comprehensive plan. The 1978 plan was based on a 15-year projected planning period, and specifically stated that installation and extension of all utilities would be consistent with the provisions of the Boulder Valley Comprehensive Plan and with responsibilities of the respective utility providers.[4] The overriding goal and approach of the comprehensive plan are based on the following policy:[5]

> The areas immediately surrounding the city can most efficiently and effectively be provided facilities and services by the city. These areas are the most logical areas for urban development. The city intends to provide, on a phased basis over the planning period, the facilities and services to accommodate this urban development.

The comprehensive plan then proceeds to divide the Boulder City and Boulder Valley areas into three sections. The first section is that within Boulder City proper for which adequate municipal facilities are already in existence, the second is that area which it is anticipated will be served by extension of utilities and other urban services during the 15-year planning period, and the remainder of the Boulder Valley is designated as land for which no urban services will be provided. The importance of the capital expenditures affecting the development of Boulder Valley is recognized by the comprehensive plan authors. They note that traditionally land use regulations had permitted urban uses and development in areas without adequate urban facilities. The result was inefficient, wasteful, and contrary to the public interest, health, safety, and welfare. To counteract this, the comprehensive plan states that:[6]

> New urban development, including all development within the city and those developments regulated in the unincorporated areas of the valley would not occur until and unless adequate urban facilities and services are available to serve the development as set out in the policy section and service standards of the comprehensive plan.

Recognition that it is essential to coordinate the public purse with land use planning to insure regulation of land uses is evident in such landmark ordinances as Ramapo, New York and other communities, which, like Boulder, have adopted a policy of phasing the expansion of urban services. Without such coordination, the resultant land use lacks control, results in sprawl and needless loss of agricultural land, as well as escalating the cost to the community.

Subdivision Regulations

Another major tool controlling land use is that of subdivision control. Some have maintained that subdivision regulation is even more significant than zoning because the pattern of a subdivision, in essence, is the pattern of a community, and the pattern of the multiple subdivisions makes up the character of the entire city.[7] The purported advantage of subdivision regulations over zoning is that subdivision regulation relies on a process based on standards of prestated regulations rather than set zones. Thus, each application is considered separately but is tied to the established regulations, the public needs, capital improvements, and its impact on offsite facilities.

The use of subdivision regulations is an old one. Prior to 1926, the purpose of subdivision regulations was simply to provide an efficient method of buying and selling land through filing a subdivision plot which numbered the individual parcels. When sold, it was a simple matter to record the owner of each of these parcels of property. In 1928 the Standard City Planning Enabling Act (SCPEA) was published by the Department of Commerce of the United States. It suggested that subdivision regulation be more than simply a means of recording sales of land, but include regulations to implement comprehensive community planning. The SCPEA placed emphasis on requiring internal improvements for the subdivision including provisions connected with

> the arrangement of streets in relation to other existing or planned streets and to the master plan, for adequate and convenient open spaces of traffice, utilities, access of fire fighting apparatus, recreation, light, and air, and for the avoidance of congestion of population, including minimum width and area of lots.[8]

During the period of 1928 to World War II, states adopted legislation allowing communities the power to engage in subdivision regulation setting standards for internal design and improvements of proposed subdivisions. After World War II, the increased growth of suburbia related to the increased role of the automobile led communities to recognition of the impact of such suburbanization on the demands for community facilities. In this period, subdivision regulations began to include provisions requiring mandatory dedication of roads, parks, school sites, open space, and similar municipal activities. When there was a need for a recreational or other urban facility beyond the confines of the actual subdivision, but which would develop as a result of several subdivisions, fees in lieu of land dedication began to be required.

In response to increasing suburbanization, urban sprawl, and leapfrogging associated with this process, communities are adopting ever-increasingly restrictive subdivision regulations. It has been suggested that the experiences of communities with phased growth, sequential installation of capital facilities, and other efforts to slow growth represent a fourth phase in subdivision regulations beginning in the 1970s.[9] The basic thrust of these new subdivision regulations is to carry those regulations beyond the internal characteristic of a specific subdivision and to consider their impact on external features of the area in which they are to be built. Thus, subdivision regulations now include restrictions on building when a subdivision would create offsite flooding, drainage problems, environmental degradation, or create an increased problem as a result of inadequate municipal facilities. The emphasis of this present revision of subdivision regulations is on expanding concern for the internal organization of the subdivision to a consideration of the relationship of the subdivision to the communities' comprehensive plan and the total environment affected by the subdivision.

The actual items controlled by the subdivision regulations are relatively standard. They are based on the rights of a community to utilize its police power to protect and provide for the public health, safety, and general welfare of the municipality. Subdivision regulations insure that the properties being developed will be protected from fire, flood, or other dangers, and minimize overcrowding and congestion. As indicated, they are increasingly used to guide the future growth and development of the community in accordance with the comprehensive plan to insure that adequate light, air, and privacy are provided to all lots in a subdivision.

A subdivision regulation ordinance normally provides a set of policies, purposes, extent of coverage statement, and similar items designed to insure that the land developer and reviewing agency carefully consider the impact of a proposed subdivision on the community. Normally, the subdivision regulation includes as its second section a statement outlining the application procedure and approval process. This involves information concerning dates for filing subdivision plats, material which needs to be presented with an application, and the process by which a preliminary subdivision proposal receives public hearing and proceeds to final approavl by the local planning commission. This section of a subdivision regulation includes requirements for plat maps, fees, bonds, required public improvements, and supporting statements from the health department, fire department, or other community agencies to insure that the subdivision meets all standards and does not result in an adverse impact on surrounding land areas. In some states it is also necessary that proposals for subdivisions be reviewed by regional or state agencies to insure that they do not have an adverse impact beyond the boundaries of the community. Notable among these are the California Coastal Management Act and the Florida Critical Environmental Areas Requirements (discussed in previous chapters).

Either in the second section on the application process or as a separate section, subdivision regulations normally set requirements for insuring that improvements are satisfactorily carried out and maintained. These normally take the form of performance bonds or escrow deposits to insure that the improvements will, in fact, be made before the property is turned over to the city for maintenance.

A major section of all subdivision regulations is that relating to the requirements for improvements, reservation of land, and design characteristics.[10] The section on requirements normally specifies details of lot size and arrangements, access to lots, grading of lots, fencing, and similar relations to the lots themselves. A second major category of requirements relates to roads within the subdivision. The standards for frontage of a subdivision on existing roads, the design plan required for grading and construction of roads, the necessity of integrating the road system of the subdivision with those of the community's general plan, and similar features are all included. Normally, subdivision regulations also include requirements for block size, width, and shape to insure that adequate access is provided for both residents and service personnel, and emergy units such as fire, police, or ambulance. Requirements are also provided for drainage and storm sewers to insure that a subdivision does not develop on-site problems of flooding or waterlogging, as well as to protect surrounding areas and the community in general from runoff associated with the subdivision. Requirements for culinary water supply and sewage are included in all subdivision regulations. These set standards for trunk lines, individual hookups, and allied aspects of the water and sewage system. Such requirements may include location of sewer manholes, cleanouts, water supply interconnections, and similar features.

Another general area of subdivision regulations is that of sidewalks. Subdivision regulations normally provide guidelines for width, location, thickness, and setback of sidewalks. Utility locations are also regulated by subdivision regulations. These may include, but are not restricted to, requirements concerning easements for both above and below ground utility corridors, and standards applicable to the specific utility. Most subdivision regulations also require specific standards for parks, playgrounds, and recreation areas. These include specific standards for individual subdivision provision of recreation or park space, or provide for fees to be paid in lieu of dedication of land.

The requirements section of a subdivision is the heart of the ordinance, and is designed to insure that all subdivisions promote the health, welfare, and safety of the occupants of the subdivision. In addition, regulations are designed to insure that the developer of the subdivision does not impose unnecessary costs upon the balance of the community in the form of requiring the community at large to provide utilities, streets, or other urban functions.

The final two sections which have been suggested as being necessary for a good subdivision regulation ordinance deal with specifications of the documents which need to be submitted by a subdivision developer, and the definitions of specific terms used in the ordinance. The specifications normally require submission of sketch plats, and preliminary and final plats showing the lot divisions, names of streets, etc. The definition section includes definitions of such things as block, lot, easement, and other terms to insure that there is no misunderstanding of the context in which they are used.

In its entirety, the subdivision plan is to the zoning ordinance what the zoning ordinance is to the comprehensive plan. The subdivision regulations allow the implementation of the characteristics specified for the individual zones, since they are designed to deal with smaller parcels.

ANNEXATION

The annexation policies of a community are of critical importance to adequately controlling land use. The annexation of property into the city imposes upon the city a burden of providing services to that land, and presupposes that it will be allowed development. Thus the degree to which a community plans for annexation reflects the degree to which development corresponds to its comprehensive plan. Historically, many communities have had legislation allowing annexation whenever a property owner requests annexation to the city. This has often resulted in a patchwork arrangement whereby the city limits may not be continuous, and in enclaves of city property within the county jurisdiction or vice versa. Where annexation is not based upon a sound policy, it may result in strip annexation as a city annexes territory into the county along roads and deprives the county of business or industrial concerns which would yield a higher tax rate. At the present time, communities and other government bodies are increasingly placing restrictions on property annexation. For example, the Boulder County Plan provides that annexation of county land to Boulder City will take place in increments over the 15-year planning cycle. Areas immediately adjacent to the city are designated as lands in which annexation will occur during the 15-year cycle on a systematic and sequential basis. Lands beyond this zone are not planned for annexation and hence will not be developed.

STATE AND NATIONAL REGULATIONS AFFECTING CONTROL OF LAND USE

The effect of federal and state regulations on land use varies dramatically from state to state (as discussed in Chapters 3 and 4). In some states (e.g., California, Hawaii, Florida, Vermont, and Oregon) there may be a fairly direct state control over land use in the form of either state zoning (Hawaii), specific zones (California, Florida), or a state review process. In similar fashion, there may exist indirect controls in the form of state requirements to qualify for funding for capital improvements, planning assistance, and similar activities. Also there may be direct regulation in the form of control of environmental degradation which can have a significant impact on land use.

At the federal level, regulations are normally more indirect, although those associated with the Environmental Protection Agency and its air and water quality standards may have a direct bearing upon land use in an individual community or rural area. In addition, the requirements of the federal government for participation in revenue sharing, urban renewal, housing assistance programs, and a host of other federally funded programs directly impact upon the land use of a particular community.

BUILDING CODES, HEALTH CODES, AND FIRE CONTROL

Several types of regulations exist that do not as directly affect land use as those discussed to this point, but they do have a role in the physical developments on land. Zoning and subdivision ordinances, public expenditures, taxation, and public facilities—all determine the specific use of a parcel of land, but code regulations play an important role in the actual organization of the space of the

~y and in the shape and function of the structures which are built. The building ~ode sets requirements for types of building material, plumbing and electrial standards, external appearance, and other features directly affecting the character of place associated with a community. In the same fashion, health and fire codes may directly affect not only the physical structures on a parcel of land, but may directly affect the use of parcels by their requirements. The building code may effectively prevent a parcel of land from being developed because of its requirements for construction. This is particularly true on environmentally sensitive lands where foundations, drains, etc. are difficult, if not impossible, to adequately provide.

Fire and health codes affect the use of a parcel of land by restricting such things as storm drainage, water supply, access for fire vehicles, and other features designed to promote the general health, welfare, and public safety of the general public. Thus a parcel of land might be disallowed for subdivision purposes in an area zoned for residential use because of excessive runoff or inaccessibility. These regulations are normally not as controversial as zoning or subdivision regulations because they tend to be highly technical in nature, and are normally accepted by the lay public as essential for their well-being.

Taken together, the land use controls discussed enable a community or rural governing body to impose a significant amount of control over the land use within their jurisdiction. Moreover, the tendency, as discussed earlier in this volume, is for increasing the extent to which such control is applied to land use in the United States. In the past 30 years, even most rural areas have changed from no regulations whatsoever to rather strict regulation of land use. Moreover, enforcement of the ordinances associated with land use is becoming increasingly strict. The experience of most areas is not innovative or pioneering, but represents the general trend of land use control in the United States. A few areas (such as California, Hawaii, Vermont, Ramapo, Petaluma, etc.) have adopted stringent controls and innovative programs in response to perceived land use pressures, but for the majority of the nation the transition to the more intensive public control of private land will follow a slower developmental process. Only in those areas where a sudden development or the cumulative effect of the slower development results in the recognition of the necessity of implementing an abrupt change will the adoption of the full range of land use controls take place. For the majority of the United States, the size of planning staffs, and the necessity to balance the optimal land use constraints against politically expedient actions, will mean that existing ordinances will only be modified slowly over time. Each succeeding revision will no doubt include more stringent controls, but rarely will they involve the quantum change associated with Boulder, Ramapo, or Mount Laurel. Nevertheless, the general tendency to move to increasing public control of private land will probably continue, although the early blush of enthusiasm associated with the concept of the quiet revolution has somewhat faded as a result of stagnating economic conditions and growing distrust of government regulations. The process by which land use controls are implemented in a community or region, although broadly similar from place to place, still reflects the character, goals, and politics of the residents of the individual place.

NOTES

[1] William I. Goodman and Eric C. Freund, *Principle and Practices of Urban Planning* (Washington, D.C.: International City Manager's Association, 1968), p. 330.

[2] A number of excellent works on zoning ordinances exist. See, for example, Arthur A. Goldberg, *Zoning and Land Use* (New York: Practicing Law Institute, 1972); Patrick J. Rohan, *Zoning and Land Use Controls* (New York: M. Bender, 1978); Norman Williams, *The Structure of Urban Zoning and its Dynamics in Urban Planning and Development* (New York: Buttenheim Publishing Corp., 1966); Robert Henry Neal, *Zoning and Property Rights: An Analysis of the American System of Land-Use Regulation* (Cambridge, Mass.: MIT Press, 1977).

[3] For more information on the role of the public spending, see Marion Clawson, *Suburban Land Conversion in the United States: An Economic and Governmental Process* (Baltimore: John Hopkins Press, 1971, for Resources for the Future).

[4] *The Boulder Valley Comprehensive Plan, June 1978* (City of Boulder and Boulder County, Colorado, 1978), p. 11.

[5] Ibid., p. 12.

[6] Ibid., p. 13.

[7] Robert H. Freilich and Peter S. Levi, *Motel Subdivision Regulation* (Chicago: American Society of Planning official, 1975), p. 13. This volume provides a complete guide for development of subdivision regulations and should be carefully read by all who are seriously interested in the planning process.

[8] Ibid., p. 2.

[9] Ibid., pp. 4–5.

[10] See Freilich and Levi, op. cit., pp. 77–129; and *A Model Land Development Code* (Washington, D.C.: American Law Institute, 1970), pp. 27–108. Although the suggestions in *A Model Land Development Code* do not conform to the specific legislation of any individual state, it provides important guidelines that usually can be implemented in developing a community's subdivision regulations.

Chapter 10

Land Use in Tomorrow's America: Today's Dilemma

In spite of opposition from some elements, public regulation of private property continues to increase. The extent of regulation of land use has implications beyond its immediate effect in the form of regulations. Decisions made today will either insure future generations a choice of how they use the land or effectively limit their actions. Because many land use activities result in irreversible changes, it is essential that the needs of future generations be considered, in any case. Although not necessarily articulated, the underlying assumption of most land use regulation at least pays lip service to this concept. Even exclusionary zoning practices restricting land use to single-family dwellings on large lots is based on the idea that it will contribute to making the community a pleasant place for present and future residents. Slow- or no-growth regulations also are defended on the grounds that they insure space will be maintained in a community for future residents. Protection of prime agricultural land, scenic and environmentally sensitive locations, and similar ordinances are partially justified on the grounds that they prevent destruction of selected areas and thus insure future generations' options in land use. The dilemma in such regulations lies in balancing present versus future needs. Exclusionary zoning may, in fact, preserve land for future use, but it does so through ignoring the needs of a segment of the existing population. Preservation of prime lands on the margins of expanding communities protects these lands for future use, but it is argued that it inflates land costs and pushes housing costs up. A secondary issue concerns the level of planning and regulation necessary to insure future alternate uses of land. Local communities tend to regulate land to insure their own interest, often at the expense of others. Few states have been e to adopt effective regulations to overcome this parochialism and to insure equate future planning on a regional or state level. Concern for this problem has generated support for a national land use program to insure that land use regulations meet minimum standards for present and future land use.

THE ROLE OF THE FEDERAL GOVERNMENT

The forces that have affected land use in the United States are the same that have given rise to the idea there is a need for control beyond the local level. All the factors which have been discussed in preceding chapters contribute to the concept of a federal regulatory agency to insure adequate protection of land and have their origin in the fundamental land use controls now in existence. The use of zoning, subdivision regulations, property tax, public expenditures, and the official map by communities represent the primary basis of land use regulation. The impact of these regulations is apparent, but they are fragmented among a bewildering array of independent or quasi-independent government and private actors. All actions of local planning agencies, local planning commissions, boards of appeal, public utilities, and private developers affect the land use, and normally do so in an unplanned and fragmented manner. The net result of the increasing urbanization of America's population and the associated expansion of suburban areas has been to increase both the number and variety of government agencies or institutions involved in attempting to regulate land, while at the same time proliferating the number, scale, and impact of private actions. As a consequence, decisions affecting land use are being made in an inefficient, crisis-related, and potentially corrupt fashion. Too often, decisions which affect relatively large sectors of the public are made on the grounds of expediency, tradition, short-term economic considerations, or other factors that may not result in land use which contributes to the well-being of the broader public.[1]

Specific criticism of the present system of land use has been made by numerous authors and includes a number of important points. First, the nature of land use problems and resultant management and decisions effecting land use increasingly affect more than the local area. Problems of pollution, traffic, energy demand, inadequate housing, and similar factors associated with land use are of regional, state, or national impact, while the regulation of the lands remains at the local level. Not only does this result in decisions which are fragmenting any comprehensive policy for land use management, but the nature of local government makes it difficult for them to effectively deal with problems of more than local impact.

A secondary criticism of existing land use regulatory devices is their complexity, overlapping, duplication, and general difficulty of comprehension because of the multiple agencies involved in administering them. In addition, several authors maintain that the local government units are the weakest points in the American democratic system and consequently the land use decisions which are made are either based on inadequate information or reflect a reaction to an immediate crisis without consideration for the long-term and offsite impact. As has bee. indicated in previous chapters, many of the people involved in the local governing process affecting land use decisions have at least conflicts of interest, and may in fact be engaged in corruption of varying levels of intensity. Many land use decisions reflect either the repayment of political debts, old friendships, or the actual acceptance of bribes or other cash remunerations. Although the United States is a democracy, the people who are actually involved in the land use decision-making process are not representative of the entire public. Those who have the greatest vested interest are the ones who normally are most actively engaged in the political process by which they may derive benefit. Thus, community planning commissions, boards of adjustment, and city councils are often dominated by developers, construction company representatives, lawyers, or others who may stand to directly benefit from land use decisions. In instances where local sentiments foster widespread support for planning and concern for land use decisions, special interest groups may come to dominate the planning process, again with unrepresentative results. The impact of the present system with its heavy reliance upon zoning ordinances and subdivision regulations is to create uniformity and to minimize the opportunity for creative or alternate land uses. In addition, the cost associated with the present permit and regulatory system contributes to the cost of development of all types.[2]

The widespread recognition of the problems associated with conventional land use management in the United States prompted emergence of interest in some type of national regulation of land use in the late 1960s and early 1970s. Interest in such regulation was reinforced by the general concern that outside of urban areas many of the nation's counties had little or no regulation whatsoever. In 1975, in North Carolina, for example, only 208 of the state's 430 municipalities had zoning ordinances, and only 140 regulated subdivisions. Of the 100 counties in North Carolina, only 6 had county-wide zoning ordinances, and only 23 had subdivision ordinances in 1975. Even in the Catskill Mountain area of New York, which was facing a boom in second home development in the mid-1970s, only 40% of the 161 communities in the 6-county region used either zoning or subdivision regulations.[3]

The forces concerned with regulating land use resulted in a number of proposals for federal land use acts in the early part of the 1970s. These consisted of proposals by various members of Congress and one proposal by the administration. The Land Use Policy and Planning Assistance Act of 1971 was passed by the Senate but failed to pass the House of Representatives in 1972. This would have created a program establishing policy guidelines for land use in the United States and authorized granting federal funds to states as an incentive to wise planning. Those states which either directly or indirectly asserted control over areas of critical environmental concern, areas impacted by key facilities such as large-scale project causing urban growth of greater than local scale, and all large-scale development, would have been eligible to receive funding from the federal government. Those states which had in existence or developed a land use program meeting the federal guidelines would be entitled to financial support under the new federal program.[4]

Although the act of 1971 was not implemented, federal land use acts were considered through 1975. The Senate Interior and Insular Affairs Committee three times reported legislation to establish a national land use act, and the Senate twice passed legislation providing states and localities with federal assistance for land resources planning and management.[5] The basic questions involved in development of a federal land use planning act focused on the underlying philosophy of the act as to whether it should be primarily a mechanism to encourage states to plan through an incentive program, or a regulatory act setting standards which states must meet, as the National Environmental Policy Act had done for air and water quality. The difficulty of implementing a federal act was compounded by the long-standing tradition for local regulation of land use decisions. Opposition to a federal regulation came from a variety of sources, representing powerful lobbying groups. The United States Chamber of Commerce opposed it on the grounds that it would affect the economic well-being of communities; the National Association of Home Builders opposed such regulations for obvious reasons; the construction trade unions, the American Farm Bureau Federation, the National Cattlemen's Association, the American Conservative Union, and the Liberty Lobby are representative of the groups who opposed implementation of a federal land use act that would have significant regulatory impact on land use decisions.

As a consequence of the opposition and actions of powerful lobbies representing vested interests and the development of issues of greater concern to the public, the potential for a national land use act seems remote. The emergence of rampant inflation and the energy crisis with its associated decline in the rate of increase in disposable income have led Americans to have less concern for issues such as land use and more concern for issues related to their direct economic situation. In addition, the mounting resentment against government in general and specific agencies such as the Environmental Protection Agency has resulted in a weakening of support for government programs which might conceivably lead to additional national regulatory agencies. The increased cost associated with taxes in an inflationary period and the resultant diminishment of purchasing power have also prompted a widespread backlash against any type of additional government spending. The enactment of the so-called Proposition Thirteen in California in 1978, which limited taxation, was a herald of changing public attitude. For the foreseeable future, a federal land use program is a dead issue. At least for the present, the federal role will continue to be restricted to indirect impact on land use through incentives provided for planning under the 701 program, the A-95 program, the 208 water quality programs, and similar types of activities. In addition, regulations associated with the NEPA result in de facto regulation of land use of certain types. The host of federal actions discussed in previous chapters illustrate that even though a national land use act has not been enacted, the role of the federal government in affecting land use decisions cannot be discounted.

Nevertheless, even in the setting of today's political climate, the problems which initially fostered interest in federal land use policies in the beginning of this decade remain. The frantic development of land in suburbia, the second home phenomenon eliminating public access to many unique and highly valued environments (such as beaches, mountains, etc.), and the continued fragmentation of land use decisions remain. There are approximately 3,000 county governments in the United States, 18,000 municipal governments, and 17,000 township governments, each of which has the power to regulate land use. At least 14,000 of them are actually engaged in land use regulation and control.[6] Since this condition continues to exist, what should be the role of the federal government in light of the preceding statements concerning the lack of potential for passage of a federal land use act? The American Planning Association has adopted a set of policies which indicate the types of actions they believe the federal government should regulate.[7] Their policy statements basically propose that the federal government be involved in a supportive role of local planning activities, and become directly involved only when the impacts of land use decisions exceed the limits of the state jurisdiction. Specifically, federal planning assistance should be provided to allow state and local governments to experiment with innovative approaches to land use problem solving, to provide training and development capabilities for state and local entities involved in managing the land resource, and to provide funds to allow state and local governing bodies access to technical expertise they might not have. In addition, the federal government should attempt to eliminate time-consuming impediments to effective planning through coordinating federal actions with state and local land use decision-making programs. In all probability, any increased role in land use divisions on the part of the federal government will be along these lines.

CHANGING DISTRIBUTION OF POPULATION AND LAND USE DECISIONS

One of the major trends which will affect land use in the future in the United States is the changing distribution of population. Loss of population in the central cities of course affects land use within the city as well as the suburbs. Continuance of the trend of the 70s for population to move to the suburbs to enjoy the "good life" will necessitate continued conversion of prime agricultural land to suburban sprawl. In addition, the general trend for population to move from the older industrialized regions of the north central and northeastern states to the south, western, and southwestern states has significant import for land use decisions. It is unfortunately a truism that most land use planning peaks after the peak period of growth. With few exceptions, communities do not grapple with the fundamental issues affecting land use decisions until the problems become so pronounced that they are difficult, if not impossible, to resolve. This is multiplied when growth occurs in areas that traditionally have been either anti-planning or lack adequate regulation, as is the case with much of the area to which growth is moving. Even when land use regulations exist in southern and western states, they may be poorly designed and enforced.

In addition, many of the communities in the rural west and south where growth is occurring lack adequate professional assistance. In 1968, the National Commission on Urban Problems reported less than one-fourth of all jurisdictions attempting to regulate land use and building practices had any full-time employees so engaged, and in only one in nine of them was such regulation directed by a full-time employee paid as much as $9,000 a year. A 1973 survey indicated that the national median for city and county planning agencies in communities with populations under 50,000 was only two authorized professional planning positions.[8]

The significance of these problems in areas of population growth is that without a significant and dramatic change, the growing areas of the United States seem doomed to repeat the same problems that have been experienced in the more urbanized regions of the United States. The recognition of problems associated with the rapid growth will almost invariably lead to some communities adopting exclusionary zoning restrictions while the older portions of such regions become the repository for the poor or others unable to afford to live in such exclusive locations. Although the efforts of Colorado and Oregon are designed to minimize some of the land use related problems associated with these high growth areas, the balance of the south and west remains unconvinced of the need to take such dramatic action. The experience of Utah in attempting to implement a state land use act is indicative of the types of problems which effectively prevent these rapid growth regions from rationally dealing with the land use related problems they are now facing or will face. The state legislature passed a state land use act in 1974 designed to mandate comprehensive planning for all 29 counties within the state, in response to the rapid growth associated with the populated Wasatch front centered on Salt Lake City. Support for this legislation was high in the rapidly urbanizing regions of the state, but there was considerable opposition to any type of state involvement in rural areas of the state. Ultra-conservative groups organized and placed the issue on the ballot through the initiative referendum process in 1976. Using emotional arguments which maintained that the land use bill would preempt property rights and contribute to the general loss of freedom associated with purported government control, these groups were successful in defeating the land use act in 1976. Since that time, in Utah, planning has been at the county and community level, with the result that many areas have no planning or regulation of land beyond minimum health standards. The implication of the experience in Utah for developing regions within the United States is that many of these areas are also characterized by rural populations who have traditionally espoused conservative political views. In such settings, it is difficult to gain acceptance of the necessity for land use regulation which exists beyond the local level. Moreover, in such communities the power of vested interest groups, particularly business and development interests, make it unlikely that the areas now experiencing population growth will be able to adequately control land use to minimize negative impacts.

ENERGY AND FUTURE LAND USE

One of the issues of the late 1970s and 1980s is that of energy demand versus supply. The American predilection for automobile travel, central heating and air conditioning, and numerous appliances results in a dramatic energy consumption factor. On a per capita basis, energy consumption in America is the highest in the world, being twice as high as that in Great Britain, two and one-half that in Germany, and four and one-half that of Japan.[9] American consumption of petroleum products has risen consistently during the post world war period, but prices and supplies in the late 1970s have become respectively higher and lower. The consequence for land use is difficult to forecast. One observer has maintained that it is impossible to project what the future impact of energy availability will be since there is the potential for rapid and wide fluctuations in availability and cost.[10] Nevertheless, certain hypotheses concerning the impact of changing energy availability on land use can be made. If gasoline supplies continue to be less than they have been in the past, use of the automobile for mass transit is threatened. Since the automobile has made America the suburban model of the world, this may serve as a mechanism to slow the flight of people to the suburbs. The new suburban areas surrounding our older metropolitan regions are characterized by a lack of mass transit alternatives, and increasing energy costs and shortages may well encourage people to move back to the central city or to refrain from fleeing. The impact of such a change on land use would be dramatic. The energy crisis may, in fact, end suburban sprawl more effectively than all of the land use regulatory mechanisms that have been tried.

Another potential outcome of limited energy supplies is in the housing market. With increasing energy cost, it is foreseeable that homes will return to the smaller size common before the last few decades. Present costs for heating a home in New England during the winter season are already alarmingly high and may well encourage new home construction focusing on smaller but more heat-efficient structures.

In a similar vein, the rush to develop alternative energy sources conceivably will have a broad-based impact on land use and land use regulation over time. The possibility for using solar energy is one example of such a potential impact on land use. If it becomes economically and technically feasible to heat a home primarily by solar energy, land use regulations to insure access to the sun's rays will become increasingly important. It is doubtful that solar or other alternate energy forms will make a noticeable impact in the short term, since the typical lifetime of a home is 50 years, and only some 1½ to 2% of the housing stock is replaced each year. The existing housing stock will continue to predominate for the next 20 to 40 years, but in anticipation of such changes many communities in the United States are adopting solar ordinances which affect land use by preventing construction of structures that would deprive neighboring property of their access to solar energy.

The changing energy situation may also affect land use in the future in the area of second home or recreational developments. Problems with such developments in Florida, Texas, Arizona, California, Oregon, and Colorado and Vermont have been the focus of attention in the past decade. With increasing prices for gasoline and shortages of same, people may well be forced to stay closer to home. This would cut the demand for recreational developments and conceivably result in a significant decline in the number of such developments in rural and environmentally unique areas. Additionally, the same forces can result in greater demand for park, recreation, and other open space facilities within the urban regions themselves.

PROTECTING THE PUBLIC INTEREST

Public action in the form of zoning regulations, community infrastructure, and location of community office buildings, as well as in the form of tax structure has a significant impact on the value of land. It has been suggested that the increase of value resulting from actions taken by the government or the community in general represents an unearned increment in value (windfall) that should be subject to some mechanism to return at least a portion of the resultant unearned increment to the public. In similar fashion, actions of the same type may result in a diminution in land values (wipeout) and it has also been suggested that there be a program to reimburse people whose property suffers such losses. One of the issues that needs to be resolved is the extent to which windfalls should be taxed and wipeouts reimbursed. The mechanism for accomplishing this could conceivably receive a great deal of planning attention in the coming decade. It has been suggested that in order to adequately resolve the windfall versus wipeout dilemma the government must instigate a program that is not a means of raising revenue, but a means of recouping the government (public) cost in such windfalls. In similar fashion, reimbursement for wipeout should not be total, but should be substantial. Several communities and states have attempted a form of windfall recapture through the use of land value taxation, business taxes for developers, etc. The legality of such devices varies from state to state and indicates the need for a comprehensive program to address this issue. Conversely, others maintain that the windfall versus wipeout is a function of the free enterprise system and one to which the government at whatever level should not address itself.

ENVIRONMENTAL CONCERN: MORE OR LESS?

The concern for the environment which resulted in the NEPA in the early 1970s has also affected and will continue to affect land use decisions in the United States. Traditional zoning mechanisms too often are inadequate to protect critical environmental areas, and it is suggested that the use of environmental impact analysis (EIS) and/or the use of carrying capacity analysis offers potential as an alternative form of land use regulation. Impact statements offer an opportunity for developments of prescribed size or nature to be critically examined to ensure that the environmental impact they generate is acceptable to the community and does not result in detrimental long-term effects. Several states have required the use of impact analysis for developments in specified zones or of specified size.

Similarly, the concept of carrying capacity can be utilized to assess density, use, and size of development. Carrying capacity is simply an analysis of the land and its ability to handle development as proposed. Use of carrying capacity analysis results in a land use regulatory mechanism which allows a community some leeway in determining land use within a zone. Thus, hillsides would have a lower carrying capacity than level land already served by urban utilities. The EIS use issue or carrying capacity singly or in combination represents a final important question concerning the future of land use of the United States. These and other innovative attempts to regulate land use are indications of the need to grapple with the basic issue of how land use regulations are applied within the nation.

EUCLIDIAN VERSUS NONTRADITIONAL LAND USE REGULATIONS

Increasingly, there is awareness of the need to ensure that land use regulations do more than ensure a repetition of past land uses. Only by innovative and creative use of existing land use controls and adoption of alternate controls can this be ensured. Against this need is the prevailing increase in sentiment against increased government regulation which handicaps attempts to increase the role of the public in managing private land use. In order to resolve this dilemma and make sure that the land resource base is wisely used, planners, government agencies, and public and private sectors will have to utilize all of the tools at their disposal to ensure that future land use will add to the quality of life within our nation. Cooperation between varying levels of government and the public and private groups involved in land use is essential to this process. Employing negotiation and compromise to resolve land use disputes instead of litigation offers potential for both increasing the wise use of land and minimizing the cost and delay associated with court challenges. Only when there is a unified and concerted attempt on the part of all who are involved in land use decisions can we hope to accomplish the goal of wise land use to guarantee present and future residents of America their demands for a high quality of life. Everyone is in favor of wise use of land, but without cooperation one or another group will invariably feel their rights and needs have been ignored. Through adequate and continued education and cooperation among the various groups affecting land use, the present land use patterns can be improved and the future of American land use ensured.

This is not a new or radical goal, but one that has been recognized by planner, public officials, and the public alike for the past century. Neither are the solutions being applied to insure that future generations have options likely to result in any major and drastic shifts in existing land use patterns. The process for making land use decisions has been determined over the course of the 200 years of the American republic's existence, and the changes which take place in a period of a few decades tend to affect this pattern in only a relatively minor way. Zoning will no doubt continue to be the preeminent tool for managing land use, and to it will be accreted the changes suggested in previous chapters as warranted. The issue of public versus private control is not new and the extent of public control will continue to increase, but probably at a marginal rate. For the foreseeable future, there seems to be no necessity to make massive alterations in the institutions or administrative arrangements for managing land use, only the need to use those tools and methods we now have in a rational and comprehensive manner. To this end, the major issue facing those involved in the land use decision-making process is probably the one of how to ensure that the existing tools and techniques are uniformly applied. The dilemma for the planner and those associated with planning in the United States today is that in spite of the seeming obvious need for application of existing regulation, numerous communities and regions persist in the delusion that private decision making is adequate alone to insure wise land use in every case. Although extensive government regulation is not always necessary, certain actions and needs can only be adequately controlled through the use of some type of government regulation and the need for such needs to be recognized. At the broader level, in order to ensure that such regulations are not unfair to individuals in specific areas of our nation, it is necessary that some type of uniformity be applied. These issues concerning the role of the public versus the private sector and the need to foster cooperation and coordination between the two will continue to attract attention, and if they are accomplished will insure that the needs of the public will be met without arbitrarily damaging the rights of private landowners.

NOTES

[1] Henry M. Jackson, *Readings on Land Use Policy* (Washington, D.C.: Government Printing Office, 1975), p. 558.

[2] Robert W. Burchell and David Listokin, *Future Land Use* (New Brunswick, N.J.: Center for Urban Policy Research, 1975), pp. 37–38.

[3] *Resources*, Number 50, October 1975, p. 3.

[4] William Reilly, "New Directions in Federal Land Use Regulation," in David Listokin, *Land Use Controls: Present Problems and Future Reform* (New Brunswick, N.J.: Center for Urban Policy Research, 1974), p. 353.

[5] Jackson, op. cit., p. iii.

[6] *Resources*, op. cit., p. 2.

[7] *Planning Policies: 77* (Washington, D.C.: American Institute of Planners, 1977), pp. 3–6.

[8] *Subdividing Rural America*, prepared for the Council on Environmental Quality by the American Society of Planning Officials (Washington, D.C.: Government Printing Office, 1976), pp. 97–101.

[9] Slan Wellesley-Miller, "Fuel Prices and Energy Technology: A Look at the Future," in Burchell and Listokin, op. cit., p. 247.

[10] George Sterliet, "Forum-The Future Is a Different United States," in Bunchell and Listokin, op. cit., p. 352.

Index

Aesthetic zoning, 200
Age restrictions, 142
Agricultural districts, 181
Agricultural zones, 161, 162, 178–182
Alabama, 120
American Planning Association, 215
Annexation, 206–207
Areas of Critical State Concern, 74
Arlington Heights, 135

Baker v. City of Milwaukie, 42
Baltimore, 95
Bedroom communities, 127
Bedroom restrictions, 136
Benefit fees, 166
Benefit taxes, 181
Black population, 130–132
Blight, 122–123
Blue Hill Avenue, 109
Boca Raton, 73, 137, 167–168
Boom towns, 120, 138–141
Boulder, 168
Boulder Colorado, 197, 203
Building codes, 207–208
Bureau of Land Management, 49
Burlington County, New Jersey, 154
Business zones, 200–201

California, 150, 175, 177
California Coastal Zone Conservation Act, 80–83

California Land Conservation Act, 187
California Land Use Regulations, 79–82
Capital expenditures, 158–59, 202–203
Capital gains tax, 79
Carrying capacity, 218
CBD, 122–125
CBD rejuvenation, 125–126
Central city, 132
Chicago, 23, 107, 109
Chicago (Historic Preservation), 156
Chlorinated hydrocarbons, 127
City Beautiful Movement, 23–24
Clean Air Act, 55, 191
Clean Water Act, 190
Cluster zoning, 152, 163
Coastal zone management, 57, 80–82
Coastal Zone Management Act (CZMA), 56–58
Code regulations, 207–208
Colorado, 82–83
Commercial land use, 107–111, 122–123
Compensable regulations, 183
Comprehensive plan, 135, 136, 197–198
Comprehensive Plan, 41–44,
    Characteristics, 41
    Housing Act of 1954, 42
    701 Funding, 42, 43, 54
    Difficulty of, 43
    Benefits, 43
Comprehensive planning, 157, 161

221

Conditional use permit, 164
Conditional zoning, 163
Conflict of interest, 213
Congestion of traffic, 111
Contract zoning, 163
Critical environmental areas, 72, 74, 150, 202
Cropland, 5-7
CZMA, 56-58

Deed restrictions, 163, 165
Deferred taxation, 167, 186
Density bonus, 156, 164
Density of development, 134
Developing communities, 136
Development of regional impact, 73-75
Development rights, 134
Development timing, 158-162
    Capital expenditures, 158-159
    Ramapo township, 159
    Justification, 159
    Moratoria, 159-160
    Land banking, 161
    Large lot zoning, 161-162
Diminishment in value, 33, 34

East Gay, Maine, 127
Elderly, 97, 108, 112, 115, 121, 142
Emery county, 140
Eminent domain, 33, 59
Encomienda, 15
Energy, 216-217
Environmental Board, 78
Environmental Impact Statement, 55, 218
Environmental Land Management Act, 73
Environmental regulations, 37-41
Euclidian zoning, 41, 124, 147, 151, 168, 219
Euclid vs. Ambler, 130
Exclusionary zoning, 87, 97, 130, 157, 160, 211, 216
Exclusive districts, 181
Expressway systems, 112
Externalities, 138, 150, 163
Exurbia, 127

Fairfax County, 137
Fair share housing, 136
Farm population, 120, 122

Farmland preservation
    California, 182, 187-188
    General, 154-155, 176-177
    Minnesota, 180
    Montana, 188
    New York, 181
    North Carolina, 187
    Pennsylvania, 181
    Taxation, 185-190
    Texas, 187
    Wisconsin, 188-189
Federal regulations
    Clean Air Act, 55
    Coastal Zone Management Act, 56, 58
    Environmental Protection Act, 55, 56
    Environmental Impact Statement, 55
    Flood plain management, 58-59
    Indirect controls, 60-61
    National Environmental Policy Act, 55
    National Land Use Act, 61
    Water Pollution Control, 56
Federal role in planning
    Agencies, 50-55
    Eminent domain, 51
    Federal Land Policy Act, 50
    Land ownership, 47-53
    Quasi-zoning, 52
    Spending, 54, 55
    Types of control, 47
Federal Water Pollution Control Act, 56
Fee in lieu of dedication, 165
Fee–simple, 151, 185
Fiscal zoning, 130
Floating zones, 164, 202
Flood Disaster Protection Act, 58-59
Floodplain, 58-59
Floodplain zones, 202
Floor area ratio, 165
Floor area rights, 156
Florida, 72-77, 120, 127, 137, 150
    Big Cypress Swamp, 38, 40
    Developments of regional impact, 41
    Environmental Land and Water Act, 40, 41
    Golden Gate Estates, 38
    Remuda Ranch Grants, 40
    Subdivisions, 36
Forest land, 8
Forest reserves, 22
Freehold tenure, 14

Golden Gate Estates, 38
Golden vs. Ramapo, 159
Governing body, 125
Government spending
    Federal Aid to Highways Act, 54
    Federal Interstate System, 54
    Housing Act of 1954, 54–55
    National Environmental Protection Act,
        54–55
Great Plains, 120–121
Greenbelt, 13, 178
Growth control, 137, 148, 211
Growth moratoria, 73

Hawaii, 66–69, 150
Hill district, 109
Historic preservation, 97–98, 152, 155–156,
    200, 201
Holding zone, 161
Housing, 130–131
Housing Act, 42, 100
Homestead Act, 19, 22
Houston, 165
HUD, 105
Huntington, 140

Idaho, 121
Impact fees, 166–167
Incentive zoning, 164
Indirect controls, 60–61
Industrial development associations, 127
Industrial land use, 107, 126, 201
Industrial parks, 127
Infrastructure, 138, 142, 148
In lieu fees, 165
Intermountain power project, 64

Jeffersonian Ethic, 18, 129, 192

Land abandonment, 6, 172
Land banking, 161, 174, 184, 185
Land capability classes, 173–174
Land rents, 125
Land resource
    Cropland, 5–7
    Distribution, 2, 3, 19–21
    Ownership, 4, 5, 14–15
    Per capita, 1
    Policies, 11–14

Land use
    Changes in use, 7, 9, 11
    Cropland, 5–7
    Issues, 12, 14
    Forest land, 8, 22
    Major uses, 6
    Ownership, 14, 15
    Policies, 11–14
    Problems, 124, 125
    Suburbs, 130–134
    Urban, 8–9, 88
Land Use Commission, 67
Land use controls
    Colonial era, 15–18
    Nuisance activities, 17
Land Use Policy Act, 213
Land and Water Conservation Act, 179
Large lot zoning, 161–162
LCDC, 71
Leapfrog development, 157
L'Enfant, Pierre, 18
Lincoln Green, 135
Lloyd, Gerald D., 152
Love Canal, 127

Macro-lots, 132
Mandatory dedication, 165
Megalopolis
    Baltimore, 95, 100, 104, 112
    Boston, 95, 109
    Housing, 136
    New York City, 94, 97, 100, 107, 109
    Philadelphia, 94, 100, 104
    Residential land use, 95–107
    Transportation, 111–113
Metropolitan Fiscal Disparities Act, 114
Metropolitan land use
    Commercial, 107–111
    Development, 88
    Industrial, 107
    Megalopolis, 94–95
    Open space, 113–114
    Problems, 93–94
    Residential, 95–107
    SMSAs, 89
    Streets, 111
    Tax base, 113, 114
    Transportation, 111–113
    Zoning, 90–93

Micropolitan
  Business districts, 123–125
  Capital investment, 122–123
  Categories, 120
  Definition, 119
  Deterioration, 123
  Housing, 121–122
  Land use, 121–127
  Migration, 120–121
  Obsolescence, 122–123
  Population growth, 120–121
  Vacancy, 123
  Zoning, 124
Migration, 120–121
Milwaukie, Oregon, 198
Minimum floor area, 162
Mining and grazing zones, 202
Minneapolis–St. Paul, 113–114
Minnesota, 113–114, 180
Minorities, 97, 108, 112, 113, 115, 121,
  130–134, 148
Mobile homes, 139
Moratoria, 148–149, 159–160
Mount Laurel, 136

National Environmental Protection Act, 55
National Flood Plain Insurance, 58–59
National Land Use Act, 61
NEPA, 54, 55
New Haven, Connecticut, 17
Newark, 98
New Jersey, 154
New towns, 127
New York City, 95, 100, 107, 109
No-growth, 85
Nonmetropolitan, 119–126
North Carolina, 213
Nuisance ordinance, 17, 27–29, 172

Obsolescence, 122–123
Ogelthorpe, James, 18
Olmsted, Frederick Law, 23
One Hundred Year Flood, 59
Open space, 113–114, 150, 152, 176
Orange County, 172
Ordinance of 1785, 19
Oregon, 69–72, 172, 182
  Baker v. City of Milwaukie, 42
  Comprehensive Planning, 42
  Land Use Act, 182
Overzoning, 92, 137
Ozarks, 121

Parking, 126
Pasture and range land, 8
Petaluma, California, 137, 168, 197
Pedestrian mall, 126
Performance bonds, 205
Performance standards, 163–164, 181
Pennsylvania, 181
Philadelphia, 17–18
Planned Unit Development, 148, 152, 163
Planning goals, 196–197
Planning policy, 196
Planning tools, 198–199
Police power, 28–29
Population caps, 73, 137
Population growth, 120–125
Population migration, 215–216
Preferential assessment, 167, 183, 185–190
Preservation of agricultural land, 65, 161,
  171–173
Prime agricultural land, 65, 67, 211
  Definition, 173, 177
  Extent, 173, 177
  Location, 173, 175
  Loss, 171–173
  Quality, 173
  Regulation, 178–179
Privatown Township, NY, 138
Property tax, 184
Property values, 132, 134
Proposition Thirteen, 214
Proposition Twenty, 80
Pruitt–Igoe, 100
Public interest, 151
Public lands, 47–53
Public nuisance, 27–29
Public purse, 202–204
Public utilities, 158

Quiet Revolution, 66, 83, 208
Quarter/quarter zoning, 180

Racial discrimination, 135
Radioactive wastes, 126–127
Ramapo, 137, 159, 164
Reclamation, 175–176
Recreation homesites, 70
Recreational zones, 202
Remuda Ranch Grants, 40
Rent supplement program, 101
Residential abandonment, 98–99
Reston, 127
Restrictive covenants, 91, 165, 167, 186

Retirement communities, 142–143
Roads, 205
Rock Springs, 139
Rollback tax, 186
Rural America
    Business district, 123–124
    Growth, 120
    Housing, 121–122
    Immigration, 120–121
    Land use, 119, 121–122, 124
    Regions, 120–125
    Services, 120–121
    Transport, 121

San Francisco, 156
Sandy, Utah, 134
Santa Fe, New Mexico, 126
Savannah, Georgia, 18
Sawtooth National Recreation Area,
    153–154
Scenic easements, 59–60, 152–164
Second homes, 217
Section 208, 56
Segregation, 136
Seigneuries, 16
Sequential growth, 158–159
Severance taxes, 140
Sliding-scale zoning, 181
Small towns, 119, 123
Social costs and benefits, 27
Social justice, 91
Solar ordinances, 217
South, 120–121
Special permits, 8–9, 164, 201
Special service districts, 140, 167
Speculation, 19–20
Spot zoning, 163
Standard City Planning Enabling Act, 42,
    204
Standard Metropolitan Statistical Areas, 88,
    89
State land use controls
    California, 65, 79–82
    Colorado, 82–83
    Development, 63
    Florida, 35–41, 72–77
    Fragmentation, 63
    Hawaii, 66–69
    Justification, 64–65
    Oregon, 69–72

Vermont, 77–79
Wyoming, 83
State zoning, 67
Strip mining, 172
Subdivision regulations
    Florida, 35–41, 204–206
Suburbanization, 174, 176, 204–205
Suburbs, 127–138
    Exclusionary zoning, 130–137
    Growth control, 137–138
    Housing, 130–132, 134
    Land use, 130
    Minorities, 130–132
Suffolk County, NY, 154
Sunbelt, 142
Sun City, 142
Sweat-equity, 104
Sweetwater County, 139

Taking issue, 13, 35, 155, 159, 184, 192
Taxation, 114, 166, 167, 191
Taylor Grazing Act, 22
Tenement House Act, 23
Timber Culture Act, 20
Timing development, 137
Toone, Tennessee, 127
Town and Country Planning Act, 152
Transfer of development rights, 151–158
    Advantages, 157
    Agricultural, 183–184
    Definition, 151
    Farmland preservation, 154–155
    Financing, 155
    Historic preservation, 155–156
    Impact, 156–157
    Open space, 152
    Requirements, 154
    Scenic, 152, 154
Transportation, 111–113

Underassessment, 191
Unique lands, 177, 214
Urban blight, 104–107
Urban flight, 217
Urban homesteading, 101, 103–105
Urban land, 8, 9, 93, 100, 101
Urban-rural fringe, 192
Urban shadow, 172
Urban sprall, 65, 91, 171, 172
Use-value assessment, 182, 185
User fees, 166–167

Vacant land, 98–100, 122, 125
Variance, 91
Vermont Act, 77, 250
Vitruvius, 15

Wasatch front, 64
Washington, 18, 23, 156
Washington Township, New Jersey, 43
Wetlands, 73
White flight, 111–113
Wild and Scenic Rivers Act, 59–60
Williamson Act, 187
Windfall, 88, 91–91, 151, 218
Wipeout, 88, 151, 218
Wisconsin Farmland Preservation Act, 188–189
Wyoming, 83, 139

Yeoman farmer, 14
York County, Pennsylvania, 171–172

Zoning
    Aesthetics, 200

Age restrictions, 142
Agricultural, 178, 182, 189
Ambler vs. Euclid, 29
Changes, 135, 168
Criticism, 90, 91, 93
Definition, 199
Euclidian, 29
Exclusionary, 32, 33, 130–137
Fiscal, 130
History, 28, 29
Implementation, 199–202
Large lot, 130
Metropolitan, 93
Ordinance, 134, 199, 202
Quarter/quarter, 180
Requirements, 31
Rural, 124
Support, 93
Weaknesses, 43
Zoning modifications, 163–165
Zoning techniques, 149